YOU KNOW THE ANSWERS—DO YOU KNOW THE QUESTION?

This taciturn president really was born on the 4th of July.

This macabre writer was once enrolled at West Point.

It's a noble gas, not a superhero's nemesis.

At one point in 1964, they had all top 5 songs on the charts.

It's the "House That Ruth Built."

It's the largest U.S. bill in circulation.

Check the questions at the bottom of the page. Congratulations! You're on your way to becoming a JEOPARDY! champion.

"The contestant everyone still remembers from the new version of the show is Chuck Forrest. . . . He was like a pitcher with a great repertoire."

—ALEX TREBEK, host of *JEOPARDY!*,
from *The JEOPARDY! Book*

Answers:

Who is Calvin Coolidge?
Who is Edgar Allan Poe?
What is Krypton?

Who are the Beatles?
What is Yankee Stadium?
What is $100?

SECRETS OF THE JEOPARDY!* CHAMPIONS

CHUCK FORREST and MARK LOWENTHAL

*This book is not authorized by Jeopardy Productions, Inc.

WARNER BOOKS

A Time Warner Company

Warner Books, Inc., 1271 Avenue of the Americas, New York, NY 10020

A Time Warner Company

Printed in the United States of America
First printing: April 1992
10 9 8 7 6 5 4 3 2 1

Library of Congress Cataloging-in-Publication Data

Forrest, Chuck.
Secrets of the Jeopardy! champions / Chuck Forrest and Mark Lowenthal.
p. cm.
ISBN 0-446-39352-5
1. Questions and answers. 2. Jeopardy (Television program)—Miscellanea. I. Lowenthal, Mark. II. Title.
AG195.F69 1992
031.02—dc20 91-39096
CIP

Cover design by Diane Luger
Cover art by Michael Racz
Book design by Giorgetta Bell McRee

ACKNOWLEDGMENTS

Jeopardy! champions rarely prepare in a sealed room or deep in the stacks of a library. Rather, they endlessly pester relatives, friends and co-workers with irrelevant facts and requests to impersonate Alex Trebek. They also lapse into a curious speech pattern of phrasing mundane statements as questions. We would be remiss if we didn't thank the following people for their help, patience and encouragement:

Chuck: Evelyn, Richard and Charles Forrest; Bill Kuesel, Blaine Renfert, Donn Rubin, Diane Faber, Bradley H. Blower, Tracy Bernstein, L. Norman Sanders and Harvey Weiss.

Mark: my wife, Cynthia, for her constant encouragement, enthusiasm and support and for being a super coach; my daughter, Sarah, for whom **Jeopardy!** was a constant feature of her first three years of life; my mother, Laura, and my sister, Marylin, who only wanted me to say her name on television; my brother-in-law and sister-in-law, Roger and Kathleen, without whom I wouldn't have known **Jeopardy!** had returned to television, and the rest of my family, friends and colleagues who did more than wish me well along the way.

CONTENTS

SECRETS OF THE JEOPARDY! CHAMPIONS

Secrets of the Jeopardy! Champions

The Mystique of Jeopardy!

Jeopardy! is more than just a game show; it has become an institution, watched every night by close to 30 million viewers in the United States and Canada. The show's "Final Jeopardy" theme music is instantly recognizable, and its perverse gimmick of requiring an answer "phrased in the form of a question" pops up in the most unexpected places, from schoolrooms to press conferences.

If you've watched the show, you've probably thought about competing yourself. That's the way **Jeopardy!** works; it's impossible to sit back and watch the show passively. The money you might win (up to $175,000) is obviously an incentive, but more important, appearing on **Jeopardy!** gives you the chance to prove to family, friends and millions of like-minded viewers just how smart you really are.

Only a small percentage of **Jeopardy!** viewers ever have the chance to compete on the program, but getting on the show is not as difficult as you may think. All you need is perseverance, a bit of luck and the willingness to take the risk. To help you develop the confidence you may lack, we've put together this book, which is about trying out for the show, preparing to play and playing. It's also intended for those millions of fans who simply enjoy the game and want to know more about it and perhaps pick up a few facts along the way.

Only Merv Griffin, the show's creator (and composer of the "Final Jeopardy" music); Alex Trebek, the current host; and the faceless but talented staff of writers who create **Jeopardy!** "answers" know all of the secrets of the game, and they are precluded from revealing them by fiscal prudence (and federal law). We hope, however, that this book will pierce the veil, dispel some of the mystery and reveal some of the innermost secrets of the show. We don't have "insider information," but we have had a certain measure of success where it really counts —on stage competing against other masters of the game. Chuck Forrest was the 1986 champion, winning $72,800 (the all-time record for years after) in the regular season and the $100,000 Tournament of Champions. Mark Lowenthal was the 1988 champion, winning a total of $149,901.

Here's how we each found ourselves competing on **Jeopardy!**:

Chuck: I remember watching the old version of the show (hosted by Art Fleming) when I came home for lunch during grade school. Later on, when I didn't get a lunch break, I looked forward to days off (or being sick) so I could watch the program. I wouldn't say that I was a fanatic, but even then **Jeopardy!** was my favorite TV show. When the show came back on the air in 1984, I was in the first year of law school. With a group of fellow students (who later became my training team), I watched the program each evening after dinner. There are few things more tedious than the first year of law school, so we eagerly looked forward to the show every day. While others in our class were interviewing for summer jobs with law firms, we planned a cross-country caravan to California to try out for **Jeopardy!** But before we could head for Hollywood, Hollywood came to us. The local station announced a **Jeopardy!** try-out in the Detroit area.

Mark: I didn't even know the show was back on the air until mid-1987, when I happened to see it while visiting relatives. I had tried out for the old version and hadn't made the cut—apparently for answering *too many* questions during the group quiz. The standards in those days were different; they were looking for more "average" players. Anyway, I started watching the new series and did pretty well at home. I had played intramural College Bowl at school and knew I had a knack for this. One night they announced that there would be local try-outs in my area. My wife urged me to give it a try.

How Do You Get on Jeopardy!?

Simple. You try out. The **Jeopardy!** crew fans out across the United States each year, conducting local try-outs. The station in your area that carries **Jeopardy!** will usually advertise the event and give the rules for applying. Each station uses its own technique for reducing the thousands of applicants to the number who are selected to try out.

Chuck: The local station gave a local phone number. I started dialing immediately (it would have helped to have touch-tone and auto redial). After about an hour-and-a-half of busy signals, I got through.

Mark: Mine was a bit more dramatic. I only heard the announcement on the last evening, and so I drove to the local television station with *one* postcard and tossed it in the box. Mine was chosen, along with 149 others. I know that some people send in hundreds of cards, but karma is karma.

Of course, you can skip this lottery by arranging to show up at the studio in Los Angeles, and trying out there. Frequent viewers will note that many of the show's contestants are introduced as "originally from" somewhere other than southern California. They do this because the majority of people trying out for the show *are* from California. Almost any day of the week you can walk in off the street and try out for **Jeopardy!** (or most other game shows). It often seems as if everyone who lives in L.A. has been on a game show at least once—partly because it's so convenient. Out-of-towners who come to L.A. to try out for **Jeopardy!** have an advantage, because the show wants contestants that the folks at home—in places other than California—can root for. So, if your postcard doesn't get picked or if the phone is always busy at your local station, head for L.A. and you are almost guaranteed a try-out.

The Try-out: Part I

The try-out consists of three parts. First is the quiz. You have 13 minutes to answer 50 questions—and no, you don't have to put down your answer in the form of a question. It's a straightforward short-answer test, covering a fairly wide range of subjects—history, chemistry, geography, current events, math, music—sort of like a quick high school refresher. When we tried out it was a written affair, but **Jeopardy!** now uses a video format from past shows to ask the questions.

Now, 13 minutes doesn't sound like a lot of time for 50 questions (more than four questions a minute), but it is. Go through the test as quickly as possible. Answer only the ones you know immediately and keep moving. Then go back over the ones you left blank. If you're not sure, go with your best guess. (There's no penalty for guessing. That's the last time we'll ever suggest guessing blindly.) Don't focus on the question to the exclusion of the category—that in itself is often a clue to the right answer. Leave yourself enough time to go over the whole quiz again before time is called. If you're up to par you'll find that you've gone over the quiz three or four times.

The **Jeopardy!** contestant coordinators, a marvelous group of folks, won't tell you what a passing score is, nor will they tell you your score. They simply call out the names of those who passed. Everyone else is asked to leave, and invited to try again some time. Lots of people try several times before getting on.

The Try-out: Part II

On to the second part of the try-out, a mock **Jeopardy!** game, on the cheap. No fancy electronic board or little buzzer—it's flip cards and the kind of bell your grade school teacher kept on her desk. Prospective contestants in groups of three play very abbreviated versions of the game. The score doesn't matter; your personality does. The staff is looking for several things here: How well do you play the game? Do you move easily from category to category? Do you project well? Are you enthusiastic?

Don't worry about dominating the game. This phase is less about smarts than it is about personality. You already proved you're bright in the quiz. Now show them how charming you'll be on the air. The best approach is to be alert but to be yourself. Remember, this isn't "Let's Make a Deal." If you've watched **Jeopardy!**, you've seen how the contestants behave—no screaming, no jumping in the air.

The Try-out: Part III

After everyone's played, the staff may ask some people to leave. They're the ones who froze, or spoke too softly, or crossed the line between enthusiasm and goofiness. For the remaining contestants, it's time for part three. Those who are left will then be interviewed and taped. You'll be asked to describe yourself, your interests, what you'd do with a lot of money. Think of things that make you stand out, that make you interesting and different. Once again, just be yourself. You've made it this far; don't try to be too cute or too clever.

And then it's over. You won't know now whether or not you made it. That's right. **Jeopardy!** will call you if they want you to come out to Los Angeles to play. And, don't call them. Our sense is that virtually everyone who gets to phase three of the try-outs eventually gets a call, but the waiting time varies widely. We both waited about two months, but we know of contestants who didn't hear for two years, although this is apparently a rarity. Out-of-town visitors to L.A. often get a break and are brought on as soon as possible.

While You're Waiting . . .

As we said, if you made it through all three parts of the try-out, assume that you're going to be on the air. What should you do while you're waiting? Well, you can do nothing. After all, this is not going to make you a media star and even if you win it all you're not going to be rich enough to quit your job. So, you might as well go on with your life. On the other hand, when you do get called, you will want to do your best, so consider using the time to study and to practice.

What Makes a Good Jeopardy! Player?

Jeopardy! is a test of three things. First, how much data have you accumulated over the years? Second, and most important, how quickly can you recall it? Third, can you do it under the pressure of competition, knowing that some 30 million people will be watching you?

> **Chuck:** Anyone with a high school education is probably acquainted with most of the information you need to play **Jeopardy!** The facts have been stored deep within your brain's recesses; you simply need a way to retrieve them. You also need to make quick connections and analogies; some of the most difficult questions are like riddles. I find it easiest to have the facts in some broader context, not just long lists, but groupings. That's one of the things we've tried to do in this book.
>
> **Mark:** What separates good **Jeopardy!** players from others who have accumulated a lot of data is really the recall speed. To a certain extent, this is simply a gift. You can improve it, however, by increasing your familiarity with the material. Studying helps, not so much in acquiring new material, but in building this sense of familiarity. On stage, **Jeopardy!** players don't spend a lot of time thinking about the answers. Their responses are fairly reflexive; they tend to know the answer, or know that they don't know it, as soon as the clue is revealed, before Alex has finished reading it.

Can You Study for Jeopardy!?

This is one of the three most asked questions for people who have been on **Jeopardy!** (more about the others later).

The answer is—absolutely! Remember, **Jeopardy!** is about the ability to recall specific information quickly, but the information has to be there to recall.

First, you have to know what to study. If you watch **Jeopardy!** regularly, you'll recognize the areas that come up most often. The second part of this book contains the basics of information—in various combinations and permutations—that we feel a **Jeopardy!** contestant has to master to play the game well. But remember, we also know a lot of good players who did very well without studying.

> **Chuck:** I began by watching the show religiously. I was fortunate to have a group of highly competitive friends with whom I watched the program, shouting out the answers. I kept track of categories, to identify areas to study. This convinced me that Sports was less important than the Bible, Presidents or Oscars. Also, I listened to "oldies" radio stations and studied 1950s and 1960s TV shows and other pop culture phenomena. I knew that this was an area where my competitors (all of whom were older than me) would probably have an advantage.

> **Mark:** I watched the show, identifying the categories that came up most often. I spent some time making lists of the things I needed to know in a notebook, and marking up an almanac. Some of the material was familiar and was largely refresher for me; other things were new. As I got closer to the game date I set aside time to study every night and had my wife quiz me randomly from my accumulated material. In the 10 **Jeopardy!** games I have played (a total of 610 questions), I can recall 20 or 30 questions that came from new material. But the main thing the studying did was to build my confidence in being able to cover a broad amount of material.

Two other things to remember if you are studying. You will never be able to learn *everything*. And there are all sorts of categories for which you cannot study—"Eleven Letter Words," "Double Double Letters," and the like.

There are also two types of **Jeopardy!** games available that are very useful for brushing up on the entire range of likely subjects: a board game and a computer game. We've used both, and we found the computer game a bit too easy. The selection of questions in the board game tended to be more demanding. There are about three editions of the home version of **Jeopardy!**, which give you a pool of thousands of questions to practice on.

> **Chuck:** The big problem I found with the home game was finding people willing to play with me. Like all games, if

you're doing extremely well, it's not a lot of fun for everyone else. I had to bribe one of my classmates to act as Emcee by offering him ½ of 1 percent of my ultimate winnings, which turned out to be a lot more money than either of us bargained for.

Mark: On the other hand, you can simply use the home game as a solitary quiz, which is what I did, going answer by answer and checking my responses in the book that accompanies the game. I found that the biggest difficulty, while studying in a prone position, was holding that red plastic panel that allows you to read the answers!

Another good way to prepare is to do crossword puzzles, double acrostics, anagrams or any other puzzles that have you draw on a pool of knowledge and think quickly. Think of them as limbering up exercises for your mind. To add the necessary element of speed, try timing yourself as you do them.

Practice Makes Perfect

If you've gone to the trouble of accumulating all of this information you ought to see how well you can use it. Being quizzed, as we suggested earlier, is one way.

But remember, on the show you don't get to answer unless you press the buzzer. The contestant buzzer takes on mythic proportions among **Jeopardy!** players. It is simply a steel cylinder, somewhat thicker than a pencil, with a little push button at the end—a lot like a retractable ballpoint pen.

The buzzer is important, but it's largely a matter of timing. You cannot ring in until Alex Trebek says the last syllable of the last word of the answer. (There is also a visual signal that it's safe to ring, but more on that later.) If you ring in too soon, your buzzer shuts down for about two-tenths of a second—a very short time, but enough for one of your opponents to ring in. Ring in too late and someone else answers first.

That's why we recommend two things. Rig up something that allows you to simulate the buzzer. Watch the show and get used to Alex's voice. He tends to speak at a very uniform speed; get used to it. And get used to pressing just as he finishes. Also, get used to *not* pressing on every question—just the ones you know or think you have a strong hunch. Remember, you lose money for every wrong answer.

Then, watch the show (every night if possible) and play along. Get your timing down; also, learn when not to press. Say your responses out loud, *phrased as a question*. Better get used to that! People often ask us how we remembered to phrase the answer in the form of a question. Don't worry, it's usually not a problem. It can be a harder habit to break than it is to acquire! Finally, brush up on the categories that give you trouble.

> **Chuck:** The buzzer has changed over the years. The old buzzer was simply a press-down system. At some point they replaced it with a new buzzer that had to be pressed down *and* let up before it would register. During "Super **Jeopardy!**" it took some getting used to after playing all my earlier games with the old buzzer. I understand that the old buzzer is now back in service. I still think the best method is to concentrate on Alex's voice as your signal for buzzing in.

> **Mark:** I had rigged a little buzzer system at home and practiced against each night's game. My buzzer had a light so I could judge if I had been "first" to answer. On the air I found that the best position for me was to hold the buzzer in my left hand (I'm a lefty) and keep my hand firmly on the podium. That prevented me from making any extraneous and time-wasting up-and-down motions with my entire hand or arm, as you sometimes see players do, often much to their undoing. It's all a question of what feels comfortable.

If, or rather, when, you do get called to be on the show, you will discover that **Jeopardy!** tapes two days a week, five shows a day. So if you are winning you can play as many as five times in one day. Stamina matters. A lot of contestants-in-waiting have been known to tape several **Jeopardy!** shows at home and play against them, back to back. We're not sure that this is a major factor, but you may want to keep it in mind. (Videotaping the show also enables you to use the remote control as a buzzer. Substitute pressing "pause" when you want to ring in.)

California, Here You Come

The call finally comes and you are off to Los Angeles—on your own money. You must pay your own way and foot your own hotel and meal bills. If you win, deduct these from your taxes. You will also be bringing three changes of clothing. As long as you're winning, you keep changing between shows to create the illusion for the folks at home of distinct days.

Taping usually takes place on Monday and Tuesday, but you will not have a firm day or time for your appearance. That all gets decided after you show up, on the days of taping. If you are coming across a few time zones, we recommend that you get to L.A. on Saturday and give yourself 24 hours to get over any jet lag. The **Jeopardy!** staff will remind you frequently that there is no guarantee that you will actually get on the show, even if you have flown cross-country to compete. After all, if **Jeopardy!** finds that you are not eligible, they are not going to put you on the air. Make sure you understand the rules and have the proper papers before you leave home.

If you've studied, you'll probably want to bring your books with you. We doubt that you will learn anything more at this late date, but as a security blanket it's probably a good idea.

Showtime

When you assemble outside the studio at the appointed hour you will meet your opponents for the first time. From watching the show you know that there is a wide range of people—doctors, lawyers, firemen, mothers, teachers, actors—who turn up. We both found that virtually all of our fellow contestants, even in the championship, were very nice, very friendly and happily free of the need to waste time psyching one another out. Some may try, but the other players tend to band together to isolate these screwballs. Relax and enjoy yourself. You'll probably never do this again.

You spend virtually the entire morning processing in, filling out forms (so the tax man can keep track of your success) and hearing the various rules and restrictions. Eventually you get down to the studio and are given a chance to practice using the infamous buzzer and the real game board. Now you will discover the visual clue we mentioned earlier about when it's time to buzz. Although you usually can't see it at home, the entire game board is surrounded by a neon light. When that light goes on, your buzzer is ready to go. This is done manually, by a crew member listening to Alex's voice. Don't bother trying to watch him; his hand is hidden behind a board.

On the Air, at Last

And then the audience files in, and the staff in charge of contestants calls out the names of those to play. Good luck!

Watching at home, looking at the categories and listening to the interviews, most people assume that categories are chosen to correspond to some of the talents or interests of the contestants. Not so. In effect, **Jeopardy!** has two separate staffs, those in charge of the players and those who make up the games; and never the twain shall meet. The games are all made up in advance and are chosen sight unseen and at random by someone from "Standards and Practices." These precautions were instituted after the quiz show scandals of the 1950s and are now required by federal law. None of these folks knows who any of the contestants are or what their backgrounds are. Similarly, the staff in charge of the players doesn't know the contents of any of the games.

Will you be nervous? Of course! Some 30 million people will be watching this, including most of your family, friends and co-workers. Just do whatever you do to keep calm. Don't get rattled if your timing is off at first. Just listen to Alex's voice and watch the light. Although at least one **Jeopardy!** contestant has fainted on the set, and others have lost their lunches during the taping, the vast majority of contestants rise to the challenge and acquit themselves honorably, win or lose. And remember, these people are all willing to risk international embarrassment if they have a very bad game, so a bit of courage is a given.

A game of **Jeopardy!** takes a lot of concentration. Most games run through virtually all the questions in both rounds—a total of 61 questions. That's a lot of thinking in a very short span of time. If you subtract the contestant introductions and interviews, commercials, prize descriptions and other interruptions, the actual competition only lasts for about 13 minutes! It's very easy to lose your concentration.

You stand up there, read the clue and say to yourself, "Oh, that's interesting." Meanwhile, someone else buzzes in, the lights in front of them flash and they pick up $800.

That's why we recommend looking at nothing except the game board. Ignore the tote boards that show the players' scores unless you hit a "Daily Double."

Now for some playing hints:

Asking a Question: Yes, you do have to phrase your response as a question. During the first round Alex will give you some leeway and a few friendly warnings. But in "Double Jeopardy" it's all or nothing, with no warnings, not even on "Daily Doubles." A wrong phrasing equals a wrong response, and down goes your score. It's not that difficult, especially if you've been practicing. But all seasoned **Jeopardy!** players remember poor Lionel Goldbart, who was eliminated from the Tournament of Champions when he forgot to phrase his response as a question on a "Daily Double."

The Format of the Clues: Almost every **Jeopardy!** clue has two parts: the item they are asking about and some sort of hint. For example, in the category "Pets": "His pet chow chow may have gotten analyzed if it sat on the couch." Let's face it, few people are knowledgeable about famous pets; but *whose* couch is famous for analysis? Freud, of course!

Often, as we've said, the hint comes from the category title itself, such as "Geography with a C" or "Eleven-Letter Words." Be sure to look for that clue, especially if you don't know the answer immediately. It's also important as a way of mentally checking that your response is correct. But don't let all this confuse you. Remember, the correct answer is invariably the most obvious one. If the category is "TV Sitcoms" and the answer begins: "This loquacious equine . . ."—don't worry about what comes next! Just get ready to say, "Who is Mr. Ed?" Be confident and don't spend time second-guessing. When you think you know it and Alex has stopped speaking, buzz in!

Moving Around the Board: The contestant with the last correct response gets to choose the next clue. This is called "controlling the board." The returning champion asks the first question of the game; in "Double Jeopardy" the player with the lowest total goes first. Control is important, because you can play to your own strengths and choose the degree of difficulty of the question (the larger amounts are more difficult). **Jeopardy!** veterans have differing views on the best strategy to use.

> **Chuck:** I pioneered the "Rubin Bounce," named for my law school friend who first suggested it. The Bounce consists of jumping around from category to category at random. This gives the show's director and camera crew headaches, since they never know where to focus next. But I think it also gave my opponents headaches, since they were a bit behind me in focusing on the next clue as it was revealed. If your competitors let their minds wander as you select, they may not even follow you at all. The basic point is, you know where you're going next and they don't.
>
> **Mark:** I prefer the more traditional method of starting at the top (the easier questions) and moving down, at least if it's a category where I'm confident. The advantage here is that if you get on a hot streak and answer three or four in a row, you may intimidate the other players even if they do know where you're going next.

"Daily Doubles": We both tended to bet very conservatively here. First, remember that the difficulty of the "Daily Double" is linked to its dollar value; "Daily Doubles" are *not* more difficult than regular clues. The **Jeopardy!** staff will keep telling you not to think of it as money, just as points, because it isn't going to be money unless you win it all. That's true, but it's also not going to be money if you throw it away. Alex likes to prod players into betting high on "Daily Doubles." After all, it makes the show more exciting. Don't worry about **Jeopardy!**'s ratings. Just do what makes you feel comfortable.

Unless it's early in the game and you can easily recoup the loss, or it's late and you're really behind, we prefer the cautious approach. Balance in your mind the value of the question (which determines its difficulty), everyone's relative scores, and your degree of confidence in the category. If it's late in the game and you have a comfortable lead, it's more sensible to sit tight rather than risk trying to pad it. Remember, it only becomes money if you're the winner.

In the Tournament of Champions or in Super **Jeopardy!** the contestants are so evenly matched that "Daily Doubles" acquire greater significance. If you make it that far be prepared to throw your previous strategy out the window.

"Final Jeopardy!": The ideal position, of course, is to have such a big lead that it doesn't matter whether you know the answer or not. But let's face it, that's not going to happen every game. It may not even happen at all.

If you're in the lead and bet the right amount, you can't lose if you answer "Final **Jeopardy!**" correctly. Even if the category is one that you aren't confident in, the odds are that you will get it right more often than not. Simply double your nearest opponent's score and add $1. Then bet the difference between that number and your score. The staff will give you as much time as you need to make up your bet, provide pencil and paper, or help with the math.

If you're behind, there are several possible strategies. You can bet it all and hope that the front runner gets it wrong and you get it right, or that he or she makes a mistake with the math. On the other hand, if you think everyone will get it wrong, you can bet nothing, hoping the leader bets too much. But your best bet, literally, is to assume that you will get it correct and the leader won't. Figure out how much the leader must bet to win if you were to bet everything. Subtract that from the leader's score and then bet enough to have $1 more than that amount. In this way, even if you are both wrong, you will probably have more than the leader at the end.

Odds and Ends: Remember the title of the game—**Jeopardy!** If you give an incorrect response you not only don't get any money, you also lose the value of the question. Every time you buzz in, you are in **Jeopardy!** That's why we warn against guessing blindly. We've seen too many players do that when they were behind. The usual result is that they dig their hole deeper and end up with the ultimate ignominy—being *minus* at the end of "Double **Jeopardy!**" and getting hustled off the stage before the final question.

If the response to a question requires a person's name, give only the last name, even if you know the first name. Except in rare cases, **Jeopardy!** only requires the last name, and if they do want the first name, Alex will ask you to "be more specific." Giving the first name only increases the chance that you will be wrong. But be careful with Spanish names, which are confusing. (For example, the middle name—as in Miguel de Cervantes Saavedra—is the family name.)

Also, between the tapings of the third and fourth games the contestants are treated to lunch on a nearby soundstage. (This tends to be late in the afternoon, however, so have some breakfast.) We both agree that unless you've already been eliminated, eat lunch sparingly, if at all. Too little food will force you to play on a grumbling stomach, but too much food makes you sluggish and tired. Stay hungry! You can eat when you get back to the hotel.

And Then It's Over

If you win, you leave the set and scurry upstairs to change clothes for the next show. If you're still winning at the end of the taping schedule, you may have to come back the next week, which can be hard on out-of-towners. If you lose, you sign some forms and quietly leave the studio. If you win five games and are retired as an undefeated champion, you sign some forms and quietly leave the studio. It seems anticlimactic, but it's not, since the show will be seen by millions of people several weeks later.

Yes, after the show airs, people *will* recognize you. Some will come up to you and ask, "Hey, aren't you . . ." Believe it or not, we have even been recognized by avid **Jeopardy!** fans as far away as Australia and Saudi Arabia! Enjoy it! This is that 15 minutes of fame that Andy Warhol promised us all.

The Tournament of Champions

Undefeated five-game winners come back in the autumn for the Tournament of Champions—the World Series, Superbowl and Olympiad of **Jeopardy!** The tournament requires 15 players, and since there are rarely 15 five-game winners, the roster is rounded out with the Teen, College and Seniors Tournament Champions, and as many four-game winners with the highest winnings as needed. A financial note: For the Tournament, **Jeopardy!** pays for your travel and your hotel, and gives you a per diem allowance.

Like the regular season, the Tournament is taped in two excruciating five-game days, but the beginning and end of the tournament have slight differences from the regular season.

In the first round, the quarter-finals, everyone plays one game. The winner of each of the five quarter-final games automatically goes on to the next round. But since there are three semi-finals, requiring nine players, four more players have to be selected. The extra four are the four players with the highest point totals among those in the quarter-finals who did not win outright. This means that you have to calculate your "Final **Jeopardy!**" bet in the quarter-finals very carefully. Bet it all and get it wrong and you're gone. Bet too little and you still may not make it. It's a fine line, since you don't know what has happened in any preceding games, as all players are sequestered until it's their turn.

The other difference is in the finals. This is actually a cumulative two-game match, with your winnings from each day added together for a total. The player with the highest total is the winner, pocketing $100,000. This means that in "Final **Jeopardy!**" in the first game you don't want to bet so much that, if you're wrong, you can't make it up in the second game.

About the Rest of This Book

That's our accumulated wit and wisdom about the mechanics of playing **Jeopardy!** We hope it's useful to those of you who play someday, and interesting to those of you who are loyal viewers. The rest of this book has the same intent. Use it to study or just test yourself against the **Jeopardy!** standard. (It also makes a good reference for crossword puzzles or acrostics!) We have tried to encompass most of the material that comes up with regularity on the show. The lists are not exhaustive, so don't be offended if some favorite fact of yours is missing. Needless to say, any mistakes are the fault of my co-author.

Finally, we promised to mention the three questions that every **Jeopardy!** winner hears the most. Well, in true **Jeopardy!** fashion, we'll give you the answers and see if you can guess the questions:

1. I don't know; you're only together on the set and never really get a chance to talk.
2. Pay taxes.
3. Yes.

And the questions? Well . . .

1. What is Alex really like?
2. What did you do with the money?
3. Did you study?

CHAPTER 1

The Presidents of the United States

Jeopardy! loves the Presidents as a category. Barely a game goes by in which some category about the Presidents does not appear—names, nicknames, wives, houses, whatever. So this is a good place to begin. It's more than just knowing who they were and in what order. There's a wealth of other information as well.

We begin with a quiz to test your knowledge of Presidential middle names (a favorite **Jeopardy!** topic).

The Clues:

1. S
2. Baines
3. Alan
4. Clark
5. Henry
6. Calvin
7. Birchard
8. Herbert Walker

9. David
10. Lynch (a very tricky one)

And now the answers:

1. What is Harry Truman's full middle name?
2. Who is Lyndon Johnson?
3. Who is Chester Arthur?
4. Who is Herbert Hoover?
5. Who is William Harrison?
6. Who is John Calvin Coolidge?
7. Who is Rutherford Hayes?
8. Who is George Bush?
9. Who is Dwight Eisenhower?
10. Who is Gerald Ford (born Leslie Lynch King, Jr.)?

The Presidents

1. George Washington (1789–97)
2. John Adams (1797–1801)
3. Thomas Jefferson (1801–09)
4. James Madison (1809–17)
5. James Monroe (1817–25)
6. John Quincy Adams (1825–29)
7. Andrew Jackson (1829–37)
8. Martin Van Buren (1837–41)
9. William Henry Harrison (1841)
10. John Tyler (1841–45)
11. James Knox Polk (1845–49)
12. Zachary Taylor (1849–50)
13. Millard Fillmore (1850–53)
14. Franklin Pierce (1853–57)
15. James Buchanan (1857–61)
16. Abraham Lincoln (1861–65)
17. Andrew Johnson (1865–69)
18. Ulysses Simpson Grant (1869–77)
19. Rutherford Birchard Hayes (1877–81)

20. James Abram Garfield (1881)
21. Chester Alan Arthur (1881–85)
22. (Stephen) Grover Cleveland (1885–89)
23. Benjamin Harrison (1889–93)
24. (Stephen) Grover Cleveland (1893–97)
25. William McKinley (1897–1901)
26. Theodore Roosevelt (1901–09)
27. William Howard Taft (1909–13)
28. (Thomas) Woodrow Wilson (1913–21)
29. Warren Gamaliel Harding (1921–23)
30. (John) Calvin Coolidge (1923–29)
31. Herbert Clark Hoover (1929–33)
32. Franklin Delano Roosevelt (1933–45)
33. Harry S Truman (1945–53)
34. Dwight David Eisenhower (1953–61)
35. John Fitzgerald Kennedy (1961–63)
36. Lyndon Baines Johnson (1963–69)
37. Richard Milhous Nixon (1969–74)
38. Gerald Rudolph Ford (1974–77)
39. Jimmy (James Earl) Carter (1977–81)
40. Ronald Wilson Reagan (1981–89)
41. George Herbert Walker Bush (1989–)

Presidents' Names

Alphabetically

First: John Adams
Last: Woodrow Wilson

Obscure First Names

Hiram Ulysses Grant (changed to Ulysses Simpson)
Stephen Grover Cleveland
Thomas Woodrow Wilson
John Calvin Coolidge
David Dwight Eisenhower (names later transposed)
Leslie Lynch King, Jr. (Gerald R. Ford)

Same First and Last Initials

Woodrow Wilson
Calvin Coolidge
Herbert Hoover
Ronald Reagan

Most Prevalent Names

First Name: James (6 Presidents)
Surname Initial: H (6 Presidents)

Presidents Who Married While in Office

Grover Cleveland
John Tyler
Woodrow Wilson

Famous First Ladies

George Washington:	Martha Custis
John Adams:	Abigail Smith
Thomas Jefferson:	Martha Skelton (died before he took office)
James Madison:	Dolley Todd
Andrew Jackson:	Rachel Donelson Robards
John Tyler:	Julia Gardiner (second wife; married while President)
Abraham Lincoln:	Mary Todd
U. S. Grant:	Julia Dent
Rutherford Hayes:	Lucy Webb ("Lemonade Lucy": she refused to serve alcohol in the White House)
Grover Cleveland:	Frances Folsom (married while President)
Theodore Roosevelt:	Edith Kermit Carow (second wife)
Woodrow Wilson:	Edith Bolling Galt (second wife; married while President)
Herbert Hoover:	Lou Henry

Franklin Roosevelt:	Anna Eleanor Roosevelt
Harry Truman:	Bess Wallace
Dwight Eisenhower:	Mamie Geneva Doud
John Kennedy:	Jacqueline Lee Bouvier
Lyndon Johnson:	Claudia Alta Taylor ("Lady Bird")
Richard Nixon:	Thelma Patricia Ryan ("Pat")
Gerald Ford:	Elizabeth Bloomer Warren ("Betty")
Jimmy Carter:	Rosalynn Smith
Ronald Reagan:	Jane Wyman; Anne Frances Davis ("Nancy")
George Bush:	Barbara Pierce

Alleged Presidential Mistresses

Thomas Jefferson:	Sally Hemmings (a slave at Monticello)
Grover Cleveland:	fathered an illegitmate child long before his election; led to Republican taunt: "Ma, Ma, where's my Pa?" and the Democrats' rejoinder: "Gone to the White House, ha, ha, ha!"
Warren Harding:	Nan Britten
Franklin Roosevelt:	Lucy Mercer Rutherford
Dwight Eisenhower:	Kay Summersby (his wartime chauffeur)
John Kennedy:	various allegations: Marilyn Monroe, Judith Campbell Exner, Angie Dickinson

Presidents Who Married Twice

John Tyler
Millard Fillmore
Benjamin Harrison
Theodore Roosevelt
Woodrow Wilson
Ronald Reagan (the only one to have been divorced)

Presidential Diseases

W. H. Harrison:	pneumonia (fatal; caught during his Inaugural)
Taylor:	acute gastroenteritis (fatal)
Lincoln:	depression, Marfan's syndrome (suspected)
Cleveland:	oral cancer (removed during a secret operation on a yacht off Long Island, while President)
Wilson:	stroke
Harding:	embolism (fatal)
Franklin Roosevelt:	polio, cerebral hemorrhage (fatal)
Eisenhower:	heart attack, ileitis
Kennedy:	Addison's disease
Johnson:	gall bladder operation
Nixon:	phlebitis
Carter:	hemorrhoids
Reagan:	skin cancer, polyps
Bush:	overactive thyroid

Presidential Firsts

First to live in the White House:	John Adams (conversely, George Washington is the only President *never* to have lived in the White House, which was completed after his term ended)
First to die in office:	William Henry Harrison
First to remarry:	John Tyler
First and only to be impeached:	Andrew Johnson (acquitted by the Senate) (The House Judiciary Committee voted articles of impeachment against Nixon, but he resigned before the House could vote)
First to marry in office:	Grover Cleveland
First to have been divorced:	Ronald Reagan

First and only to resign:	Richard Nixon
First to have been adopted:	Gerald R. Ford (born Leslie Lynch King, Jr.)

Presidents Who Died in Office

Natural Causes

William Henry Harrison (pneumonia)
Zachary Taylor (acute gastroenteritis)
Warren G. Harding (embolism)
Franklin D. Roosevelt (cerebral hemorrhage)

Assassination

Abraham Lincoln by John Wilkes Booth (Ford's Theatre, Washington)

James A. Garfield by Charles Guiteau (B&O Rail Station, Washington)

William McKinley by Leon Czolgosz (Pan-American Exposition, Buffalo, New York)

John F. Kennedy by Lee Harvey Oswald (Dallas, Texas)

> **"Curse of Tecumseh":** According to legend, the defeated Shawnee leader Tecumseh uttered this curse when he was killed in 1813 (supposedly by future Vice President Richard Johnson). Every President elected in a year ending in "0" from 1840 to 1960 failed to survive his Presidency: W. H. Harrison (1840); Lincoln (1860); Garfield (1880); McKinley (1900); Harding (1920); F. D. Roosevelt (1940); Kennedy (1960). The "curse" was broken by Reagan, who was elected in 1980 but lived out his Presidency and even survived an assassination attempt.

Attempted Assassinations

Andrew Jackson	(1835, by Richard Lawrence, a deranged house painter, in the Capitol Rotunda; first assassination attempt against a president)

Theodore Roosevelt	(after his term, while running as the Bull Moose candidate, in Milwaukee)
Franklin Roosevelt	(while President-elect, by Giuseppe Zangara, in Miami; Chicago Mayor Anton Cermak was killed in the attack)
Harry Truman	(by Puerto Rican nationalists, while living at Blair House during the White House reconstruction)
Gerald Ford	(twice: by Lynette "Squeaky" Fromme and Sara Jane Moore)
Ronald Reagan	(by John Hinckley, at the Washington Hilton)

Presidential Terms and Ages

Longest Serving:	Franklin Roosevelt (12 years, 39 days)
Shortest Serving:	William Henry Harrison (32 days)
Oldest President:	Reagan (age at election 69; 77 when he left office)
Youngest President:	Theodore Roosevelt (42)
Youngest When Elected:	John F. Kennedy (43)
Oldest at Death:	John Adams (90 years, 247 days)
Longest Lived after Term:	Herbert Hoover (31 years, 231 days)

Presidents in the Military

French and Indian War
Washington

American Revolution
Washington
Monroe

War of 1812; Indian Wars
Jackson
W. H. Harrison
Taylor

Black Hawk (Indian) War
Lincoln

Mexican War
Taylor
Pierce
Grant

Civil War
(A. Johnson was given the rank of Brigadier General while Military Governor of Tennessee)
Grant
Hayes
Garfield
B. Harrison
McKinley

Spanish-American War
T. Roosevelt

World War I
Truman
Eisenhower

World War II
Eisenhower
Kennedy (commanded PT-109, sunk by Japanese destroyer)
L. Johnson
Nixon
Ford
Reagan (served in Hollywood as a reserve officer)
Bush (youngest pilot in the Navy; shot down by Japanese)

Public Careers After Presidency

J. Q. Adams:	Congressman from Massachusetts
Tyler:	elected to Confederate Congress
A. Johnson:	elected to U.S. Senate from Tennessee
Taft:	Chief Justice of the United States

Presidential Homes

Washington:	Mount Vernon (Virginia)
Jefferson:	Monticello (Virginia)
Madison:	Montpelier (Virginia)
Monroe:	Ash Lawn (Virginia)
Jackson:	The Hermitage (Tennessee)
Buchanan:	Wheatland (Pennsylvania)
T. Roosevelt:	Sagamore Hill (New York)
F. Roosevelt:	Hyde Park (New York)
Eisenhower:	Gettysburg (Pennsylvania)
Kennedy:	Hyannisport (Massachusetts)
L. Johnson:	LBJ Ranch (Texas)
Nixon:	Casa Pacifica (California)
Reagan:	Rancho Cielo (California)
Bush:	Walker's Point (Kennebunkport, Maine)

Presidential Birthplaces, Birth Dates

State claiming most Presidents: Virginia—8; (followed by Ohio—7; New York—4)
Only states of the 13 original states that have produced no Presidents: Maryland, Delaware
Born on the 4th of July: Coolidge
Died on the 4th of July: Jefferson and John Adams, on the same day (1826); Monroe (1831)
First President born in the independent USA: Van Buren (1784)
First President born in the 19th Century: Pierce (1804)
First President born in the 20th Century: Kennedy (1917)
First President born west of the Mississippi: Hoover
Last President born in a log cabin: Garfield

Colleges Claiming the Most Presidents

Harvard (5: J. Adams, J. Q. Adams, T. Roosevelt, F. Roosevelt, Kennedy)
William and Mary (3: Jefferson, Monroe, Tyler)

Presidential Nicknames

Washington:	Father of His Country, American Fabius, Atlas of America, Sage of Mount Vernon, Surveyor President, Old Fox
J. Adams:	Duke of Braintree, Father of the American Navy, His Rotundity, Old Sink or Swim
Jefferson:	Father of the Declaration of Independence, Father of the University of Virginia, Long Tom, Pen of the Revolution, Red Fox (for his red hair), Sage of Monticello
Madison:	Father of the Constitution, Sage of Montpelier (his home)
Monroe:	Last of the Cocked Hats
J. Q. Adams:	Accidental President, Old Man Eloquent, Second John
Jackson:	Old Hickory, Sage of the Hermitage, Duel Fighter, Mischievous Andy, Land Hero of 1812
Van Buren:	Kinderhook Fox, Little Magician, Red Fox of Kinderhook, Little Van
W. H. Harrison:	Farmer President, Log Cabin President, Old Tippecanoe (for his 1811 Indiana victory over Indians)
Tyler:	Accidental President, His Accidency
Polk:	First Dark Horse, Young Hickory
Taylor:	Old Rough and Ready, Old Buena Vista (his Mexican War victory)
Fillmore:	Accidental President, His Accidency, Wool Carder President
Pierce:	Handsome Frank
Buchanan:	Bachelor President, Sage of Wheatland, Old Buck
Lincoln:	Great Emancipator, Honest Abe, Ancient, Rail Splitter, Sage of Springfield, Illinois Baboon
A. Johnson:	Old Veto, Tennessee Tailor, His Accidency
Grant:	Butcher from Galena (Illinois), Galena Tanner, Uncle Sam, Unconditional Surrender
Hayes:	Fraud President, His Fraudulency (refers to the disputed 1876 election)
Garfield:	Canal Boy, Preacher President, Teacher President
Arthur:	America's First Gentleman, Dude President, His Accidency

Cleveland:	Buffalo Hangman, Buffalo Sheriff, Old Veto, Sage of Princeton
B. Harrison:	Grandfather's Hat (after cartoons showing him dwarfed by Wm. H. Harrison's hat)
McKinley:	Stocking Foot Orator
T. Roosevelt:	TR, Rough Rider, Trust Buster, Bull Moose, Happy Warrior
Wilson:	Schoolmaster in Politics
Harding:	Shadow of Blooming Grove
Coolidge:	Silent Cal, Red
Hoover:	Friend of Helpless Children, Hermit Author of Palo Alto, Man of Great Heart
F. Roosevelt:	FDR, Boss, Dr. New Deal, Sphinx, Squire of Hyde Park, That Man in the White House
Truman:	Give 'Em Hell Harry, Man from Missouri, Man from Independence
Eisenhower:	Ike
Kennedy:	JFK
L. Johnson:	LBJ
Nixon:	Tricky Dick
Carter:	Peanut Farmer, Grits
Reagan:	Great Communicator, Dutch, The Gipper
Bush:	Poppy (his family nickname)

Related Presidents

John Adams and John Quincy Adams (father and son)

William Henry Harrison and Benjamin Harrison (grandfather and grandson)

Franklin Roosevelt and Theodore Roosevelt (cousins)

Other Noted Presidential Relatives

Lincoln:	sons Willie (died in White House), Tad, Robert (later Secretary of War)
Cleveland:	daughter Ruth (candy bar "Baby Ruth" named for her, *not* Babe Ruth)

T. Roosevelt:	daughter Alice (color "Alice Blue" is named for her); son Theodore, WWII general
Taft:	son Senator Robert Taft; grandson also Senator Robert Taft
F. Roosevelt:	sons James (a Congressman), Elliot (mayor of Miami Beach and writer of mystery novels featuring his mother, Eleanor)
Truman:	daughter Margaret (now a mystery writer; Harry got involved in a controversy with a music critic who panned one of her early recitals)
Eisenhower:	son John (Army officer, ambassador to Belgium, military historian); grandson David (historian, married to Julie Nixon)
Kennedy:	brothers Joe (killed in WWII), Robert (JFK's Attorney General, later a U.S. Senator from New York, also assassinated), Ted (U.S. Senator from Massachusetts); daughter Caroline, son John, Jr. (called John-John as a boy) (both lawyers); brothers-in-law Sargent Shriver (first head of the Peace Corps, Democrats' 1972 vice presidential candidate after Sen. Eagleton resigned), Peter Lawford (actor)
L. Johnson:	brother Sam Houston Johnson; daughters Lynda Bird (wife of Senator Charles Robb of Virginia) and Luci Baines
Nixon:	daughters Tricia and Julie (married to Eisenhower's grandson David)
Carter:	mother Lillian (an elderly Peace Corps volunteer); brother Billy ("Billy Beer" was named for him); daughter Amy (political activist), son Chip
Reagan:	son Michael and daughter Maureen by first marriage; son Ronald and daughter Patti by second marriage
Bush:	son Neil (implicated in the savings-and-loan scandal)

Presidential Pets

T. Roosevelt:	his children kept a menagerie, including snakes
Wilson:	sheep used to crop White House lawn to free manpower for WWI

F. Roosevelt:	Fala, a terrier
Kennedy:	Macaroni, daughter Caroline's pony
L. Johnson:	Him and Her, beagles; LBJ outraged the public when he picked up his dogs by their ears
Nixon:	Checkers, spaniel made famous in 1952 speech; King Timahoe (an Irish setter)
Ford:	Liberty, a golden retriever
Reagan:	Lucky, a French sheep dog
Bush:	Millie, a springer spaniel and best-selling author

Presidential Elections and Party Affiliations

1789:	Washington (Federalist)	vs.	(unopposed)
1792:	Washington (Federalist)	vs.	(unopposed)
1796:	Adams (Federalist)	vs.	Thomas Jefferson (Democratic-Republican)
1800:	Jefferson (Democratic-Republican)	vs.	John Adams (Federalist)
1804:	Jefferson (Democratic-Republican)	vs.	Charles Pinckney (Federalist)
1808:	Madison (Democratic-Republican)	vs.	Charles Pinckney (Federalist)
1812:	Madison (Democratic-Republican)	vs.	De Witt Clinton (Federalist)
1816:	Monroe (Democratic-Republican)	vs.	Rufus King
1820:	Monroe (Democratic-Republican)	vs.	(unopposed; 1 vote cast for J. Q. Adams)
1824:	J. Quincy Adams (National Republican)	vs.	Andrew Jackson, Henry Clay, William Crawford (Democrats)

1828: Jackson (Democrat)	vs.	John Quincy Adams (National Republican)
1832: Jackson (Democrat)	vs.	Henry Clay (National Republican)
1836: Van Buren (Democrat)	vs.	William Henry Harrison (Whig)
1840: Wm. H. Harrison (Whig)	vs.	Martin Van Buren (Democrat)
1844: Polk (Democrat)	vs.	Henry Clay (Whig)
1848: Taylor (Whig)	vs.	Lewis Cass (Democrat)
1852: Pierce (Democrat)	vs.	Winfield Scott (Whig) ("Old Fuss & Feathers"; last Whig candidate)
1856: Buchanan (Democrat)	vs.	John C. Fremont (Republican; first nominee of that party)
1860: Lincoln (Republican)	vs.	Stephen Douglas (Northern Democrat), John Breckinridge (Southern Democrat), John Bell (Constitutional Union)
1864: Lincoln (Republican/National Union)	vs.	George McClellan (Democrat; Union general)

1868: Grant (Republican)	vs.	Horatio Seymour (Democrat)
1872: Grant (Republican)	vs.	Horace Greeley (Democrat/Liberal Republican; died before Electoral College met)
1876: Hayes (Republican)	vs.	Samuel J. Tilden (Democrat)
1880: Garfield (Republican)	vs.	Winfield Scott Hancock (Democrat; Union general)
1884: Cleveland (Democrat)	vs.	James G. Blaine (Republican)
1888: B. Harrison (Republican)	vs.	Grover Cleveland (Democrat)
1892: Cleveland (Democrat)	vs.	Benjamin Harrison (Republican); James Weaver (Populist)
1896: McKinley (Republican)	vs.	William Jennings Bryan (Democrat; "Boy Orator of the Platte"; won nomination with "Cross of Gold" speech)
1900: McKinley (Republican)	vs.	William Jennings Bryan (Democrat)
1904: T. Roosevelt (Republican)	vs.	Alton Parker (Democrat)

1908: Taft (Republican)	vs.	William Jennings Bryan (Democrat)
1912: Wilson (Democrat)	vs.	William Howard Taft (Republican), T. Roosevelt (Progressive—"Bull Moose")
1916: Wilson (Democrat)	vs.	Charles Evans Hughes (Republican; later Chief Justice)
1920: Harding (Republican)	vs.	James Cox & F. Roosevelt (Democrat)
1924: Coolidge (Republican)	vs.	John W. Davis (Democrat)
1928: Hoover (Republican)	vs.	Al Smith (Democrat; 1st Catholic nominee)
1932: F. Roosevelt (Democrat)	vs.	Herbert Hoover (Republican)
1936: F. Roosevelt (Democrat)	vs.	Alf Landon (Republican; Governor of Kansas)
1940: F. Roosevelt (Democrat)	vs.	Wendell Willkie (Republican)
1944: F. Roosevelt (Democrat)	vs.	Thomas E. Dewey (Republican; "Gangbuster" as NY district attorney; Governor of New York)
1948: Truman & Barkley (Democrat)	vs.	Thomas E. Dewey & Earl Warren (Re-

		publican); Strom Thurmond (States Rights); Henry Wallace (Progressive)
1952: Eisenhower & Nixon (Republican)	vs.	Adlai Stevenson & John Sparkman (Democrat)
1956: Eisenhower & Nixon (Republican)	vs.	Adlai Stevenson & Estes Kefauver (Democrat)
1960: Kennedy & Johnson (Democrat)	vs.	Richard Nixon & Henry Cabot Lodge (Republican)
1964: Johnson & Humphrey (Democrat)	vs.	Barry Goldwater & William Miller (Republican)
1968: Nixon & Agnew (Republican)	vs.	Hubert Humphrey & Edmund Muskie (Democrat); George C. Wallace & Curtis Lemay (American Independent)
1972: Nixon & Agnew (Republican)	vs.	George McGovern & Sargent Shriver (replacing Thomas Eagleton, who resigned) (Democrat)
1976: Carter & Mondale (Democrat)	vs.	Gerald Ford &

		Robert Dole (Republican)
1980: Reagan & Bush (Republican)	vs.	Jimmy Carter & Walter Mondale (Democrat); John Anderson & Patrick Lucey (Independent)
1984: Reagan & Bush (Republican)	vs.	Walter Mondale & Geraldine Ferraro (Democrat)
1988: Bush & Quayle (Republican)	vs.	Michael Dukakis & Lloyd Bentsen (Democrat)

Party Affiliation

Republican:	18
Democrat:	13 (Cleveland counts twice, as both the 22d and 24th President)
Whig:	4
Democratic Republican:	4
Federalist:	2
National Republican:	1

Presidents Who Ran Unopposed

Washington	(1789, 1792)
Monroe	(1820; 1 Elector cast a vote for John Quincy Adams, to preserve for Washington the only totally unanimous vote)

*Presidents Defeated for Reelection**

J. Adams	B. Harrison
J. Q. Adams	Taft
Van Buren	Hoover
Cleveland	Carter

*(**Note:** Ford was defeated for a *second term* in 1976, but not for "reelection" since he had not been elected President or Vice President. He was appointed Vice President after Agnew's resignation and became President upon Nixon's resignation.)

Presidential Election Re-matches

Adams vs. Jefferson (1796, 1800)
Cleveland vs. B. Harrison (1888, 1892)
McKinley vs. Bryan (1896, 1900)
Eisenhower vs. Stevenson (1952, 1956)

Major Party Candidates Who Lost More Than Once

Three-time Losers	*Two-time Losers*
Clay (1824, 1832, 1844)	Pinckney (1804, 1808)
Bryan (1896, 1900, 1908)	Dewey (1944, 1948)
	Stevenson (1952, 1956)

Presidential Conventions

City to host most conventions: Chicago (24)
Greatest number of ballots: Democrats, 1924 (103 ballots)
First city to host convention: Baltimore (1831)

Major Third-Party Candidates

1860: Bell (Constitutional Union Party)
1892: Weaver (Populist)
1912: Theodore Roosevelt (Progressive or "Bull Moose")
1924: La Follette (Progressive)
1948: Henry Wallace (Progressive); Thurmond (States' Rights)
1968: George Wallace (American Independent Party)
1980: Anderson (Independent)

Elections Not Settled by Electoral College

(The Constitution requires that a candidate receive a majority of electoral votes; if no one does, the House of Representatives elects the President, each state having one vote, and the Senate elects the Vice President.)

1800: Jefferson elected by House of Representatives
1824: J. Q. Adams elected by House of Representatives
1876: Hayes elected by Congressional Committee

Other Election Facts

Total number of electoral votes: 538 (= 435 House seats; 100 Senators; 3 for Washington, D.C.)
Number of electoral votes needed to win: 270
Minimum number of states needed for 270 electoral votes: 12
State with most electoral votes: California (54)
Minimum electoral votes per state: 3 (7 States: Alaska, Delaware, Montana, North Dakota, South Dakota, Vermont, Wyoming; 1 non-State: Washington, D.C.)
Candidate who won most electoral votes: Reagan, 525 (1984)
Candidate with more popular votes but fewer electoral votes: Cleveland (vs. B. Harrison, 1888)
Only election featuring incumbent President vs. incumbent Vice President: 1800 (J. Adams vs. Jefferson)

The Vice Presidents

President	Vice President
Washington	**1.** John Adams (2 terms)
J. Adams	**2.** Thomas Jefferson
Jefferson	**3.** Aaron Burr
	4. George Clinton
Madison	George Clinton
	5. Elbridge Gerry ("Gerrymander," politically distorting election districts named for him)
Monroe	**6.** Daniel Tompkins (2 terms)

J. Q. Adams	**7.** John C. Calhoun
Jackson	John C. Calhoun (resigned)
	8. Martin Van Buren
Van Buren	**9.** Richard Johnson (allegedly killed Shawnee Chief Tecumseh; ran on the slogan: "Rumpsey dumpsey, rumpsey dumpsey; Colonel Johnson killed Tecumseh.")
Wm. H. Harrison	**10.** John Tyler
Tyler	(none)
Polk	**11.** George M. Dallas (Dallas, Texas, was named for him)
Taylor	**12.** Millard Fillmore
Fillmore	(none)
Pierce	**13.** William Rufus King (took oath in Cuba; died before returning to United States)
Buchanan	**14.** John C. Breckinridge (youngest Vice President)
Lincoln	**15.** Hannibal Hamlin
	16. Andrew Johnson
Andrew Johnson	(none)
Grant	**17.** Schuyler Colfax
	18. Henry Wilson (name at birth was Jeremiah Colbaith)
Hayes	**19.** William A. Wheeler
Garfield	**20.** Chester Alan Arthur
Arthur	(none)
Cleveland	**21.** Thomas A. Hendricks
B. Harrison	**22.** Levi P. Morton (oldest Vice President)
Cleveland	**23.** Adlai E. Stevenson (grandfather of Adlai Stevenson, the Democratic presidential nominee in 1952 and 1956)
McKinley	**24.** Garrett A. Hobart
McKinley	**25.** T. Roosevelt
T. Roosevelt	(none)
	26. Charles W. Fairbanks (Fairbanks, Alaska, was named for him)
Taft	**27.** James S. Sherman (known as "Sunny Jim")
Wilson	**28.** Thomas R. Marshall (2 terms) (source of: "What this country needs is a good five-cent cigar.")

Harding	**29.** Calvin Coolidge
Coolidge	(none)
	30. Charles G. Dawes (wrote the music for the song "It's All in the Game," a hit in 1958)
Hoover	**31.** Charles Curtis
F. Roosevelt	**32.** John Nance Garner (2 terms)
	33. Henry A. Wallace (in 1948, ran for President on Progressive Party)
	34. Harry S Truman
Truman	(none)
	35. Alben W. Barkley (known as "The Veep")
Eisenhower	**36.** Richard M. Nixon (2 terms)
Kennedy	**37.** Lyndon Johnson
L. Johnson	(none) (1964 was the last full year in which there was no Vice President)
	38. Hubert Humphrey
Nixon	**39.** Spiro Agnew (elected to 2 terms; resigned 1973)
	40. Gerald Ford (first Vice President appointed under the 25th Amendment)
Ford	**41.** Nelson Rockefeller (second Vice President appointed under the 25th Amendment)
Carter	**42.** Walter Mondale
Reagan	**43.** George Bush (2 terms)
Bush	**44.** (James Danforth) Dan Quayle

Facts About Vice Presidents

VPs serving under 2 different Presidents:
Clinton (Jefferson and Madison)
Calhoun (J. Q. Adams and Jackson)

VPs who resigned: Calhoun, Agnew

VPs who were appointed to office: Ford, Rockefeller

Oldest VP: Levi Morton (75, VP to B. Harrison)

Youngest VP: John Breckinridge (36, VP to Buchanan)

VPs who ran successfully for President: Adams (1796), Jefferson (1800), Van Buren (1836), Bush (1988)

Incumbent VPs who lost for President: Breckinridge (1860), Nixon (1960), Humphrey (1968)

Only incumbent VP to defeat incumbent President: Jefferson (over Adams, 1800)
Major cities named for VP's:
Dallas, Texas (George Dallas, Polk's VP)
Fairbanks, Alaska (Charles Fairbanks, T. Roosevelt's VP)
Shortest term as VP: Tyler (32 days)
State producing the most VPs: New York (8)
Only VP of the Confederacy: Alexander Stephens (of Georgia)

Quiz 1: THE PRESIDENTS OF THE UNITED STATES

Clues:

1. He was the only man to serve non-consecutive terms as President.
2. This taciturn Yankee really was born on the 4th of July.
3. This President never lived in the White House.
4. The only President never to win a national election for President or Vice President.
5. The last President in office when the United States formally declared war.
6. Lincoln was nominated at the Wigwam, in the city that has hosted the most conventions.
7. Jefferson, Monroe and Tyler were all alumni of this college in their home state.
8. The only incumbent Vice President to defeat the incumbent President.
9. The number of Presidents with six-letter first names beginning with "G."
10. He was called "The Galena Tanner."

Answers:

1. Who is Grover Cleveland?
2. Who is Calvin Coolidge?
3. Who is George Washington?
4. Who is Gerald Ford?
5. Who is Franklin Roosevelt (1941)?
6. What is Chicago?
7. What is William and Mary?
8. Who is Jefferson (defeated John Adams, 1800)?
9. What is 4 (Washington, Cleveland, Ford, Bush)?
10. Who is Ulysses S. Grant?

CHAPTER 2

The United States

After the Presidents, facts about the United States and each individual state are another sure bet for virtually each **Jeopardy!** game. Again, there's a lot of information here. There are some things that are probably not worth studying: state birds, flags, mottoes. It's not that these topics don't come up; they do. But the more obscure facts are usually phrased in such a way that the answer is more or less hinted at in the clue. If your capacity for memorization is unlimited, go for it!

All About the States

THE 50 STATES

State (Abbrev.)	Capital	Largest City	Nickname
Alabama (AL)	Montgomery	Birmingham	Heart of Dixie, Camelia State
Alaska (AK)	Juneau	Anchorage	Last Frontier
Arizona (AZ)	Phoenix	Phoenix	Grand Canyon State

State (Abbrev.)	Capital	Largest City	Nickname
Arkansas (AR)	Little Rock	Little Rock	Land of Opportunity
California (CA)	Sacramento	Los Angeles	Golden State
Colorado (CO)	Denver	Denver	Centennial State
Connecticut (CT)	Hartford	Bridgeport	Constitution State, Nutmeg State
Delaware (DE)	Dover	Wilmington	First State, Diamond State
Florida (FL)	Tallahassee	Jacksonville	Sunshine State
Georgia (GA)	Atlanta	Atlanta	Peach State, Empire State of the South
Hawaii (HI)	Honolulu	Honolulu	Aloha State
Idaho (ID)	Boise	Boise	Gem State
Illinois (IL)	Springfield	Chicago	Prairie State
Indiana (IN)	Indianapolis	Indianapolis	Hoosier State
Iowa (IA)	Des Moines	Des Moines	Hawkeye State
Kansas (KS)	Topeka	Wichita	Sunflower State
Kentucky (KY)	Frankfort	Louisville	Bluegrass State
Louisiana (LA)	Baton Rouge	New Orleans	Pelican State
Maine (ME)	Augusta	Portland	Pine Tree State
Maryland (MD)	Annapolis	Baltimore	Old Line State, Free State
Massachusetts (MA)	Boston	Boston	Bay State, Old Colony
Michigan (MI)	Lansing	Detroit	Great Lake State, Wolverine State
Minnesota (MN)	St. Paul	Minneapolis	North Star State, Gopher State

State (Abbrev.)	Capital	Largest City	Nickname
Mississippi (MS)	Jackson	Jackson	Magnolia State
Missouri (MO)	Jefferson City	Kansas City	Show Me State
Montana (MT)	Helena	Billings	Treasure State
Nebraska (NE)	Lincoln	Omaha	Cornhusker State
Nevada (NV)	Carson City	Las Vegas	Sagebrush State, Battle Born State, Silver State
New Hampshire (NH)	Concord	Manchester	Granite State
New Jersey (NJ)	Trenton	Newark	Garden State
New Mexico (NM)	Santa Fe	Albuquerque	Land of Enchantment
New York (NY)	Albany	New York	Empire State
North Carolina (NC)	Raleigh	Charlotte	Tarheel State, Old North State
North Dakota (ND)	Bismarck	Fargo	Peace Garden State
Ohio (OH)	Columbus	Columbus	Buckeye State
Oklahoma (OK)	Oklahoma City	Oklahoma City	Sooner State
Oregon (OR)	Salem	Portland	Beaver State
Rhode Island (RI)	Providence	Providence	Ocean State
Pennsylvania (PA)	Harrisburg	Philadelphia	Keystone State
South Carolina (SC)	Columbia	Columbia	Palmetto State
South Dakota (SD)	Pierre	Sioux Falls	Coyote State, Sunshine State
Tennessee (TN)	Nashville	Memphis	Volunteer State
Texas (TX)	Austin	Houston	Lone Star State
Utah (UT)	Salt Lake City	Salt Lake City	Beehive State
Vermont (VT)	Montpelier	Burlington	Green Mountain State
Virginia (VA)	Richmond	Virginia Beach	Old Dominion

State (Abbrev.)	Capital	Largest City	Nickname
Washington (WA)	Olympia	Seattle	Evergreen State
West Virginia (WV)	Charleston	Charleston	Mountain State
Wisconsin (WI)	Madison	Milwaukee	Badger State
Wyoming (WY)	Cheyenne	Casper	Equality State

State Nicknames

Connecticut: *Nutmeg State* is said to refer to the fraudulent practice of Connecticut merchants of selling scented sawdust as "nutmeg"

Colorado: *Centennial State* refers to Colorado's admission to the Union in 1876, the U.S. centennial

Nevada: *Battle Born State* refers to its admission during the Civil War

North Carolina: *Tarheel* was the way in which N.C. troops were said to hold their lines during the Civil War

Oklahoma: *Sooner State* refers to those who sneaked into the Indian Territory "sooner" than the law allowed

Wyoming: *Equality State* refers to its role as the first state to allow women to vote

State Names

Most letters: Massachusetts, North Carolina and South Carolina
Least letters: Iowa, Ohio, Utah
Only name ending in 3 vowels: Hawaii
Only name ending in 3 consonants: Massachusetts
State names using only 1 of the 5 vowels: Alabama, Alaska, Arkansas, Kansas, Mississippi, New Jersey, Tennessee
Longest official state name: Rhode Island and Providence Plantations
Only single-syllable state name: Maine

States Named for People

Delaware: Lord De La Warr
Georgia: King George II of Britain
Louisiana: King Louis XIV of France

Maryland:	Queen Henrietta Maria, wife of King Charles I of England
New York:	Duke of York, later James II
North and South Carolina:	King Charles I of England
Pennsylvania:	William Penn
Virginia (and West Virginia):	Queen Elizabeth I (The Virgin Queen)
Washington:	George Washington

(Note: Of the states named for people, Louisiana and Washington are the only ones that were not one of the 13 colonies.)

States That Are Commonwealths

Kentucky, Massachusetts, Pennsylvania, Virginia

Only State to Secede from Another State

West Virginia (seceded from Virginia, 1863, during the Civil War)

States That Seceded to Form the Confederacy

Alabama, Arkansas, Florida, Georgia, Louisiana, Mississippi, North Carolina, South Carolina, Tennessee, Texas, Virginia

Only State with a Unicameral Legislature

Nebraska (members are called Senators)

Only State Whose Governor Has No Veto Power

North Carolina

States That Have Been Independent Countries

Vermont (1777–91)
Texas (1836–45)
Hawaii (1894–98)

(Note: The "California Republic," commemorated on the state's flag, lasted only three weeks. The declaration of the republic was a provocative act by a group of settlers seeking annexation by the United States, and did not constitute a real republic.)

World's First Written Constitution

Connecticut (Fundamental Orders, 1639)

States Whose Governors Became President

California:	Reagan
Georgia:	Carter
Massachusetts:	Coolidge
New Jersey:	Wilson
New York:	Van Buren, Cleveland, T. Roosevelt, F. Roosevelt
Ohio:	McKinley
Tennessee:	Polk, A. Johnson

(Taft served as Governor of the Philippines, then a U.S. colony)

State with the Largest Indian Population

Arizona

Can you name the seven state capitals with two-word names? (By the way, their states are virtually all contiguous.) How about the only three-word state capital? Or the only one-word state capital to contain the entire name of the state?

State Capitals

Largest population: Phoenix
Smallest population: Montpelier
Oldest: Santa Fe, New Mexico (founded 1610)
Farthest north (all 50 states): Juneau, Alaska
Farthest north (continental 48 states): Bismarck, N. Dakota
Farthest south (all 50 states): Honolulu, Hawaii
Farthest south (continental 48 states): Austin, Texas
Farthest east (all 50 states): Augusta, Maine

Farthest east (continental 48 states): Augusta, Maine
Farthest west (all 50 states): Honolulu, Hawaii
Farthest west (continental 48 states): Salem, Oregon

Capitals with Two-word Names:

Baton Rouge
Carson City
Des Moines
Jefferson City
Little Rock
Oklahoma City
Santa Fe

Capital with Three-word Name:

Salt Lake City

Which four Presidents have state capitals named for them? Which other capitals are named for famous figures?

Capitals Named for Presidents:

Jackson, Mississippi
Jefferson City, Missouri
Lincoln, Nebraska
Madison, Wisconsin

Capitals Named for Other People:

Albany, New York (James II, Duke of York and Albany, later King of England)
Annapolis, Maryland (Queen Anne)
Austin, Texas (Stephen Austin, "The Father of Texas")
Bismarck, North Dakota (Otto von Bismarck)
Carson City, Nevada (Kit Carson)
Columbus, Ohio
Raleigh, North Carolina (Sir Walter Raleigh)
St. Paul, Minnesota

Only One-Word State Capital to Contain the Name of the State: Indianapolis, Indiana

State Capitals That Served As Capitals of the Confederacy

Montgomery, Alabama (February–July 1861)
Richmond, Virginia (July 1861–April 1865)
(Last capital of the Confederacy: Danville, Virginia, April–May 1865)

U.S. Geography

Highest point: Mt. McKinley, Alaska (20,320 feet; called Denali by Native Americans)
Lowest point: Death Valley, California (282 feet below sea level)
Largest state: Alaska
Smallest state: Rhode Island
Most populous state: California
Least populous state: Wyoming
Highest state (average elevation): Colorado
Lowest state: Delaware
Driest state: Nevada (7 inches average rainfall annually)
Only continental state to border only one other state: Maine
Only state with no straight lines in its boundaries: Hawaii
Four Corners: Arizona, Colorado, New Mexico and Utah touch corners.
State with longest coastline: Alaska (which has more than half of the total U.S. seacoast)
Longest river: Mississippi River
States with land below sea level:
- California
- Louisiana

Great Lakes: Huron, Ontario, Michigan, Erie, Superior (remember "HOMES")
- Largest: Superior
- Smallest: Ontario
- Only lake entirely in the United States: Michigan

Geographic center:
- 50 States: South Dakota
- 48 States: Kansas

Geographic center of U.S. population: Missouri

U.S. Cities

10 Largest Cities by Population (county names in parentheses)

1. New York (7.3 million) (Bronx; Kings [Brooklyn]; New York [Manhattan]; Queens; Richmond [Staten Island])
2. Los Angeles (3.5 million) (Los Angeles)
3. Chicago (2.8 million) (Cook)
4. Houston (1.7 million) (Harris)
5. Philadelphia (1.6 million) (Philadelphia)
6. San Diego (1.1 million) (San Diego)
7. Detroit (1 million) (Wayne)
8. Dallas (1 million) (Dallas)
9. Phoenix (0.9 million) (Maricopa)
10. San Antonio (0.9 million) (Bexar)

Cities and Their Rivers

Albuquerque: Rio Grande
Atlanta: Chattahoochee
Austin: Colorado
Boston: Charles
Buffalo: Niagara
Chicago: Chicago
Cincinnati: Ohio
Cleveland: Cuyahoga
Dallas: Trinity
Denver: South Platte
Detroit: Detroit
El Paso: Rio Grande
Hartford: Connecticut
Houston: Houston Ship Channel
Jacksonville: St. Johns
Little Rock: Arkansas
Memphis: Mississippi
Minneapolis: Mississippi
Miami: Miami
New Haven: Quinnipiac

New Orleans:	Mississippi
New York:	East, Harlem, Hudson
Oklahoma City:	N. Canadian
Omaha:	Missouri
Philadelphia:	Delaware, Schuylkill
Phoenix:	Salt
Pittsburgh:	Allegheny, Monongahela, Ohio
Portland:	Columbia
Richmond:	James
St. Louis:	Mississippi
Salt Lake City:	Jordan
San Antonio:	San Antonio
Tulsa:	Arkansas
Washington:	Potomac

Cities and Airports

Your luggage may never disappear at any of these airports, but it's still good to know where they are. We've included the official abbreviation used by each airport as well.

Atlanta:	William B. Hartsfield International (ATL)
Baltimore:	Baltimore Washington International (BWI)
Boston:	Gen. Edward Lawrence Logan International (BOS)
Chicago:	O'Hare International (ORD—originally Orchard Field; world's busiest airport); Midway (MDW)
Cleveland:	Cleveland Hopkins (CLE)
Dallas:	Dallas/Fort Worth Regional (DFW); Love Field (DAL)
Denver:	Stapleton (DEN)
Detroit:	Detroit Metropolitan Wayne County (DTW); City Airport (DET)
Hartford/Springfield:	Bradley International (BDL)
Houston:	Houston International (IAH); William P. Hobby (HOU)
Las Vegas:	McCarran International (LAS)
Los Angeles:	Los Angeles International (LAX)

Milwaukee:	General Mitchell Field (MKE; named for air force pioneer Billy Mitchell)
New Orleans:	New Orleans International (MSY; formerly Moisant Field)
New York:	John F. Kennedy International (JFK; formerly Idlewild); La Guardia (LGA)
Oklahoma City:	Will Rogers World Airport (OKC)
Phoenix	Phoenix Sky Harbor International (PHX)
St. Louis:	St. Louis-Lambert International (STL)
San Diego:	San Diego International (SAN: also called Lindbergh Field, for famed aviator Charles Lindbergh)
San Francisco:	San Francisco International (SFO)
Washington:	National (DCA); Dulles International (IAD; named for Secretary of State John Foster Dulles)

Oldest Permanent City in the United States

St. Augustine, Florida (founded 1565)

City Nicknames

Boston:	The Hub of the Universe, Beantown
Brooklyn:	City of Churches
Chicago:	City That Works, Windy City, City of Broad Shoulders; Chi-town, Second City
Cincinnati:	Queen City
Dallas:	Big D
Denver:	Mile High City
Detroit:	Motown, Motor City
Flint:	Vehicle City
Los Angeles:	City of Angels
Nashville:	Music City, USA
New Orleans:	Crescent City, Big Easy
New York:	Big Apple
Philadelphia:	City of Brotherly Love
Pittsburgh:	Iron City
San Francisco:	The City by the Bay, Baghdad by the Bay, Frisco (a nickname that residents apparently hate)

U.S. Geographic Position

Finally, some of the most common questions about U.S. geography deal with these "unknown" facts. If you don't believe us, check a map:

- Reno, Nevada is *west* of Los Angeles.
- The northernmost point in the continental United States is in Minnesota, not Maine.
- Most of South America lies far east of the United States. If you fly due south from Miami, you just graze the west coast of Peru. Fly due south from Detroit and you miss South America entirely.
- The southernmost point in Hawaii is about as far south as Mexico City.
- All of England is north of the continental United States. Detroit lies on the same latitude as Rome. Cairo is as far north as New Orleans. Philadelphia and Beijing are near the same latitude.

Quiz 2:
THE UNITED STATES

Clues:

1. The four states that touch at Four Corners in the southwest.
2. In a failed bid for German investments, North Dakota named its capital for him.
3. The *two* Sunshine States.
4. The only Commonwealth not one of the original thirteen states.
5. The Confederate capital before Richmond.
6. Largest city in America named for a bird.
7. The only Great Lake entirely within the United States.
8. The world's busiest airport used to be called Orchard Field.
9. America's Jordan River flows into this body of water, not the Dead Sea.
10. This state's nickname celebrates women's suffrage.

Answers:

1. What are Colorado, Utah, Arizona, New Mexico?
2. Who is Bismarck?
3. What are Florida, South Dakota?
4. What is Kentucky?
5. What is Montgomery, Alabama?
6. What is Phoenix?
7. What is Lake Michigan?
8. What is O'Hare, Chicago (symbol ORD)?
9. What is the Great Salt Lake?
10. Why is Wyoming the Equality State?

CHAPTER 3

World Geography

It's time to expand your horizons. It's a big world out there, and that means there are a lot of other facts about geography that **Jeopardy!** draws on regularly for its answers.

The Continents

CONTINENTAL SUPERLATIVES

	Highest Mountain	Longest River	Largest Nation	Most Populous	Largest City
Antarctica	Vinson Massif	(none)	(none)	(none)	(none)
Africa	Kilimanjaro (Tanzania)	Nile	Sudan	Nigeria	Cairo, Egypt
Asia	Everest (Nepal)	Chiang Jiang (Yangtze)	USSR	China	Tokyo-Yokohama, Japan

	Highest Mountain	Longest River	Largest Nation	Most Populous	Largest City
Australia	Kosciusko	Murray-Darling	Australia	Australia	Sydney
Europe	Mt. Blanc (France/Italy)	Danube	USSR	USSR	Moscow
N. America	McKinley (USA)	Mississippi	Canada	United States	Mexico City
S. America	Aconcagua (Argentina/Chile)	Amazon	Brazil	Brazil	Sao Paolo, Brazil

Landlocked Nations

Africa (14): Botswana, Burkina Faso, Burundi, Central African Republic, Chad, Lesotho, Malawi, Mali, Niger, Rwanda, Swaziland, Uganda, Zambia, Zimbabwe
Asia (5): Afghanistan, Bhutan, Laos, Mongolia, Nepal
Australia: (none)
Europe (8): Andorra, Austria, Czechoslovakia, Hungary, Liechtenstein, Luxembourg, San Marino, Switzerland
North America: (*none*—North America is the only *multination* continent with no landlocked countries; El Salvador is the only North American nation with no Atlantic/Caribbean coast; Belize is the only one with no Pacific coast)
South America (2): Bolivia, Paraguay

Nations Spanning More Than One Continent

Egypt: Africa and Asia
U.S.S.R: Europe and Asia
Turkey: Europe and Asia

Geographic Features:

Largest peninsula:	Arabia
Largest island:	Greenland (known to its inhabitants as Kalaallit Nunaat)
Largest atoll:	Kwajalein (Republic of the Marshall Islands)
Largest reef:	Great Barrier Reef (Australia)
Largest archipelago:	Indonesia
Largest delta:	Ganges River (India, Bangladesh)
Largest gorge:	Grand Canyon (U.S.)
Largest swamp:	Mato Grosso (Brazil)
Largest gulf:	Gulf of Mexico
Largest bay:	Hudson Bay (Canada)
Largest freshwater lake:	Lake Superior (Canada, U.S.)
Deepest lake:	Lake Baikal (USSR; 5,712 feet deep)
Largest underground lake:	Tennessee
Deepest cave:	France
Highest point on Earth:	Mt. Everest (29,028 feet)
Deepest point on Earth:	Mariana Trench, Pacific (35,840 feet deep)
Greatest tides:	Bay of Fundy (Canada)
Highest volcano:	Aconcagua (Argentina, Chile)
Largest active volcano:	Mauna Loa (Hawaii)
Largest desert:	Sahara (North Africa)
Continents with no desert:	Europe, Antarctica

Countries on the Equator

Ecuador, Colombia, Brazil, Sao Tome and Principe, Gabon, Congo, Zaire, Uganda, Kenya, Somalia, Indonesia

Continents the Equator Passes Through

South America, Africa

Capital Cities:

Africa

Algeria:	Algiers	Benin:	Porto-Novo
Angola:	Luanda	Botswana:	Gaborone

Africa

Burkina Faso:	Ouagadougou
Burundi:	Bujumbura
Cameroon:	Yaounde
Cape Verde:	Praia
Central African Republic:	Bangui
Chad:	N'djamena
Comoros:	Moroni
Congo:	Brazzaville
Cote d'Ivoire:	Abidjan
Djibouti:	Djibouti
Egypt:	Cairo
Ethiopia:	Addis Ababa
Gabon:	Libreville
The Gambia:	Banjul (formerly Bathhurst)
Ghana:	Accra
Guinea:	Conakry
Guinea-Bissau:	Bissau
Kenya:	Nairobi
Liberia:	Monrovia (named for James Monroe)
Lesotho:	Maseru
Libya:	Tripoli
Madagascar:	Antananarivo (formerly Tananarive)
Malawi:	Lilongwe
Mali:	Bamako
Mauritania:	Nouakchott
Mauritius:	Port Louis
Morocco:	Rabat
Mozambique:	Maputo
Namibia:	Windhoek
Niger:	Niamey
Nigeria:	Lagos
Rwanda:	Kigali
Sao Tome and Principe:	Sao Tome
Senegal:	Dakar
Seychelles:	Victoria
Sierra Leone:	Freetown
Somalia:	Mogadishu
Sudan:	Khartoum
Swaziland:	Mbabane
Tanzania:	Dar-es-Salaam
Togo:	Lome
Tunisia:	Tunis
Uganda:	Kampala
Zaire:	Kinshasa (formerly Leopoldville)
Zambia:	Lusaka
Zimbabwe:	Harare (formerly Salisbury)
South Africa (3 capitals):	Cape Town (legislative) Pretoria (executive) Bloemfontein (judicial)

Asia

Afghanistan:	Kabul
Bahrain:	Manama
Bangladesh:	Dhaka
Bhutan:	Thimphu

Asia

Country	Capital	Country	Capital
Brunei Darussalam:	Bandar Seri Begawan	Maldives:	Male
Burma:*	Rangoon*	Mongolia:	Ulaan Bataar
Cambodia:	Phnom Penh	Nepal:	Kathmandu
China:	Beijing (formerly Peking, Peiping)	Pakistan:	Islamabad
India:	New Delhi	Philippines:	Quezon City (Manila *de facto*)
Indonesia:	Djakarta (formerly Batavia)	Qatar:	Doha
Iran:	Teheran	Saudi Arabia:	Riyadh
Iraq:	Baghdad	Singapore:	Singapore
Israel:	Jerusalem**	Sri Lanka:	Colombo
Japan:	Tokyo	Syria:	Damascus
Jordan:	Amman	Taiwan:	Taipei
N. Korea:	Pyongyang	Thailand:	Bangkok
S. Korea:	Seoul	United Arab Emirates:	Abu Dhabi
Kuwait:	Kuwait City	Vietnam:	Hanoi
Laos:	Vientiane	Yemen:	Sanaa (North Yemen and South Yemen merged in 1990)
Lebanon:	Beirut		
Malaysia:	Kuala Lumpur		

*In 1989 Burma announced it had changed its name to Myanmar, with its capital to be called Yangon.
**Although Israel claims Jerusalem as its capital, most nations continue to recognize Tel Aviv.

Australia and Pacific Nations†

Country	Capital	Country	Capital
Australia:	Canberra	Nauru:	Yaren
Fiji:	Suva	New Zealand:	Wellington
Kiribati:	Tarawa	Papau New Guinea:	Port Moresby
Micronesia:‡	Pohnpei		

†Note: each of these is an island nation.
‡Micronesia, officially, is the Federated States of Micronesia.

Australia and Pacific Nations

Republic of the Marshall Islands:	Majuro
Solomon Islands:	Honiara
Tonga:	Nuku'alofa
Tuvalu:	Funafuti
Vanuatu:	Vila
Western Samoa:	Apia

Europe

Albania:	Tirana
Andorra:	Andorra la Vella
Austria:	Vienna (Wien to natives)
Belgium:	Brussels (Bruxelles)
Bulgaria:	Sofia
Cyprus:	Nicosia
Czechoslovakia:	Prague (Praha)
Denmark:	Copenhagen (Köbenhavn)
Estonia:	Tallinn
Finland:	Helsinki
France:	Paris
Germany:	Berlin
Greece:	Athens (Athinai)
Hungary:	Budapest
Iceland:	Reykjavik
Ireland:	Dublin (Baile Atha Cliath)
Italy:	Rome (Roma)
Latvia:	Riga
Liechtenstein:	Vaduz
Lithuania:	Vilnius
Luxembourg:	Luxembourg
Malta:	Valletta
Monaco:	Monaco-Ville
Netherlands:	Amsterdam
Norway:	Oslo
Poland:	Warsaw (Warszawa)
Portugal:	Lisbon (Lisboa)
Romania:	Bucharest
Spain:	Madrid
Sweden:	Stockholm
Switzerland:	Bern
Turkey:	Ankara (ancient Angora)
USSR:	Moscow (Moskva)
United Kingdom:	London
Yugoslavia:	Belgrade

North America and Caribbean Nations

Antigua and Barbuda:	St. John's
The Bahamas:	Nassau
Barbados:	Bridgetown
Belize:	Belmopan
Canada:	Ottawa
Costa Rica:	San Jose
Cuba:	Havana

North America and Caribbean Nations

Dominica:	Roseau
Dominican Republic:	Santo Domingo
El Salvador:	San Salvador
Grenada:	St. George's
Guatemala:	Guatemala City
Haiti:	Port-au-Prince
Honduras:	Tegucigalpa
Jamaica:	Kingston
Mexico:	Mexico City
Nicaragua:	Managua
Panama:	Panama City
St. Christopher (St. Kitts) and Nevis:	Basseterre
St. Lucia:	Castries
St. Vincent and the Grenadines:	Kingstown
Trinidad and Tobago:	Port-of-Spain
United States:	Washington, D.C.

South America

Argentina:	Buenos Aires
Bolivia:	Sucre (La Paz *de facto*)
Brazil:	Brasilia
Colombia:	Bogota
Chile:	Santiago
Ecuador:	Quito
Guyana:	Georgetown
Paraguay:	Asuncion
Peru:	Lima
Suriname:	Paramaribo
Uruguay:	Montevideo
Venezuela:	Caracas

Permanent Members of the United Nations Security Council

Britain, China, France, United States, Soviet Union

Countries That Do Not Belong to the United Nations

Andorra
Kiribati
Monaco
Nauru
San Marino
Switzerland
Taiwan
Tonga
Tuvalu
Vatican City

Famous Official Buildings

OFFICIAL RESIDENCES

Argentina: Casa Rosada
Canada: 24 Sussex Drive
Chile: La Moneda Palace
France: Elysée Palace
Italy: Quirinale Palace
South Korea: Blue House
United Kingdom: 10 Downing Street; Chequers (leisure)
United States: White House, 1600 Pennsylvania Ave; Camp David (leisure)

FOREIGN POLICY CENTERS

France: Quai D'Orsay
Ottoman Empire: Sublime Porte
United Kingdom: Whitehall (entire government area; Foreign Office is in Downing Street)
United States: Foggy Bottom

Colonial Empires

Lots of places around the globe once belonged to someone else, especially during the heyday of colonial empires. Here is who ruled what, listed by current name with the colonial name noted afterward.

Africa

Belgium: Burundi; Rwanda (*Ruanda*); Zaire (*Belgian Congo*)

Britain: Botswana (*Bechuanaland*); Egypt (a protectorate); Gambia; Ghana; Kenya; Lesotho (*Basutoland*); Malawi (*Nyasaland*); Nigeria; Sierra Leone; South Africa (in part from the Netherlands); Sudan (*Anglo-Egyptian Sudan*); Swaziland; Tanzania (*Tanganyika and Zanzibar*); Uganda; Zambia (*N. Rhodesia*); Zimbabwe (*S. Rhodesia*)

France: Algeria; Benin (*formerly Togo*); Burkina Faso (*FWA*)*; Cameroon (*FEQ; from Germany*)*; Central African Republic (*FEQ*)*; Chad (*FEQ*)*; Comoros; Congo (*FEQ*)*; Cote d'Ivoire (*FWA*)*; Djibouti (*French Somaliland*)*; Gabon (*FEQ*)*; Guinea (*FWA*)*;

Madagascar; Mali (*FWA*)*; Morocco; Niger (*FWA*)*; Senegal (*FWA*)*; Togo; Tunisia
*(*FEQ* = French Equatorial Africa; *FWA* = French West Africa)

Germany: Cameroon; Namibia (*German Southwest Africa*); Tanganyika (*German East Africa*); Togo

Italy: Ethiopia (*during WWII*); Libya; Somalia

Netherlands: South Africa (*Cape Colony, 1652–1814*)

Portugal: Angola; Cape Verde; Guinea-Bissau (*Portuguese Guinea*); Mozambique; Sao Tome and Principe

South Africa: Namibia (*League of Nations mandate from Germany*)

Spain: Rio de Oro (*later Spanish Sahara, now annexed by Morocco*); Equatorial Guinea (*Rio Muni*)

Asia

Britain: Bangladesh (*part of India*); Brunei; Burma (now called Myanmar); Hong Kong (still a Crown Colony; reverts to China, 1997); India; Israel (*part of the mandate Palestine*); Jordan (*part of the mandate Transjordan*); Malaysia (*made up of the colonies Malaya, N. Borneo, Sarawak*); Pakistan (*part of India*); Singapore; Sri Lanka (*Ceylon*); (South) Yemen (*Aden, Federation of S. Arabia*)

France: Cambodia (*part of French Indochina*); Laos (*part of French Indochina*); Lebanon; Syria; Vietnam (*part of French Indochina*)

Japan: Korea (*from Russia, 1905; lost 1945*); Taiwan (*from China, 1894; lost 1945*)

Netherlands: Indonesia (*Netherlands East Indies*)

Portugal: East Timor (seized by Indonesia, 1975); Goa (seized by India, 1961); Macao (reverts to China, 1997)

Spain: Philippines (*lost to United States, 1898*)

United States: Philippines (*from Spain, 1898; independent, 1945*)

Australia and Pacific

Britain: Australia; Fiji; New Zealand

United States: Guam; American Samoa

Europe

Britain: Gibraltar (*from Spain, 1714; still a colony*); Ireland; Malta

North America and the Caribbean

Britain: Antigua and Barbuda; The Bahamas; Barbados; Belize (*British Honduras*); Canada (*Quebec from France, 1763*); Grenada; Jamaica; St. Christopher and Nevis; St. Lucia; St. Vincent and the Grenadines; Trinidad and Tobago; United States

Denmark: Virgin Islands (*sold to the United States, 1917*)

France: Canada (*Quebec; lost to Britain, 1763*); Guadaloupe; Haiti; Louisiana Territory (*sold to the United States, 1803*); Martinique; St. Martin*

Netherlands: New York (*New Netherlands*); St. Maarten*

Russia: Alaska (*Russian America*)

Spain: Costa Rica; Cuba; Dominican Republic; El Salvador; Honduras; Mexico; Nicaragua; Panama; Puerto Rico (*lost to the United States, 1898*)

Sweden: Delaware (*Ft. Christiana*)

United States: Puerto Rico (*from Spain, 1898*); Virgin Islands (*bought from Denmark, 1917*)

*The Dutch/French colony of St. Maarten/St. Martin is the smallest island in the world owned by more than one nation.

South America

Britain: Guyana (*British Guiana*); River Plate (now part of Argentina)

France: French Guiana (an "overseas department" of France)

Netherlands: Suriname (*Dutch Guiana*)

Portugal: Brazil; Uruguay (1680–1778; 1817–25)

Spain: Argentina; Bolivia; Chile; Colombia (*New Granada*); Paraguay; Peru; Uruguay (1778–1811); Venezuela

Remaining Colonies

This can be controversial. For example, Puerto Rico is a self-governing Commonwealth, whose citizens are U.S. citizens; it is not considered a colony, nor is Guam. France calls its dependencies "overseas departments"; they elect Deputies to the national legislature in Paris.

Britain: Anguilla; Bermuda; Cayman Islands; Falkland Islands; Gibraltar; Hong Kong (reverts to China, 1997); Montserrat; Pitcairn Island (of *Mutiny on the Bounty* fame); St. Helena (Napoleon's final exile); Turks and Caicos Islands

Denmark: Greenland

France: Mayotte (between Madagascar and Africa); New Caledonia; Polynesia; St. Martin

Netherlands: Aruba; Netherlands Antilles; St. Maarten

Portugal: Macao (reverts to China, 1997)

United States: American Samoa; Caroline Islands; Mariana Island; Virgin Islands

Countries Named for People

Bolivia: Simon Bolivar
Colombia: Christopher Columbus
Mauritius: Maurice of Nassau (Dutch head of state at time of discovery)
Philippines: King Philip II of Spain
Republic of the Marshall Islands: Capt. Marshall, their discoverer
St. Kitts: St. Christopher
St. Lucia
San Marino: St. Martin
Sao Tome: St. Thomas
St. Vincent
Saudi Arabia: for the Saud family
Solomon Islands: King Solomon
United States of America: Amerigo Vespucci

Countries That Have Changed Names in the 20th Century

Benin: Dahomey
Burkina Faso: Upper Volta

Cambodia: Kampuchea (briefly)
Central African Republic: Central African Empire (briefly)
Cote d'Ivoire: Ivory Coast
Egypt: formerly part of the United Arab Republic, with Syria
Iran: Persia
Myanmar: Burma
Sri Lanka: Ceylon
Syria: formerly part of the United Arab Republic, with Egypt
Thailand: Siam
Turkey: Ottoman Empire
USSR: Russia
Zaire: Congo

Countries' Names in Their Own Tongue

Belgie/Belgique: Belgium (in its 2 official languages, Flemish and French, spoken respectively by Flemings and Walloons)
Chosen: Korea
Deutschland: Germany
Druk-yul: Bhutan
Eire: Ireland
Ellas: Greece
Espana: Spain
Island: Iceland
Kalaallit Nunaat: Greenland
Kypriaki/Kibris: Cyprus
al-Maghrib: Morocco
Magyar: Hungary
Misr: Egypt
Nippon: Japan
Norge: Norway
Osterreich: Austria
Schweiz, Suisse, Suizzera, Suizra: Switzerland (which has 4 official languages: German, French, Italian and Romansch)
Shqiperia: Albania
Suomi: Finland
Sverige: Sweden

Oceans

Arctic Ocean
Atlantic Ocean
Indian Ocean
Pacific Ocean

Seas

What are the three seas named for colors? Sail on.

Andaman Sea (s. of Burma)
Arabian Sea
Arafura Sea (Australia/New Guinea)
Aral Sea (USSR—a landlocked sea)
Sea of Azov (USSR, e. of Crimea)
Baltic Sea (Scandinavia/USSR)
Banda Sea (Indonesia)
Barents Sea (n. of Norway)
Beaufort Sea (n. of Canada)
Bellinghausen Sea (Antarctica)
Bering Sea (Alaska/Siberia)
Black Sea (Turkey/USSR)
Caribbean Sea
Caspian Sea (Iran/USSR—a landlocked sea)
Celebes Sea (Indonesia/Philippines)
Chukchi Sea (n. of USSR)
Coral Sea (e. of Australia)
East China Sea
East Siberian Sea (n.e. of Siberia)
Flores Sea (Indonesia)
Greenland Sea
Sea of Japan
Java Sea (Indonesia)
Kara Sea (n. of USSR)
Laptev Sea (n. of USSR)
Mediterranean Sea
Mollucca Sea (Indonesia)
North Sea
Norwegian Sea
Sea of Okhotsk (e. of Siberia)
Philippine Sea
Red Sea
Ross Sea (Antarctica)
Scotia Sea (Falkland Islands)
South China Sea
Sulu Sea (southeast of Philippines)
Tasman Sea (s.e. of Australia)
Timor Sea (n.e. of Australia)
Weddell Sea (Antarctica)
Yellow Sea (e. of China)

Seas Named for People

Barents: Willem Barents (Dutch)
Beaufort: Sir Francis Beaufort (British)

Bellinghausen: Fabian Bellinghausen (Russian; first to circumnavigate Antarctica)
Bering: Vitus Bering (Danish)
Laptev: Kharion and Dmitry Laptev (Russian; brothers)
Ross: James Clark Ross (British)
Philippine: King Philip of Spain
Tasman: Abel Tasman (Dutch)
Weddell: James Weddell (British)

World Cities

A lot of this may seem obscure but, believe it or not, most of these facts have appeared on **Jeopardy!** at one time or another. Also, this is just the sort of information that is often provided to flesh out a **Jeopardy!** question, giving you just that much of an advantage if it looks at all familiar. (Here's a sample: "Paris is on the Seine, but Belgium's capital is on the Senne.")

Cities Whose Names Have Changed

North and South America

New York:	New Amsterdam
Mexico City:	Tenochtitlan
Toronto:	Fort York

Africa

Maputo (Mozambique):	Lourenço Marques
Harare (Zimbabwe):	Salisbury
Lubumbashi (Zaire):	Elizabethville
Kinshasa (Zaire):	Leopoldville
N'Djamena (Chad):	Ft. Lamy
Banjul (Gambia):	Bathurst
Antananarivo (Madagascar):	Tananarive

Europe

St. Petersburg:	Leningrad, Petrograd
Gdansk (Poland):	Danzig

Szczecin (Poland):	Stettin
Wroclaw (Poland):	Breslau
Chemnitz (Germany):	Karl-Marx Stadt
Volgograd (USSR):	Stalingrad, Tsaritsyn
Gorki (USSR):	Nizhni Novgorod
Sverdlovsk (USSR):	Ekaterinburg
Oslo:	Christiania

Asia

Ankara:	Angora
Istanbul:	Constantinople, Byzantium
al-Madina (Saudi Arabia):	Yathrib
Amman:	Philadelphia
Beijing:	Peking, Peiping
Guangzhou:	Canton
Yangon:	Rangoon
Ho Chi Minh City:	Saigon
Djakarta:	Jakarta, Batavia
Tokyo:	Edo

Rivers Running Through Major Cities

Bangkok:	Chao Praya
Belgrade:	Danube
Berlin:	Spree
Brussels:	Senne
Buenos Aires:	Rio de la Plata
Bucharest:	Dombovita
Budapest:	Danube
Cairo:	Nile
Calcutta:	Hooghly
Canberra:	Molonglo
Damascus:	Barada
Delhi:	Yamuna
Florence:	Arno
Frankfurt:	Main
Kiev:	Dniepr
Khartoum:	Nile (confluence Blue and White Niles)
Lima:	Rimac
Lisbon:	Tagus
Liverpool:	Mersey
London:	Thames
Madrid:	Manzanares
Milan:	Olna
Montreal:	St. Lawrence
Moscow:	Moscow
Munich:	Isar
Ottawa:	Ottawa
Paris:	Seine

City	River
Prague:	Vlatava
Rome:	Tiber
Santiago:	Mapocho
Sao Paulo:	Tiete
Seoul:	Han
Shanghai:	Huangpo, Wusong
St. Petersburg	Neva
Toronto:	Don
Vienna:	Danube
Warsaw:	Vistula

Airports Serving Major Cities

Amsterdam:	Schipol
Barcelona:	del Prat
Berlin:	Tegel
Bogota:	El Dorado
Brussels:	Zavantem
Bucharest:	Otopeni
Budapest:	Ferihagy
Calcutta:	Dum Dum
Cape Town:	D.F. Malan
Djakarta:	Soekarno-Hatta
Frankfurt:	Rhein-Main
Genoa:	Cristoforo Colombo
Havana:	Jose Marti
Hong Kong:	Kai Tak
Istanbul:	Ataturk
Jeddah:	King Abdulaziz
Johannesburg:	Jan Smuts
London:	Heathrow,* Gatwick, Stansted
Madrid:	Barajas
Manila:	Ninoy Aquino
Montreal:	Mirabel
Moscow:	Sheremetyevo
Nairobi:	Jomo Kenyatta
Panama:	Omar Torrijos
Papeete, Tahiti:	Faaa
Paris:	Charles de Gaulle, Orly, Le Bourget**
Pisa:	Galileo Galilei
Reykjavik:	Keflavik
Riyadh:	King Khalid
Rome:	Leonardo Da Vinci
Seoul:	Kimpo
Shanghai:	Hongqiao
Singapore:	Changi
St. Petersburg:	Pulkovo
Stockholm:	Arlanda
Sydney:	Kingsford Smith
Teheran:	Mehrabad
Tokyo:	Narita, Haneda
Toronto:	Lester Pearson
Venice:	Marco Polo
Vienna:	Vienna-Schwechat
Zurich:	Kloten

*London's Heathrow is the world's busiest *non-U.S.* airport.

**Lindbergh landed at Le Bourget in 1927, having made the first nonstop flight across the Atlantic.

Quiz 3:
WORLD GEOGRAPHY

Clues:

1. The only multinational continent with no landlocked nations.
2. These two continents have their highest peaks named for famous figures in American history.
3. Snow-capped Puncak Jaya, located on this tropical land mass, is the highest mountain on an island.
4. Tanzania is a merger of these two place names.
5. The place to be for an authentic Angora sweater.
6. Natives call it "Suomi."
7. These African nations and their capitals begin with the same letters.
8. The capitals of Antigua and Barbuda and Newfoundland have the same name.
9. Portugal's last colony, it reverts to China in 1997.
10. It's the last colony in Europe.

Answers:

1. What is North America?
2. What are North America (McKinley) and Australia (Kosciusko)?
3. What is New Guinea?
4. What are Tanganyika and Zanzibar?
5. What is Ankara, Turkey?
6. What is Finland?
7. What are Algiers, Algeria; Bujumbura, Burundi; Djibouti, Djibouti; Maputo, Mozambique; Niamey, Niger; Sao Tome, Sao Tome and Principe?
8. What is St. John's?
9. What is Macao?
10. What is Gibraltar?

CHAPTER 4

The Body Human

It's time to go from the wide world outside to the one inside you. Basically, it's simple anatomy and a little biology. You don't have to be a medical student to get through this, and it may even make you feel better.

The Parts of the Body

Skeleton

Humans are *vertebrates,* as are all other species with bones. Human skeletons have 206 bones. Bones are joined together by ligaments. The bones also manufacture red and white blood cells.

Muscles

Muscles are the tissues that make limbs move. Humans and other vertebrates have three types of muscles:

Skeletal: the most abundant type of muscle, making up 40–50% of total human body weight. Also known as *striated* or *voluntary* muscles. (In animals, this is what constitutes "meat" for consumption.)

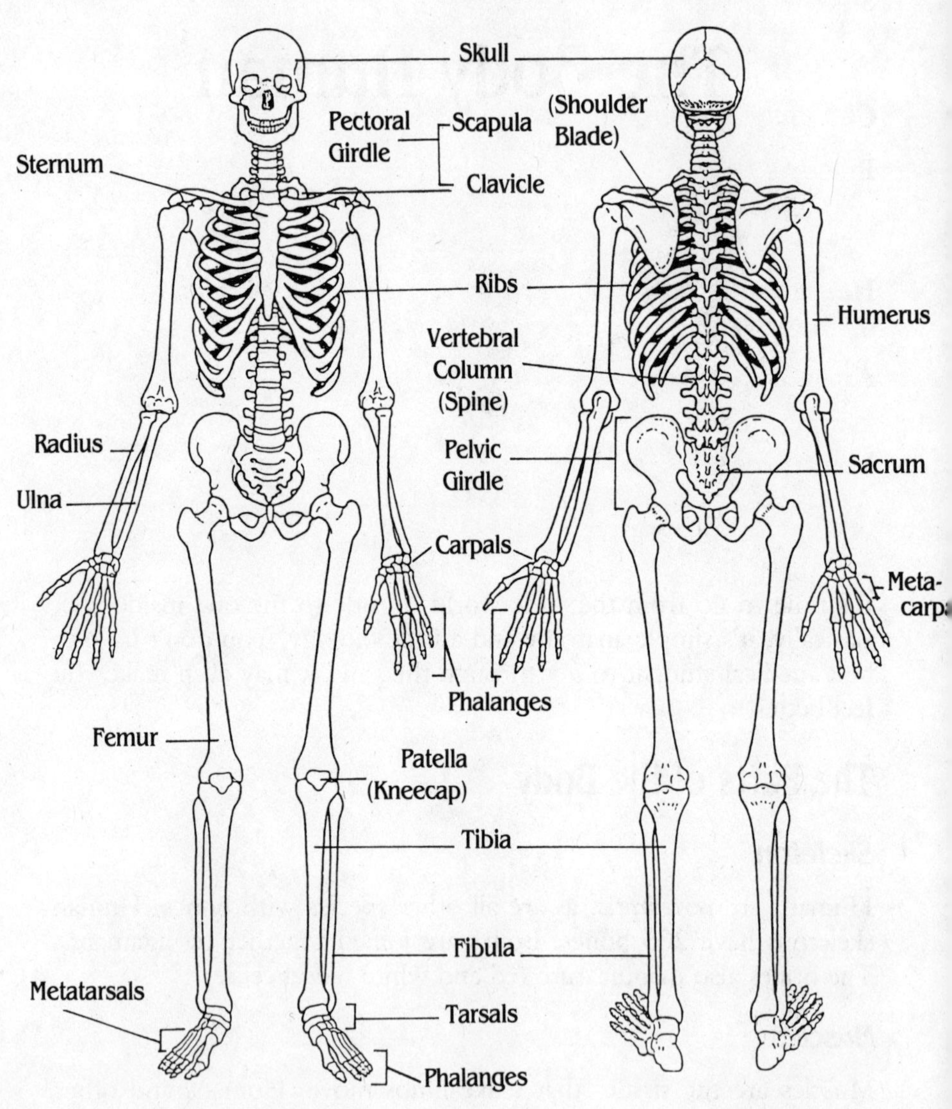
Skull
Pectoral Girdle
Scapula
(Shoulder Blade)
Sternum
Clavicle
Ribs
Humerus
Vertebral Column (Spine)
Radius
Pelvic Girdle
Sacrum
Ulna
Carpals
Meta-
carp
Phalanges
Femur
Patella (Kneecap)
Tibia
Fibula
Metatarsals
Tarsals
Phalanges

Cardiac: as the name suggests, this type of muscle is only found in the heart.

Smooth: found throughout the body.

Circulatory System

Blood: the basic fluid that carries nutrition to cells and waste away from them, carries oxygen to tissues, and regulates body temperature. Blood has red cells (erythrocytes) and white cells (leukocytes).

Heart: center of circulation, a muscular pump with four chambers (left and right ventricles and atriums).

Arteries: blood vessels that take blood away from the heart. The largest artery is the *aorta.*

Veins: blood vessels that bring blood back to the heart. There are two large veins, the *superior* and *inferior vena cava,* which bring blood from the upper (superior) and lower (inferior) body and extremities.

Capillaries: smaller blood vessels.

Respiratory System

Nostrils: they take in air, as does the mouth. Small hairs in the nose filter out dirt.

Nasal passages: they warm the air and add moisture to it.

Pharynx: passageway down from the mouth.

Trachea: the windpipe, the air passage down to the lungs. The trachea carries air down and dust upward to the mouth.

Bronchi: two branches (each one is a *bronchus*) that go from the trachea to the lungs.

Lungs: two spongy organs where *external respiration* takes place, the transfer of oxygen to the blood and carbon dioxide and water from the blood. This actually happens in countless *bronchioles,* which end in capillary-surrounded protrusions called *alveoli.*

Digestive System

You are what you eat, as the saying goes, but you have to break down all that food into its constituent nutrients. The entire set of digestive organs is called the alimentary canal. Here's how it's done:

Mouth: the teeth grind and tear the food; *saliva* (produced by *parotid, submaxillary* and *sublingual* glands) begins to break it down via enzymes. The mass of food leaving the mouth is called *bolus,* i.e., a soft ball.

Esophagus: a muscular tube leading from the mouth to the stomach. It moves the food down via contractions called "peristalsis."

Stomach: the stomach churns the food via contractions and secretes powerful acids and enzymes to break it down further. Food at this stage is called *chyme.*

Small Intestine: 22–28 feet long, comprised of three sections: *duodenum, jejunum* and *ileum*. The small intestine completes the digestion of food and absorbs the nutrient contents.

Pancreas: a small organ attached to the small intestine, it reduces the acid content of the chyme and secretes enzymes to break down proteins, fats and carbohydrates.

Liver: the largest internal organ, it produces bile, which aids in digestion.

Gallbladder: this small organ stores and concentrates the bile, and sends it into the small intestine.

Large Intestine: also called the colon, this organ stores undigested food residues prior to their elimination as waste.

Nervous System

You actually have three different nervous systems: *central, peripheral* and *autonomic.* Don't be nervous, just read along.

Central Nervous System

BRAIN: the control center for all bodily activities and functions. It weighs about three pounds and has three main sections: *Cerebrum,* the largest part, up front; controls voluntary muscles, including those connected with the senses; also controls intelligence and emotions. *Cerebellum,* below and behind the cerebrum; assists in coordinating voluntary muscles. *Brain stem,* or *medulla oblongata,* controls involuntary muscles, as in breathing, heartbeat, gland secretion. The brain's cover is the *cerebral cortex.*

SPINAL CORD: carries nerve impulses to and from the brain.

Peripheral Nervous System: two sets of nerves, *cranial,* which communicate with special sensory organs and other parts of head; and *spinal,* which carry impulses to and from the spinal cord.

Autonomic Nervous System: involuntary, comprised of two systems, *sympathetic,* which regulates heart, gland secretions, digestive organs; and *parasympathetic,* which supports the sympathetic system.

Endocrine System

These are ductless glands producing hormones that regulate many body functions.

Thyroid: located in the throat, it regulates the rate of metabolism.

Pituitary: a small wonder of a gland, located at the bottom of the brain, it regulates skeleton growth, development of sex organs, milk production by mammary glands, thyroid activity, blood pressure, kidney function. Among its hormones is ACTH.

Adrenals: near the liver and pancreas, influences metabolism, certain white blood cell production, blood vessel changes, increased heart action (via adrenalin), liver and nervous system.

Pancreas: produces *insulin,* which enables liver to store sugar and regulates use of sugar in the body. Associated glands are the *islets of Langerhans.*

Testes, Ovaries: the organs producing, respectively, hormones that determine male and female secondary sex characteristics.

Excretory System

In addition to the large intestine, mentioned in *Digestive System,* there are some other organs.

Kidneys: two organs that filter wastes, including excess water, chemicals and salts out of blood.

Bladder: sac that stores urine.

Ureters: ducts leading from kidneys to bladder.

Urethera: tube from bladder to outside of body.

Integumentary System

This is the outer you, hair, nails and your skin—the largest single organ of the body. It has three layers:

Epidermis: the outermost layer, includes skin, hair and nails. Serves as a protective layer against dirt, disease, injury. Produces *melanin,* which creates skin color.

Dermis: middle layer, responds to changes in temperature, touch, pressure, pain, emotion and infection. Secretes perspiration and oil.

Subcutaneous: the fatty bottom layer, comprising fat cells, blood vessels, nerve endings.

Vitamins and Minerals

Closely related to anatomy are the nutrients you take in and how they work, or what happens if you're not getting your RDA (Recommended Daily Allowance).

VITAMINS AND MINERALS: ROLES AND ILLNESSES

Vitamin	Function	Deficiency
Vitamin A	Eyes, skin, mouth, respiration	Night blindness
B Complex		
Vitamin B1 (Thiamine)	Brain, nerves, heart	Beriberi
Vitamin B2 (Riboflavin)	Skin, mouth, eyes, liver, nerves	
Niacin	Gastrointestinal, skin, brain	Pellagra

VITAMINS AND MINERALS: ROLES AND ILLNESSES

Vitamin	Function	Deficiency
B Complex		
Vitamin B6	Skin, red blood cells, brain, kidneys, adrenals	
Pantothenic Acid	Adrenals, kidney, skin, brain, spinal cord	
Biotin	Skin, muscles	
Folic Acid	Red blood cells	Anemia
Vitamin B12	Red blood cells	Pernicious anemia
Vitamin C (Ascorbic acid)	Bones, joints, mouth, capillaries	Scurvy
Vitamin D	Bones, teeth	Rickets
Vitamin E	Reproduction, muscles, red blood cells, liver, brain	
Vitamin K	Blood	

Mineral	Function
Calcium	Primary role is in bone formation
Magnesium	Helps transmit electric nerve messages
Phosphorus	Bones and teeth; also metabolism
Sodium, Potassium, Chlorine	Various functions

Other minerals and elements are needed only in trace amounts. They include selenium, iron (to avoid anemia), chromium, copper, fluorine, iodine (for the thyroid gland) and zinc.

Famous Figures in Medicine and Biology

Time for a check-up of your knowledge of medical pioneers. Do you know which diseases were conquered by Edward Jenner, Robert Koch or Louis Pasteur? Who discovered insulin? DNA? penicillin?

Sir Frederick Banting, Charles H. Best and J.J.R. MacLeod (Canada):	discovered insulin
Christiaan Barnard (South Africa):	performed the first successful human heart transplant
F. H. Crick (Britain) and James Watson (U.S.):	discovered structure of DNA, the basic component of all genetic material
Alexander Fleming (Britain):	discovered penicillin
Galen (Greco-Roman):	the greatest ancient physician; seen as the founder of the rational school (vs. superstition) of medicine
William Harvey (Britain):	discovered course of blood circulation
Hippocrates (ancient Greece):	"father of medicine"; the Hippocratic oath taken by new doctors is named for him
Robert Hooke (17th-century Britain):	discovered existence of cells
Edward Jenner (Britain):	pioneered use of inoculation; cured smallpox
Robert Koch (German):	discovered cause of tuberculosis
Anton van Leeuwenhoek (Netherlands):	discovered existence of bacteria
Joseph Lister (Britain):	antiseptic surgery
Gregor Mendel (Austria):	laws of heredity
Louis Pasteur (France):	discovered antibiodies, cured rabies
Ivan Pavlov (Russia):	conditioned reflex
Albert Sabin (U.S.):	formulated polio vaccine (oral)
Jonas Salk (U.S.):	formulated polio vaccine
Andreas Vesalius (16th-century Italy):	studied human anatomy
August von Wasserman (German):	discovered cause of syphilis

Quiz 4: THE BODY HUMAN

Clues:

1. The common name for the patella.
2. Integumentary refers to this part of the body.
3. Rickets is a disease caused by a deficiency of this.
4. This gland produces insulin.
5. 40–50 percent of your body weight is made up of this type of tissue.
6. Hormones are produced by this system of glands.
7. The majority of the bones in your body are located here.
8. If you're surrounded by alveoli, you must be here.
9. Vitamin B2 is also called this.
10. The vessels that take blood away from the heart.

Answers

1. What is the kneecap?
2. What is skin?
3. What is Vitamin D?
4. What is the pancreas?
5. What are muscles?
6. What is the endocrine system?
7. What are the hands?
8. What are the lungs?
9. What is riboflavin?
10. What are the arteries?

CHAPTER 5

The U.S. Government and the Constitution

The Cabinet

Besides knowing the various departments of the Cabinet, you should learn some of their major sub-components. It's another one of those areas that **Jeopardy!** keeps coming back to. We haven't listed the names of the various Cabinet Secretaries as these change every several years. You can easily update that information on your own. We've listed the Cabinet departments in order of seniority, which also determines the order that the Cabinet Secretaries have in Presidential succession after the *Vice President,* the *Speaker of the House* and the *President Pro Tem of the Senate.* Note: The Post Office was removed from the Cabinet in 1970.

State Department (1789; established as Department of Foreign Affairs)

Treasury Department (1789)

Bureau of Alcohol, Tobacco and Firearms
Customs

Bureau of Engraving and Printing
Internal Revenue Service
Mint
Secret Service

Defense Department (1947; formed from Department of War [1789] and Department of the Navy [1798])

Justice Department (1789; established as Office of the Attorney General; Justice Department founded 1870)

Federal Bureau of Investigation
Bureau of Prisons
Immigration and Naturalization Service

Interior Department (1849)

Bureau of Indian Affairs
Bureau of Mines
Fish and Wildlife Service
Geological Survey
National Park Service

Agriculture Department (1862)

Food Stamps
Forestry Service

Commerce Department (1903; established as Department of Commerce and Labor; became Department of Commerce, 1913)

Bureau of the Census
National Bureau of Standards
Travel and Tourism

Labor Department (1913)

Health and Human Services Department (1953; established as Department of Health, Education and Welfare [HEW]; Education Department split off and HEW was renamed, 1979)

Housing and Urban Development Department (1965)

Transportation Department (1966)

Coast Guard
St. Lawrence Seaway

Energy Department (1977)

Education Department (1979)

Veterans Affairs Department (1989)

The Supreme Court

Current number of members: 9 (Congress sets the number of Justices; it originally was 6)
First Chief Justice: John Jay
Longest-serving Chief Justice: John Marshall (1801–35)
First Jewish Justice: Louis Brandeis (appointed 1916)
First black Justice: Thurgood Marshall (appointed 1967)
First female Justice: Sandra Day O'Connor (appointed 1981)
Longest-serving Justice: William O. Douglas (1939–75)
President who appointed the most Justices: Washington (10); (Franklin Roosevelt is second with 9)
Presidents who had no Supreme Court appointees: Wm. H. Harrison; Taylor; A. Johnson (Congress reduced the number of Justices to prevent him from making any appointments); Carter
Only President to become Chief Justice: William Howard Taft

Quiz 5A:
THE U.S. GOVERNMENT

Clues:

1. These bodyguards were originally employed to catch counterfeiters.
2. The Defense Department was created by merging these two departments.
3. Despite its name, this department is in charge of the "outdoors."
4. Thomas Jefferson was the first to head this department.
5. The only department head not called "Secretary."
6. The four departments that made up Washington's Cabinet.
7. This department controls the census.
8. He's next in line of Presidential succession after the Vice President.
9. It's the smallest department.
10. Day to day, this secretary commands the Coast Guard.

Answers:

1. What is the Secret Service?
2. What are the War and Navy departments?
3. What is the Interior?
4. What is the State Department?
5. Who is the Attorney General (Justice Department)?
6. What are State, Treasury, War and the Attorney General?
7. What is the Commerce Department?
8. Who is the Speaker of the House?
9. What is the State Department?
10. Who is the Secretary of Transportation?

The U.S. Constitution

Here's another **Jeopardy!** favorite, the Constitution. We've included the dates the amendments were added to the Constitution, and some information about the Declaration of Independence as well.

Articles

1. Congress's powers
2. President's powers
3. Judiciary's powers
4. Recognition of each State's Acts; admission of new States; republican form of government guaranteed
5. Amendment process
6. Supremacy of Constitution; no religious test required for office
7. Ratification process for Constitution

Amendments

Bill of Rights (Amendments 1–10) (1791)

1. Freedom of speech, press, petition, religion
2. Right to bear arms
3. Limits on quartering troops in homes
4. Regulation of search and seizure
5. Prosecution, double jeopardy; due process; compensation for private property
6. Speedy trial; right to call witnesses
7. Trial by jury
8. No excessive bail or cruel and unusual punishment
9. "Rule of construction": enumeration of rights in Constitution does not deny rights retained by the people
10. Rights not delegated by the Constitution are retained by the states or the people
11. Limits on federal judicial powers (1795)
12. Separate electoral ballots for President and Vice President (1804)

Civil War Amendments (13–15)

13. Abolition of Slavery (1865)
14. Rights of citizenship unabridged (1868) (extended 5th Amendment due process limits to states)
15. Race no bar to voting rights (1870)
16. Federal income tax permitted (1913)
17. Direct elections of U.S. senators (1913) (previously, state legislatures elected senators)
18. Prohibition of liquor (1919)
19. Women's suffrage (1920)
20. "Lame Duck" Amendment: moves Presidential term to begin January 20; Congress to begin January 3 (as of 1933; previously, Presidents were inaugurated on March 4)
21. Repeals prohibition on liquor (18th Amendment) (1933)
22. President limited to two terms (1951)
23. District of Columbia can vote in Presidential elections (1961)
24. Bans poll tax in federal elections (1964)
25. Presidential disability and succession (1967)
26. Voting age set at 18 (1971)

Facts about the Constitution

Year of signing: 1787
Number of signers: 39
State with most signers: Pennsylvania (8)
State with fewest signers: New York (1)
State with no signers: Rhode Island
Some famous signers: George Washington, Benjamin Franklin, Alexander Hamilton, James Madison ("Father of the Constitution"), Rufus King, Roger Sherman, Gouverneur Morris
First state to ratify: Delaware

Declaration of Independence

Year of signing: 1776
Number of signers: 56
State with most signers: Pennsylvania (8)
State with fewest signers: Rhode Island (2)

Some famous signers: John Adams (a co-drafter), Samuel Adams, Benjamin Franklin (a co-drafter), Elbridge Gerry, Button Gwinnett, John Hancock (President of Congress), Thomas Jefferson (principal drafter), Richard Henry Lee (Robert E. Lee's father), Roger Sherman

Quiz 5B: THE U.S. CONSTITUTION

Clues:

1. The only crime defined in the Constitution.
2. Speaker Foley might object, but Article 4 guarantees each state this form of government.
3. Before the Civil War, how each slave counted for the census.
4. The only amendment to repeal another amendment.
5. Without this amendment, Gerald Ford would never have been President.
6. The three things pledged by signers of the Declaration of Independence.
7. Trial by jury is guaranteed in all cases involving more than this sum.
8. Horrors! This amendment forbids "Double Jeopardy."
9. This state refused to sign the Constitution, saying the other 12 seceded from it.
10. These two future Presidents both signed the Constitution.

Answers:

1. What is treason?
2. What is "republican" form of government?
3. What is as three-fifths of a person?
4. What is the 21st Amendment (repealed the 18th)?
5. What is the 25th Amendment?
6. What is their "Lives, Fortunes and Sacred Honor"?
7. What is $25?
8. What is the 5th Amendment?
9. What is Rhode Island?
10. Who are Washington and Madison?

CHAPTER 6

Academy Awards

This can be a toughie. There's a lot of information here, and some of it is, well, obscure. We've listed all the major Oscars (you can skip Best Foreign Film, Best Song, Best Art Direction), and grouped the Oscars by multiple winners as well.

MAJOR OSCAR WINNERS 1927–1990

	1927–28	1928–29	1929–30
Best Actor	Emil Jannings *(Way of All Flesh)*	Warner Baxter *(In Old Arizona)*	George Arliss
Best Actress	Janet Gaynor *(Seventh Heaven)*	Mary Pickford *(Coquette)*	Norma Shearer *(The Divorce)*

Best Director	Frank Borzage *(Seventh Heaven)* Lewis Milestone *(Two Arabian Knights)*	Frank Lloyd *(The Divine Lady)*	Lewis Milestone *(All Quiet on the Western Front)*
Best Picture	*Wings*	*Broadway Melody*	*All Quiet on the Western Front*

	1930–31	**1931–32**	**1932–33**
Best Actor	Lionel Barrymore *(Free Soul)*	Frederic March *(Dr. Jekyll and Mr. Hyde)* Wallace Beery *(The Champ)*	Charles Laughton *(Private Life of Henry VIII)*
Best Actress	Marie Dressler *(Min and Bill)*	Helen Hayes *(The Sin of Madelon Claudet)*	Katharine Hepburn *(Morning Glory)*
Best Director	Norman Taurog *(Skippy)*	Frank Borzage *(Bad Girl)*	Frank Lloyd *(Cavalcade)*
Best Picture	*Cimarron*	*Grand Hotel*	*Cavalcade*

	1934	**1935**	**1936**
Best Actor	Clark Gable *(It Happened One Night)*	Victor McLaglen *(The Informer)*	Paul Muni *(Story of Louis Pasteur)*
Best Actress	Claudette Colbert *(It Happened One Night)*	Bette Davis *(Dangerous)*	Luise Rainer *(The Great Ziegfeld)*

Best Sup. Actor	—	—	Walter Brennan *(Come and Get It)*
Best Sup. Actress	—	—	Gale Sondergaard *(Anthony Adverse)*
Best Director	Frank Capra *(It Happened One Night)*	John Ford *(The Informer)*	Frank Capra *(Mr. Deeds Goes to Town)*
Best Picture	*It Happened One Night*	*Mutiny on the Bounty*	*The Great Ziegfeld*

	1937	**1938**	**1939**
Best Actor	Spencer Tracy *(Captains Courageous)*	Spencer Tracy *(Boys Town)*	Robert Donat *(Goodbye Mr. Chips)*
Best Actress	Luise Rainer *(The Good Earth)*	Bette Davis *(Jezebel)*	Vivien Leigh *(Gone with the Wind)*
Best Sup. Actor	Joseph Schildkraut *(The Life of Emile Zola)*	Walter Brennan *(Kentucky)*	Thomas Mitchell *(Stagecoach)*
Best Sup. Actress	Alice Brady *(In Old Chicago)*	Fay Bainter *(Jezebel)*	Hattie McDaniel *(Gone with the Wind)*
Best Director	Leo McCarey *(The Awful Truth)*	Frank Capra *(You Can't Take It With You)*	Victor Fleming *(Gone with the Wind)*
Best Picture	*The Life of Emile Zola*	*You Can't Take It With You*	*Gone with the Wind*

	1940	1941	1942
Best Actor	James Stewart *(Philadelphia Story)*	Gary Cooper *(Sergeant York)*	James Cagney *(Yankee Doodle Dandy)*
Best Actress	Ginger Rogers *(Kitty Foyle)*	Joan Fontaine *(Suspicion)*	Greer Garson *(Mrs. Miniver)*
Best Sup. Actor	Walter Brennan *(The Westerner)*	Donald Crisp *(How Green Was My Valley)*	Van Heflin *(Johnny Eager)*
Best Sup. Actress	Jane Darwell *(Grapes of Wrath)*	Mary Astor *(The Great Lie)*	Teresa Wright *(Mrs. Miniver)*
Best Director	John Ford *(Grapes of Wrath)*	John Ford *(How Green Was My Valley)*	William Wyler *(Mrs. Miniver)*
Best Picture	*Rebecca*	*How Green Was My Valley*	*Mrs. Miniver*

	1943	1944	1945
Best Actor	Paul Lukas *(Watch on the Rhine)*	Bing Crosby *(Going My Way)*	Ray Milland *(Lost Weekend)*
Best Actress	Jennifer Jones *(Song of Bernadette)*	Ingrid Bergman *(Gaslight)*	Joan Crawford *(Mildred Pierce)*
Best. Sup. Actor	Charles Coburn *(The More the Merrier)*	Barry Fitzgerald *(Going My Way)*	James Dunn *(A Tree Grows in Brooklyn)*
Best Sup. Actress	Katina Paxinou *(For Whom the Bell Tolls)*	Ethel Barrymore *(None But the Lonely Heart)*	Anne Revere *(National Velvet)*

Best Director	Michael Curtiz *(Casablanca)*	Leo McCarey *(Going My Way)*	Billy Wilder *(Lost Weekend)*
Best Picture	*Casablanca*	*Going My Way*	*Lost Weekend*

	1946	**1947**	**1948**
Best Actor	Frederic March *(Best Years of Our Lives)*	Ronald Colman *(A Double Life)*	Laurence Olivier *(Hamlet)*
Best Actress	Olivia de Havilland *(To Each His Own)*	Loretta Young *(Farmer's Daughter)*	Jane Wyman *(Johnny Belinda)*
Best Sup. Actor	Harold Russell *(Best Years of Our Lives)*	Edmund Gwenn *(Miracle on 34th Street)*	Walter Huston *(Treasure of the Sierra Madre)*
Best Sup. Actress	Anne Baxter *(The Razor's Edge)*	Celeste Holm *(Gentlemen's Agreement)*	Claire Trevor *(Key Largo)*
Best Director	William Wyler *(Best Years of Our Lives)*	Elia Kazan *(Gentlemen's Agreement)*	John Huston *(Treasure of the Sierra Madre)*
Best Picture	*Best Years of Our Lives*	*Gentlemen's Agreement*	*Hamlet*

	1949	**1950**	**1951**
Best Actor	Broderick Crawford *(All the King's Men)*	Jose Ferrer *(Cyrano de Bergerac)*	Humphrey Bogart *(African Queen)*
Best Actress	Olivia de Havilland *(The Heiress)*	Judy Holliday *(Born Yesterday)*	Vivien Leigh *(A Streetcar Named Desire)*

Best Sup. Actor	Dean Jagger *(12 O'Clock High)*	George Sanders *(All About Eve)*	Karl Malden *(A Streetcar Named Desire)*
Best Sup. Actress	Mercedes McCambridge *(All the King's Men)*	Josephine Hull *(Harvey)*	Kim Hunter *(A Streetcar Named Desire)*
Best Director	Joseph L. Mankiewicz *(Letter to Three Wives)*	Joseph L. Mankiewicz *(All About Eve)*	George Stevens *(A Place in the Sun)*
Best Picture	*All the King's Men*	*All About Eve*	*An American in Paris*

	1952	**1953**	**1954**
Best Actor	Gary Cooper *(High Noon)*	William Holden *(Stalag 17)*	Marlon Brando *(On the Waterfront)*
Best Actress	Shirley Booth *(Come Back, Little Sheba)*	Audrey Hepburn *(Roman Holiday)*	Grace Kelly *(The Country Girl)*
Best Sup. Actor	Anthony Quinn *(Viva Zapata)*	Frank Sinatra *(From Here to Eternity)*	Edmond O'Brien *(Barefoot Contessa)*
Best Sup. Actress	Gloria Grahame *(The Bad and the Beautiful)*	Donna Reed *(From Here to Eternity)*	Eva Marie Saint *(On the Waterfront)*
Best Director	John Ford *(The Quiet Man)*	Fred Zinnemann *(From Here to Eternity)*	Elia Kazan *(On the Waterfront)*

Best Picture	*Greatest Show on Earth*	*From Here to Eternity*	*On the Waterfront*

	1955	1956	1957
Best Actor	Ernest Borgnine *(Marty)*	Yul Brynner *(The King and I)*	Alec Guinness *(Bridge on the River Kwai)*
Best Actress	Anna Magnani *(The Rose Tattoo)*	Ingrid Bergman *(Anastasia)*	Joanne Woodward *(Three Faces of Eve)*
Best Sup. Actor	Jack Lemmon *(Mr. Roberts)*	Anthony Quinn *(Lust for Life)*	Red Buttons *(Sayonara)*
Best Sup. Actress	Jo Van Fleet *(East of Eden)*	Dorothy Malone *(Written on the Wind)*	Miyoshi Umeki *(Sayonara)*
Best Director	Delbert Mann *(Marty)*	George Stevens *(Giant)*	David Lean *(Bridge on the River Kwai)*
Best Picture	*Marty*	*Around the World in 80 Days*	*Bridge on the River Kwai*

	1958	1959	1960
Best Actor	David Niven *(Separate Tables)*	Charlton Heston *(Ben-Hur)*	Burt Lancaster *(Elmer Gantry)*
Best Actress	Susan Hayward *(I Want to Live)*	Simone Signoret *(Room at the Top)*	Elizabeth Taylor *(Butterfield 8)*
Best Sup. Actor	Burl Ives *(The Big Country)*	Hugh Griffith *(Ben-Hur)*	Peter Ustinov *(Spartacus)*

Best Sup. Actress	Wendy Hiller *(Separate Tables)*	Shelley Winters *(Diary of Anne Frank)*	Shirley Jones *(Elmer Gantry)*
Best Director	Vincente Minnelli *(Gigi)*	William Wyler *(Ben-Hur)*	Billy Wilder *(The Apartment)*
Best Picture	*Gigi*	*Ben-Hur*	*The Apartment*

	1961	**1962**	**1963**
Best Actor	Maximilian Schell *(Judgment at Nuremberg)*	Gregory Peck *(To Kill a Mockingbird)*	Sidney Poitier *(Lilies of the Field)*
Best Actress	Sophia Loren *(Two Women)*	Anne Bancroft *(The Miracle Worker)*	Patricia Neal *(Hud)*
Best Sup. Actor	George Chakiris *(West Side Story)*	Ed Begley *(Sweet Bird of Youth)*	Melvyn Douglas *(Hud)*
Best Sup. Actress	Rita Moreno *(West Side Story)*	Patty Duke *(The Miracle Worker)*	Margaret Rutherford *(The VIPs)*
Best Director	Jerome Robbins *(West Side Story)*	David Lean *(Lawrence of Arabia)*	Tom Richardson *(Tom Jones)*
Best Picture	*West Side Story*	*Lawrence of Arabia*	*Tom Jones*

	1964	**1965**	**1966**
Best Actor	Rex Harrison *(My Fair Lady)*	Lee Marvin *(Cat Ballou)*	Paul Scofield *(A Man for All Seasons)*

Best Actress	Julie Andrews *(Mary Poppins)*	Julie Christie *(Darling)*	Elizabeth Taylor *(Who's Afraid of Virginia Woolf?)*
Best Sup. Actor	Peter Ustinov *(Topkapi)*	Martin Balsam *(A Thousand Clowns)*	Walter Matthau *(The Fortune Cookie)*
Best Sup. Actress	Lila Kedrova *(Zorba the Greek)*	Shelley Winters *(A Patch of Blue)*	Sandy Dennis *(Who's Afraid of Virginia Woolf?)*
Best Director	George Cukor *(My Fair Lady)*	Robert Wise *(The Sound of Music)*	Fred Zinnemann *(A Man for All Seasons)*
Best Picture	*My Fair Lady*	*The Sound of Music*	*A Man for All Seasons*

	1967	**1968**	**1969**
Best Actor	Rod Steiger *(In the Heat of the Night)*	Cliff Robertson *(Charly)*	John Wayne *(True Grit)*
Best Actress	Katharine Hepburn *(Guess Who's Coming to Dinner)*	Katharine Hepburn *(The Lion in Winter)* Barbra Streisand *(Funny Girl)*	Maggie Smith *(The Prime of Miss Jean Brodie)*
Best Sup. Actor	George Kennedy *(Cool Hand Luke)*	Jack Albertson *(The Subject Was Roses)*	Gig Young *(They Shoot Horses, Don't They?)*

Best Sup. Actress	Estelle Parsons *(Bonnie and Clyde)*	Ruth Gordon *(Rosemary's Baby)*	Goldie Hawn *(Cactus Flower)*
Best Director	Mike Nichols *(The Graduate)*	Sir Carol Reed *(Oliver)*	John Schlesinger *(Midnight Cowboy)*
Best Picture	*In the Heat of the Night*	*Oliver*	*Midnight Cowboy*

	1970	**1971**	**1972**
Best Actor	George C. Scott *(Patton*—refused)	Gene Hackman *(The French Connection)*	Marlon Brando *(The Godfather*—refused)
Best Actress	Glenda Jackson *(Women in Love)*	Jane Fonda *(Klute)*	Liza Minnelli *(Cabaret)*
Best Sup. Actor	John Mills *(Ryan's Daughter)*	Ben Johnson *(The Last Picture Show)*	Joel Grey *(Cabaret)*
Best Sup. Actress	Helen Hayes *(Airport)*	Cloris Leachman *(The Last Picture Show)*	Eileen Heckart *(Butterflies Are Free)*
Best Director	Franklin Schaffner *(Patton)*	William Friedkin *(The French Connection)*	Bob Fosse *(Cabaret)*
Best Picture	*Patton*	*The French Connection*	*The Godfather*

	1973	1974	1975
Best Actor	Jack Lemmon *(Save the Tiger)*	Art Carney *(Harry and Tonto)*	Jack Nicholson *(One Flew Over the Cuckoo's Nest)*
Best Actress	Glenda Jackson *(A Touch of Class)*	Ellen Burstyn *(Alice Doesn't Live Here Anymore)*	Louise Fletcher *(One Flew Over the Cuckoo's Nest)*
Best Sup. Actor	John Houseman *(The Paper Chase)*	Robert De Niro *(The Godfather, Part II)*	George Burns *(The Sunshine Boys)*
Best Sup. Actress	Tatum O'Neal *(Paper Moon)*	Ingrid Bergman *(Murder on the Orient Express)*	Lee Grant *(Shampoo)*
Best Director	George Roy Hill *(The Sting)*	Francis Ford Coppola *(The Godfather, Part II)*	Milos Forman *(One Flew Over the Cuckoo's Nest)*
Best Picture	*The Sting*	*The Godfather, Part II*	*One Flew Over the Cuckoo's Nest*

	1976	1977	1978
Best Actor	Peter Finch *(Network)*	Richard Dreyfuss *(The Goodbye Girl)*	Jon Voight *(Coming Home)*

Best Actress	Faye Dunaway *(Network)*	Diane Keaton *(Annie Hall)*	Jane Fonda *(Coming Home)*
Best Sup. Actor	Jason Robards *(All the President's Men)*	Jason Robards *(Julia)*	Christopher Walken *(The Deer Hunter)*
Best Sup. Actress	Beatrice Straight *(Network)*	Vanessa Redgrave *(Julia)*	Maggie Smith *(California Suite)*
Best Director	John G. Avildsen *(Rocky)*	Woody Allen *(Annie Hall)*	Michael Cimino *(The Deer Hunter)*
Best Picture	*Rocky*	*Annie Hall*	*The Deer Hunter*

	1979	**1980**	**1981**
Best Actor	Dustin Hoffman *(Kramer vs. Kramer)*	Robert DeNiro *(Raging Bull)*	Henry Fonda *(On Golden Pond)*
Best Actress	Sally Field *(Norma Rae)*	Sissy Spacek *(Coal Miner's Daughter)*	Katharine Hepburn *(On Golden Pond)*
Best Sup. Actor	Melvyn Douglas *(Being There)*	Timothy Hutton *(Ordinary People)*	John Gielgud *(Arthur)*
Best Sup. Actress	Meryl Streep *(Kramer vs. Kramer)*	Mary Steenburgen *(Melvin and Howard)*	Maureen Stapleton *(Reds)*
Best Director	Robert Benton *(Kramer vs. Kramer)*	Robert Redford *(Ordinary People)*	Warren Beatty *(Reds)*

Best Picture	*Kramer vs. Kramer*	*Ordinary People*	*Chariots of Fire*

	1982	**1983**	**1984**
Best Actor	Ben Kingsley *(Gandhi)*	Robert Duvall *(Tender Mercies)*	F. Murray Abraham *(Amadeus)*
Best Actress	Meryl Streep *(Sophie's Choice)*	Shirley MacLaine *(Terms of Endearment)*	Sally Field *(Places in the Heart)*
Best Sup. Actor	Louis Gosset Jr. *(An Officer and a Gentleman)*	Jack Nicholson *(Terms of Endearment)*	Haing S. Ngor *(The Killing Fields)*
Best Sup. Actress	Jessica Lange *(Tootsie)*	Linda Hunt *(Year of Living Dangerously)*	Peggy Ashcroft *(A Passage to India)*
Best Director	Richard Attenborough *(Gandhi)*	James L. Brooks *(Terms of Endearment)*	Milos Forman *(Amadeus)*
Best Picture	*Gandhi*	*Terms of Endearment*	*Amadeus*

	1985	**1986**	**1987**
Best Actor	William Hurt *(Kiss of the Spider Woman)*	Paul Newman *(The Color of Money)*	Michael Douglas *(Wall Street)*
Best Actress	Geraldine Page *(Trip to Bountiful)*	Marlee Matlin *(Children of a Lesser God)*	Cher *(Moonstruck)*
Best Sup. Actor	Don Ameche *(Cocoon)*	Michael Caine *(Hannah and Her Sisters)*	Sean Connery *(The Untouchables)*

Best Sup. Actress	Anjelica Huston *(Prizzi's Honor)*	Dianne Wiest *(Hannah and Her Sisters)*	Olympia Dukakis *(Moonstruck)*
Best Director	Sydney Pollack *(Out of Africa)*	Oliver Stone *(Platoon)*	Bernardo Bertolucci *(The Last Emperor)*
Best Picture	*Out of Africa*	*Platoon*	*The Last Emperor*

	1988	**1989**	**1990**
Best Actor	Dustin Hoffman *(Rain Man)*	Daniel Day-Lewis *(My Left Foot)*	Jeremy Irons *(Reversal of Fortune)*
Best Actress	Jodie Foster *(The Accused)*	Jessica Tandy *(Driving Miss Daisy)*	Kathy Bates *(Misery)*
Best Sup. Actor	Kevin Kline *(A Fish Called Wanda)*	Denzel Washington *(Glory)*	Joe Pesci *(Goodfellas)*
Best Sup. Actress	Geena Davis *(The Accidental Tourist)*	Brenda Fricker *(My Left Foot)*	Whoopi Goldberg *(Ghost)*
Best Director	Barry Levinson *(Rain Man)*	Oliver Stone *(Born on the 4th of July)*	Kevin Costner *(Dances with Wolves)*
Best Picture	*Rain Man*	*Driving Miss Daisy*	*Dances with Wolves*

Multiple Oscar Winners

(Note: "BP" indicates film was also Best Picture)

Ingrid Bergman

Actress: *Gaslight* (1944)
Actress: *Anastasia* (1956)
Sup. Actress: *Murder on the Orient Express* (1974)

Marlon Brando

Actor: *On the Waterfront* (1954, BP)
Actor: *The Godfather* (refused; 1972, BP)

Walter Brennan

Sup. Actor: *Come and Get It* (1936)
Sup. Actor: *Kentucky* (1938)
Sup. Actor: *The Westerner* (1940)

Frank Borzage (Director)

Seventh Heaven (1927–28)
Bad Girl (1931–32)

Frank Capra (Director)

It Happened One Night (1934, BP)
Mr. Deeds Goes to Town (1936)
You Can't Take It with You (1938)

Gary Cooper

Actor: *Sergeant York* (1941)
Actor: *High Noon* (1952)

Bette Davis

Actress: *Dangerous* (1935)
Actress: *Jezebel* (1938)

Olivia de Havilland

Actress: *To Each His Own* (1946)
Actress: *The Heiress* (1949)

Robert De Niro

Sup. Actor: *Godfather, Part II* (1974, BP)
Actor: *Raging Bull* (1980)

Sally Field

Actress: *Norma Rae* (1979)
Actress: *Places in the Heart* (1984)

Melvyn Douglas

Sup. Actor: *Hud* (1963)
Sup. Actor: *Being There* (1979)

Jane Fonda

Actress: *Klute* (1971)
Actress: *Coming Home* (1978)

John Ford (Director)

The Informer (1935)
The Grapes of Wrath (1940)
How Green Was My Valley (1941, BP)
The Quiet Man (1952)

Milos Forman (Director)

One Flew Over the Cuckoo's Nest (1975, BP)
Amadeus (1984, BP)

Helen Hayes

Actress: *Sin of Madelon Claudet* (1931–32)
Sup. Actress: *Airport* (1974)

Katharine Hepburn

Actress: *Morning Glory* (1932–33)
Actress: *Guess Who's Coming to Dinner* (1967)
Actress: *The Lion in Winter* (1968)
Actress: *On Golden Pond* (1981)

Dustin Hoffman

Actor: *Kramer vs. Kramer* (1979, BP)
Actor: *Rain Man* (1988, BP)

Glenda Jackson

Actress: *Women in Love* (1970)
Actress: *A Touch of Class* (1973)

Elia Kazan (Director)

Gentleman's Agreement (1947, BP)
On the Waterfront (1954, BP)

David Lean (Director)

Bridge on the River Kwai (1957, BP)
Lawrence of Arabia (1962, BP)

Vivien Leigh

Actress: *Gone with the Wind* (1939, BP)
Actress: *A Streetcar Named Desire* (1951)

Jack Lemmon

Sup. Actor: *Mr. Roberts* (1955)
Actor: *Save the Tiger* (1973)

Frank Lloyd (Director)

The Divine Lady (1928–29)
Cavalcade (1932–33, BP)

Joseph L. Mankiewicz (Director)

Letter to Three Wives (1949)
All About Eve (1950, BP)

Frederic March

Actor: *Dr. Jekyll and Mr. Hyde* (1931–32)
Actor: *The Best Years of Our Lives* (1946, BP)

Leo McCarey (Director)

The Awful Truth (1937)
Going My Way (1944, BP)

Lewis Milestone (Director)

Two Arabian Knights (1927–28)
All Quiet on the Western Front (1929–30, BP)

Jack Nicholson

Actor: *One Flew Over the Cuckoo's Nest* (1975, BP)
Sup. Actor: *Terms of Endearment* (1983, BP)

Anthony Quinn

Sup. Actor: *Viva Zapata!* (1952)
Sup. Actor: *Lust for Life* (1956)

Luise Rainer

Actress: *The Great Ziegfeld* (1936, BP)
Actress: *The Good Earth* (1937)

Jason Robards

Sup. Actor: *All the President's Men* (1976)
Sup. Actor: *Julia* (1977)

Maggie Smith

Actress: *The Prime of Miss Jean Brodie* (1969)
Sup. Actress: *California Suite* (1978)

George Stevens (Director)

A Place in the Sun (1951)
Giant (1956)

Meryl Streep

Sup. Actress: *Kramer vs. Kramer* (1979, BP)
Actress: *Sophie's Choice* (1982)

Oliver Stone (Director)

Platoon (1986, BP)
Born on the 4th of July (1989)

Elizabeth Taylor

Actress: *Butterfield 8* (1960)
Actress: *Who's Afraid of Virginia Woolf?* (1966)

Spencer Tracy

Actor: *Captains Courageous* (1937)
Actor: *Boys Town* (1938)

Peter Ustinov

Sup. Actor: *Spartacus* (1960)
Sup. Actor: *Topkapi* (1964)

Billy Wilder (Director)

The Lost Weekend (1945, BP)
The Apartment (1960, BP)

Shelley Winters

Sup. Actress: *Diary of Anne Frank* (1959)
Sup. Actress: *A Patch of Blue* (1965)

William Wyler (Director)

Mrs. Miniver (1942, BP)
The Best Years of Our Lives (1946, BP)
Ben-Hur (1959, BP)

Fred Zinnemann (Director)

From Here to Eternity (1953, BP)
A Man for All Seasons (1966, BP)

Oscar Data

Film with most Oscar nominations: *All About Eve* (14)
Film with most Oscars: *Ben-Hur* (11)
Most Oscars, Best Actress: Katharine Hepburn (4)
Most Oscars, Best Actor:
  Frederic March (2)
  Gary Cooper (2)
  Spencer Tracy (2)
  Marlon Brando (2—but 1 was declined)
  Dustin Hoffman (2)
Most Oscars, Best Supporting Actor: Walter Brennan (3)
Most Oscars, Best Director: John Ford (4)
Only films to win all four major awards (Best Picture, Director, Actor, Actress):
  It Happened One Night (1934)
  One Flew Over the Cuckoo's Nest (1975)
Youngest Oscar winner: Tatum O'Neal, *Paper Moon,* 1973 (10 years old)
Oldest Oscar winner: Jessica Tandy, *Driving Miss Daisy,* 1989 (80 years old)
Actors who refused Oscars:
  George C. Scott (*Patton*)
  Marlon Brando (*The Godfather*)
Only sequel to win Best Picture: *The Godfather, Part II*
Only Westerns to win Best Picture: *Cimarron* (1930–31) and *Dances with Wolves* (1990)
Only major Oscar for a foreign film: Sophia Loren, Best Actress (*Two Women,* 1961)
Ties for awards:
  Best Actor, 1931–32:
    Frederic March (*Dr. Jekyll and Mr. Hyde*)
    Wallace Beery (*The Champ*)
  Best Actress, 1968:
    Katharine Hepburn (*The Lion in Winter*)
    Barbra Streisand (*Funny Girl*)
  Best Director, 1927–28:
    Frank Borzage (*Seventh Heaven*)
    Lewis Milestone (*Two Arabian Nights*)

Quiz 6: THE ACADEMY AWARDS

Clues:

1. Jane Wyman and Marlee Matlin both were Best Actress winners for characters with this disability.
2. The only tie for Best Actress.
3. The only man chosen Best Supporting Actor three times.
4. Her first and last Best Actress awards came 47 years apart.
5. Only back-to-back Best Actor winner.
6. Before San Francisco streetcars, Karl Malden rode this one to an Oscar.
7. The first black Oscar winner.
8. These two actors refused Oscars.
9. The only two movies to win all four top Oscar awards.
10. The only single name performer to win an Oscar.

Answers:

1. What is deafness (*Johnny Belinda; Children of a Lesser God*)?
2. Who are Katharine Hepburn and Barbra Streisand (1968)?
3. Who is Walter Brennan?
4. Who is Katharine Hepburn?
5. Who is Spencer Tracy?
6. What is *A Streetcar Named Desire?*
7. Who is Hattie McDaniel (*Gone with the Wind*)?
8. Who are George C. Scott (*Patton*) and Marlon Brando (*The Godfather*)?
9. What are *It Happened One Night* and *One Flew Over the Cuckoo's Nest?*
10. Who is Cher (*Moonstruck*)?

CHAPTER 7

Shakespeare

As they sing in *Kiss Me Kate* (Quick! This Broadway musical is based on what play?), "Brush Up Your Shakespeare." Even if Shakespeare was not one of your favorites in school, his work is a major source of **Jeopardy!** questions. After all, it offers countless plots, characters, locations and quotations. (The answer to the question: *The Taming of the Shrew*.)

The Plays

Histories

King John
Richard II
Henry IV, Parts I and II
Henry V
Henry VI, Parts I, II and III
Richard III
Henry VIII

Tragedies

Antony and Cleopatra
Coriolanus
Hamlet
Julius Caesar
King Lear
Macbeth

Tragedies (cont.)

The Merchant of Venice (sometimes considered, technically, a comedy)
Othello
Romeo and Juliet
Timon of Athens
Titus Andronicus
Troilus and Cressida

Comedies

All's Well That Ends Well
As You Like It
Comedy of Errors
Love's Labour's Lost
Measure for Measure
The Merry Wives of Windsor
A Midsummer Night's Dream
Much Ado About Nothing
The Taming of the Shrew
Twelfth Night
The Two Gentlemen of Verona

Romances

The Tempest
The Winter's Tale
Cymbeline
Pericles, Prince of Tyre

Locales of Shakespeare's Plays

Athens

A Midsummer Night's Dream
Timon of Athens

Bohemia

The Winter's Tale

Britain

King John
Henry IV, Parts I and II
Henry V (part)
Henry VI, Parts I, II and III (part)
Henry VIII
Richard II
Richard III
King Lear
Cymbeline (part)
The Merry Wives of Windsor

Cyprus

Othello (part)

Egypt

Antony and Cleopatra (part)

Ephesus (Asia Minor)

Comedy of Errors
Pericles, Prince of Tyre (part)

Florence

All's Well That Ends Well (part)

France

As You Like It (Forest of Arden)
All's Well That Ends Well (Rousillon)
Henry V (part)
Henry VI, Parts I, II and III (part)

Illyria (Yugoslavia)

Twelfth Night

Mitylene (Greece)

Pericles, Prince of Tyre (part)

Navarre (French–Spanish border)

Love's Labour's Lost

Padua (Italy)

The Taming of the Shrew

Pentapolis (fictional)

Pericles, Prince of Tyre (part)

Rome

Coriolanus
Cymbeline (part)
Julius Caesar
Titus Andronicus
Antony and Cleopatra (part)

Scotland

Macbeth

Sicily

Much Ado About Nothing (Messina)
The Winter's Tale

Troy

Troilus and Cressida

Tyre (Lebanon)

Pericles, Prince of Tyre (part)

Venice

The Merchant of Venice
Othello (part)

Verona

The Two Gentlemen of Verona
Romeo and Juliet
The Taming of the Shrew (part)

Vienna

Measure for Measure

Plots and Quotes from Shakespeare

As Hamlet notes, "The play's the thing . . ." Here are synopses of all of Shakespeare's plays, followed by famous quotations.

All's Well That Ends Well

(Setting: Rousillon, France; Florence)

Main characters:

Bertram, Count of Rousillon, *a royal ward;* Helena, *a physician's daughter;* King of France.

Plot:

Helena loves Bertram, who leaves to attend the King. Helena goes to Paris to try to cure the King's fistula, which has resisted all cures. If she fails, she will be executed; if she succeeds, she may marry any courtier. She succeeds, but Bertram spurns her unless she can obtain his ring, which she does through a ruse.

Antony and Cleopatra

(Setting: Egypt and other parts of the ancient world)

Main characters:

Mark Antony, *one of the triumvirs ruling the Roman Empire;* Cleopatra; Octavius Caesar, *Antony's rival;* Enobarbus, *Antony's lieutenant;* Charmian and Iras, *Cleopatra's servants.*

Plot:

The story of Antony and Cleopatra's love affair, and of the final Roman civil war, ending with Octavius' victory at Actium. Antony commits suicide when he falsely hears that Cleopatra is dead; she kills herself with the bite of an asp rather than be made a captive by Octavius.

> "Age cannot wither her, nor custom stale
> Her infinite variety . . ." (Enobarbus)
>
> "I am dying, Egypt, dying . . ." (Antony)

As You Like It

(Setting: The Forest of Arden)

Main characters:

Oliver and Orlando, *brothers and rivals;* Duke Frederick; Rosalind, *his niece;* Jaques, *a jester.*

Plot:

A complicated tale of sibling rivalry: Oliver vs. Orlando; Duke Frederick vs. his brother. Orlando is in exile, as is the disguised Rosalind. In the end, all rivals are reconciled; Orlando and Rosalind marry.

> "All the world's a stage,
> And all the men and women merely players: . . .
> And one man in his time plays many parts,
> His acts being seven ages." (Jaques)

The Comedy of Errors

(Setting: Ephesus)

Main characters:

Aegeon, *a merchant; his twin sons, both named* Antipholus; *their twin servants, both named* Dromio.

Plot:

Mistaken identities among the two sets of twins, as Aegeon tries to reunite his family long separated by a storm at sea: one set of master and servant from Ephesus, the other from Syracuse. Based on the Latin comedy *The Twins,* by Plautus.

Coriolanus

(Setting: Rome)

Main characters:

Caius Marcius Coriolanus, *a Roman soldier;* Volumnia, *his mother;* Virgilia, *his wife;* Tullus Aufidius, *leader of the Volsci;* Sicinius and Brutus, *two tribunes.*

Plot:

Brave but modest Marcius, called Coriolanus for his victory over the Volsci at Corioli, cannot bring himself to campaign for votes in the election for consul; Sicinius and Brutus use this to turn the people against him. Coriolanus allies himself with Tullus, his former foe, against Rome. Their march on Rome is turned back by Volumnia's pleas to her son; in the Volscian camp he allows himself to be killed in a conspiracy led by Tullus, who only recognizes Coriolanus' nobility after he is dead.

Cymbeline

(Setting: ancient Britain and Rome)

Main characters:

Cymbeline, *King of Britain;* Imogen, *his daughter;* the Queen, *his second wife;* Cloten, *the Queen's son;* Posthumus, *secretly married to Imogen.*

Plot:

Cymbeline's wife plots against Imogen, his daughter by his first marriage. Cymbeline banishes Posthumus, who comes to doubt Imogen's faithfulness to him during his exile in Rome and plots to kill her. Imogen disguises herself as a man and is helped by her long-lost brothers, without knowing who they are. The Queen instigates a Roman invasion of Britain, which the brothers and Posthumus defeat; the Queen dies and all are reconciled.

Hamlet

(Setting: Elsinore Castle, Denmark)

Main characters:

Hamlet, *Prince of Denmark;* Queen Gertrude, *his mother;* King Claudius, *his uncle;* Polonius, *counsellor to the King;* Laertes and Ophelia, *Polonius' son and daughter;* Horatio, *Hamlet's friend;* Rosencrantz and Guildenstern, *courtiers.*

Plot:

Hamlet is upset that, upon his father's apparently accidental death, his uncle Claudius usurped the throne and married his mother. His father's ghost appears, revealing that Claudius murdered him and seduced Gertrude; the ghost tells Hamlet to seek revenge. Hamlet feigns madness to mask his purposes. He stages a play, *The Murder of Gonzago,* re-creating his father's murder and proving Claudius' guilt by his reaction. When Hamlet confronts the Queen, he kills Polonius, who had hidden in her room. Hamlet survives assassination when sent with Rosencrantz and Guildenstern to England. Laertes joins Claudius in a plot to kill Hamlet during a fencing match, either via a poisioned blade or drink. Ophelia, rejected by Hamlet, goes mad upon the death of her father, and drowns in a stream. At the fencing match Gertrude unknowingly drinks from the poisoned cup and Laertes wounds Hamlet. The blades get switched and Hamlet stabs Laertes fatally with the poisoned one. Gertrude now falls from her poison and dies. Laertes reveals the plot and Hamlet kills Claudius. Hamlet wills his kingdom to Fortinbras, Prince of Norway, and dies in Horatio's arms. *Hamlet* is Shakespeare's longest play; the title role is Shakespeare's longest part.

"O! that this too too solid flesh would melt, . . ." (Hamlet)

"Frailty, thy name is woman!" (Hamlet)

"Neither a borrower nor a lender be;" (Polonius)

"This above all, to thine own self be true, . . ." (Polonius)

"Something is rotten in the state of Denmark." (Marcellus)

"Brevity is the soul of wit." (Polonius)

"The play's the thing
Wherein I'll catch the conscience of the king." (Hamlet)

"To be, or not to be: that is the question:
Whether 'tis nobler in the mind to suffer
The slings and arrows of outrageous fortune,

Or to take arms against a sea of troubles, . . ." (Hamlet)

"To sleep: perchance to dream:" (Hamlet)

"Get thee to a nunnery." (Hamlet)

"The lady doth protest too much, methinks." (Queen Gertrude)

"Alas, poor Yorick, I knew him, Horatio; a fellow of infinite jest, . . ." (Hamlet)

"The rest is silence." (Hamlet, his last words)

"Good night, sweet prince,
And flights of angels sing thee to thy rest!" (Horatio)

Henry IV, Parts I and II

(Setting: Britain, early 15th century)

Main characters:

King Henry IV; Prince Hal, *his son;* Falstaff, *Hal's companion;* Owen Glendower, *a rebel;* Henry Percy (Hotspur).

Plot:

Having deposed Richard II (see below), Henry must face various threats to his rule. Hal, however, leads a riotous life with the cowardly, blustering Falstaff and various lowlifes at the Boar's Head Tavern in Eastcheap. Finally, Hal rises to his station, killing rebellious Hotspur in battle. When he succeeds to the throne, Hal, now Henry V, dismisses Falstaff and turns to the duties of kingship.

"Banish plump Jack, and banish all the world." (Falstaff)

"We have heard the chimes at midnight." (Falstaff)

"The better part of valor is discretion." (Falstaff)

Henry V

(Setting: England and France, early 15th century)

Main characters:

King Henry V; the Dauphin (crown prince) of France; King Charles VI of France; Montjoy, *a French herald;* Princess Katherine, *daughter of Charles.*

Plot:

Henry has a potential claim to the French throne; the Dauphin insults him for this pretension, provoking a war. Henry invades France, barely winning the siege of Harfleur. A large French army traps Henry and his outnumbered troops at Agincourt, where he wins a crushing victory. Henry successfully woos Princess Katherine. As an aside, Falstaff dies as his friends prepare to leave with the army for France.

> "Once more unto the breach, dear friends, once more; . . ." (Henry V)
>
> "A little touch of Harry in the night." (Chorus)
>
> "This day is called the feast of Crispian . . ." (Henry V)
>
> "We few, we happy few, we band of brothers; . . ." (Henry V)

Henry VI, Parts I, II and III

(Setting: England and France, 1422–1471)

Main characters:

King Henry VI; Joan of Arc; Queen Margaret of Anjou, *Henry's wife;* the Duke of York; the Duke of Suffolk, *his rival;* Edward (later IV) and Richard (later III), *York's sons;* Edward, Prince of Wales, *son of Henry VI.*

Plot:

The story of the War of the Roses between the House of York (White Rose) and the House of Lancaster (Red Rose), and of the Hundred Years' War between England and France. Under weak King Henry, the two branches of the royal house vie for power while France regains its lost territory. Ultimately, the Dukes of York and Suffolk,

Prince Edward and Henry VI are all killed. Edward IV ascends the throne. (The play *Richard III* completes the story.)

"The first thing we do, let's kill all the lawyers." (Dick the Butcher)

Henry VIII

(Setting: Britain)

Main characters:	**Plot:**
King Henry VIII; Thomas Cardinal Wolsey, *Chancellor;* Queen Katharine; Anne Boleyn; Archbishop Thomas Cranmer.	A retelling of Henry VIII's first divorce, from Katharine, in his search for an heir. Henry falls in love with Anne Boleyn; Wolsey will arrange the divorce but cannot support the remarriage. Wolsey falls from office but dies before he can be tried. Cranmer supports the King, including his break with Rome. This was the last play performed at the Globe before the theater burned after an errant shot by a stage cannon.

"Had I but serv'd my God with half the zeal
I serv'd my king, he would not in mine age
Have left me naked to mine enemies." (Cardinal Wolsey)

Julius Caesar

(Setting: ancient Rome)

Main characters:	**Plot:**
Julius Caesar, *ruler of Rome;* Casca, Brutus, Cassius, *conspirators against Caesar;* Mark Antony,	Cassius and others plot to kill Caesar, fearing his dictatorial tendencies. Cassius induces Brutus ("the noblest Roman"), Caesar's friend, to join the plot.

Caesar's lieutenant;
Octavius, *Caesar's nephew.*

They kill Caesar on the Ides of March, but Antony turns the Romans against the assassins with his funeral oration. Anthony allies with Caesar's young nephew, Octavius. They defeat the assassins at Phillippi; Cassius and Brutus commit suicide.

"Beware the ides of March." (Soothsayer)

"The fault, dear Brutus, is not in our stars,
But in ourselves, that we are underlings." (Cassius)

"Let me have men about me that are fat; . . .
Yond' Cassius has a lean and hungry look;
He thinks too much: such men are dangerous." (Julius Caesar)

"But for my own part, it was Greek to me." (Casca)

"When beggars die, there are no comets seen;
The heavens themselves blaze forth the death of princes . . . (Calpurnia)

"Cowards die many times their deaths;
The valiant never taste of death but once." (Caesar)

". . . I am as constant as the northern star, . . ." (Caesar)

"Cry 'Havoc!' and let slip the dogs of war." (Mark Antony)

"I come to bury Caesar, not to praise him.
The evil that men do lives after them,
The good is oft interred with their bones." (Antony)

"This was the most unkindest cut of all." (Antony)

"There is a tide in the affairs of men,
Which, taken at the flood, leads on to fortune;" (Brutus)

"This [Brutus] was the noblest Roman of them all." (Antony)

King John

(Setting: England and France)

Main characters:

King John; Arthur, *his nephew;* Constance, *Arthur's mother.*

Plot:

The story of John's seizure of the throne after the death of his brother, Richard the Lionheart, and despite the claims of Arthur. John has Arthur blinded; he later dies trying to escape. John is poisoned by a monk.

King Lear

(Setting: ancient Britain)

Main characters:

Lear, *King of Britain;* Goneril, Regan, Cordelia, *his daughters;* the Earl of Kent; the Earl of Gloucester; Edgar, Gloucester's *rightful heir* and Edmund, *his bastard;* Lear's Fool *(jester).*

Plot:

Lear plans to divide his kingdom among his daughters, asking each to proclaim their love for him. Goneril and Regan flatter him; Cordelia refuses to do more than offer him the proper love and devotion. Outraged, Lear denies Cordelia her portion and exiles her and her defender, the Earl of Kent. Edmund tricks Gloucester into exiling Edgar. Goneril and Regan strip away Lear's remaining rights; he goes mad and is alone except for his Fool. Cordelia invades with a French army and finds the mad Lear, but she is defeated by her sisters and Edmund. The victors fall out among themselves; Goneril kills Regan and commits suicide; Edmund's treachery is unmasked. Lear enters, carrying Cordelia, whom Edmund had hanged. Then he dies as well.

"Nothing will come of nothing." (Lear)

"How sharper than a serpent's tooth it is
To have a thankless child!" (Lear)

"Blow, winds, and crack your cheeks!" (Lear)

"I am a man
More sinn'd against than sinning." (Lear)

"Ay, every inch a king." (Lear)

The Life of Timon of Athens

(Setting: Athens)

Main characters:

Timon, *a wealthy man;* Alcibiades, *an Athenian noble;* Apemantus, *a philosopher.*

Plot:

Wealthy Timon, a patron of the arts and banquet-giver, is easily flattered, as Apemantus warns him. A rumor spreads questioning Timon's wealth; his creditors demand payment and his former guests all refuse to help. Timon invites them to a final feast, where he decries their conduct and withdraws from Athens to live in a cave, hating all mankind. Timon discovers a hoard of gold but remains bitter and refuses to help Athens against the ambitious, unscrupulous Alcibiades. News of Timon's death closes the play.

Love's Labour's Lost

(Setting: Navarre)

Main characters:

Ferdinand, *King of Navarre;* the Princess of France.

Plot:

Ferdinand and his courtiers pledge to turn the court into an academy and to forgo women for three years while they study, but they fall in love with the Princess and respective members of her court, and try to keep this secret from one another. The King of France dies and the Princess must go home; the other couples also must each separate for a year.

Macbeth

(Setting: Scotland, mid-11th century)

Main characters:

Macbeth, *Thane of Glamis;* Banquo, *his friend;* Lady Macbeth; King Duncan; Malcolm, Donalbain, *his sons;* Macduff, *Thane of Fife;* the three witches.

Plot:

Macbeth and Banquo meet three witches who foretell of Macbeth's eventual ascendancy to the throne. This stirs Macbeth's and his wife's ambition. Macbeth murders Duncan when the King stays at Macbeth's castle, Dunsinane. Macbeth seizes the throne; now he becomes suspicious of everyone. First he has Banquo murdered; then Macduff's family. Lady Macbeth, consumed by guilt, sleepwalks at night trying to clean imaginary blood from her hand; she dies. Macduff leads an army against Macbeth and kills him; Malcolm is proclaimed king. In theater legend, *Macbeth* is considered an unlucky play to perform, and is never referred to by name, but as "the Scottish play."

"When shall we three meet again?
In thunder, lightning, or in rain?" (First Witch)

"Fair is foul, and foul is fair . . ." (Three Witches)

"If it were done when 'tis done, then 'twere well
It were done quickly; . . ." (Macbeth)

"But screw your courage to the sticking-place, . . ." (Lady Macbeth)

"Is this a dagger which I see before me,
The handle toward my hand?" (Macbeth)

"Macbeth does murder sleep, the innocent sleep,
Sleep that knits up the ravel'd sleave of care, . . ." (Macbeth)

"Double, double toil and trouble;
Fire burn and cauldron bubble. . . ." (Three Witches)

"Eye of newt, and toe of frog,
Wool of bat, and tongue of dog." (Second Witch)

"Great Birnam wood to high Dunsinane hill
Shall come against him." (Third Apparition)

"Out, damned spot! out, I say!" (Lady Macbeth)

"All the perfumes of Arabia will not sweeten this little hand." (Lady Macbeth)

"Tomorrow, and tomorrow, and tomorrow,
Creeps in this petty pace from day to day,
To the last syllable of recorded time; . . .
It is a tale
Told by an idiot, full of sound and fury,
Signifying nothing." (Macbeth)

"Lay on, Macduff,
And damn'd be him that first cries,
'Hold, enough.' " (Macbeth)

Measure for Measure

(Setting: Vienna)

Main characters:

Vincentio, *Duke of Vienna;* Angelo, *one of the Duke's deputies;* Claudio and Juliet, *lovers;* Isabella, *Claudio's sister.*

Plot:

Vincentio suddenly gives Angelo control of Vienna. Angelo orders strict enforcement of the old law ordering death for lovers living together before marriage. Claudio is the first to be sentenced. When Isabella pleads with Angelo for her brother's life, Angelo finds himself lusting for her. He hypocritically offers to spare Claudio if Isabella will become his mistress. Vincentio, disguised as a friar, reappears and sets everything right, and weds Isabella.

The Merchant of Venice

(Setting: Venice)

Main characters:

Antonio, *a merchant of Venice;* Shylock, *a Jewish moneylender;* Jessica, *his daughter;* Portia, *an heiress;* Bassanio and Lorenzo, *friends of Antonio.*

Plot:

Antonio borrows money from Shylock; the security is "a pound of flesh." Portia, wooed by many, asks each suitor to choose among caskets of gold, silver and lead for permission to marry her; Bassanio correctly chooses the leaden one. When Antonio's loan is due and Shylock tries to collect, Balthazar, a lawyer (Portia in disguise) argues that Shylock is entitled only to the flesh but no blood. Shylock relents and says he will take the money Bassanio offered for his friend. But by threatening a Venetian's life, Shylock must forfeit half his goods to Venice and half to Antonio, and must convert. Jessica marries Lorenzo.

"It is a wise father that knows his own child." (Launcelot Gobbo)

"If you prick us, do we not bleed?" (Shylock)

"All that glisters is not gold . . ." (Prince of Morocco)

"The quality of mercy is not strain'd, . . ." (Portia)

The Merry Wives of Windsor

(Setting: The Garter Inn)

Main characters:

Sir John Falstaff and various of his friends and wenches.

Plot:

More of Falstaff's cavorting; largely a play written to revive this popular character.

A Midsummer Night's Dream

(Setting: Athens and the nearby woods)

Main characters:

Theseus, *Duke of Athens;* Hipploxta, *Queen of the Amazons;* Oberon, *King of the Fairies;* Titania, *his wife;* Puck, *a fairy;* Hermia, Helena, Demetrius, Lysander, *young Athenians;* Bottom, Flute, Snout, Quince, Snug, Starveling, *Athenian tradesmen.*

Plot:

Theseus woos his captive, Hipploxta, as their wedding nears. Oberon argues with Titania. Hermia refuses to wed Demetrius, risking execution; she loves Lysander; Helena loves Demetrius. In the woods, their relationships are confused as Puck administers a love potion to the wrong lovers. He also gives some to Titania, who falls in love with Bottom, whom Oberon had given the head of an ass. In the end, the couples are happily sorted out; the tradesmen perform *Pyramus and Thisbe* at the royal wedding.

"Lord, what fools these mortals be!" (Puck)

Much Ado About Nothing

(Setting: Messina)

Main characters:

Beatrice; Benedick.

Plot:

The stormy and comic romance of Beatrice, who has long spurned men, and Benedick, her acerbic equal, aided by their various friends and relations.

Othello

(Setting: Venice, Cyprus)

Main characters:

Othello, *a Moor;* Desdemona, *a Venetian noble, his wife;* Iago and Cassio, *Othello's lieutenants;* Emilia, *Iago's wife and Desdemona's waiting-woman.*

Plot:

Othello is a commander in the Venetian military and is sent to defend Cyprus against the Turks. Iago, passed over for promotion in favor of Cassio, plots to ruin his rival and Othello. He tricks Cassio into drunkenness and arouses Othello's jealousy, hinting that Cassio and Desdemona were lovers. As his jealously consumes him, Othello smothers the innocent Desdemona. Othello then learns the truth and kills himself; Cassio brings Iago to justice.

"O! beware, my lord, of jealousy;
It is the green-eyed monster . . ." (Iago)

"Put out the light, and then put out the light: . . ." (Othello)

"Then must you speak
Of one that loved not wisely but too well." (Othello)

Pericles, Prince of Tyre

(Setting: Tyre, Pentapolis, Mytilene Ephesus)

Main characters:

Pericles, *Prince of Tyre;* Thaisa, *his wife;* Marina, *their daughter;* Gower, *poet and play's narrator.*

Plot:

Pericles marries Thaisa; she is separated from him and Marina, who is in turn separated from Pericles. She spends time in a brothel, where her virtue preserves her innocence. They are all happily reunited in the end.

Richard II

(Setting: Britain, late 14th century)

Main characters:

King Richard II; John of Gaunt, Duke of Lancaster, *his uncle;* Henry Bolingbroke, *Gaunt's son.*

Plot:

Richard exiles Bolingbroke, a rival. For upbraiding him about his misrule, Richard confiscates all of Gaunt's property after his death. While Richard is in Ireland, Bolingbroke returns and leads a rebellion. Richard is taken prisoner and deposed. Bolingbroke becomes Henry IV. Richard is killed at Pontefract Castle.

"This royal throne of kings, this scepter'd isle, . . .
This other Eden, demi-paradise, . . .
This happy breed of men, this little world,
This precious stone set in the silver sea, . . .
This blessed plot, this earth, this realm, this England, . . ."
(Richard II)

". . . let us sit upon the ground
And tell sad stories of the death of kings: . . .
All murder'd: for within the hollow crown . . .
Keeps Death his court." (Richard II)

"O! that I were as great
As my grief, or lesser than my name, . . ." (Richard II)

"Mount, mount, my soul! thy seat is up on high, . . ." (Richard II)

Richard III

(Setting: Britain, late 15th century)

Main characters:

King Edward IV; Edward and Richard, *his sons;* Richard, Duke of Gloucester and George, Duke of Clarence, *King Edward's brothers;* Duke of Buckingham, *Richard's ally;* Henry Tudor, Earl of Richmond.

Plot:

Richard, Duke of Gloucester, plots to remove all those who stand between him and the throne. He has Clarence sent to the Tower, where he is later murdered. Named protector and guardian of young Edward V upon the King's death, Richard sends him and his younger brother to the Tower "for their safety." After he usurps the throne, with Buckingham's help, he has the two princes killed. Henry Tudor, a descendant of Edward III, lands a rebel army in Britain and defeats and kills Richard at Bosworth Field. Henry is proclaimed Henry VII, ending the War of the Roses.

"Now is the winter of our discontent
Made glorious summer by this sun of York." (Richard III)

"I am not in the giving vein today." (Richard III)

"A horse! A horse! my kingdom for a horse!" (Richard III)

Romeo and Juliet

(Setting: Verona)

Main characters:

Romeo Montague; Juliet Capulet; Tybalt, *her cousin;* Mercutio, *Romeo's friend;* Friar Lawrence; Juliet's Nurse.

Plot:

The Montagues and Capulets have a longstanding, bloody feud. Romeo and Juliet fall in love and secretly marry, even as the feud claims Tybalt and Mercutio. Romeo is banished for Tybalt's death. Juliet feigns her death via a drug as a ruse to escape to join Romeo. Unaware of her plan, Romeo returns, finds her "dead," and takes poison. She awakens, sees Romeo's body, and kills herself with his dagger. Their deaths force the two families to end the feud.

This play is the inspiration for Leonard Bernstein's *West Side Story*.

"A pair of star-cross'd lovers." (Prologue)

"But soft! what light through yonder window breaks?
It is the east and Juliet is the sun!" (Romeo)

"What's in a name? That which we call a rose
By any other name would smell as sweet." (Juliet)

"O! swear not by the moon, . . ." (Juliet)

"Good night, good night! parting is such sweet sorrow, . . ."
(Juliet)

The Taming of the Shrew

(Setting: Padua, Verona)

Main characters:

Katherina (*the shrew*) and Bianca, *sisters;* Petruchio, *a gentleman from Verona.*

Plot:

Bianca, the younger sister, cannot marry until Katherina does, but she disdains all suitors. Petruchio gains their father's consent to marry Katherina. He wins her heart by feigning indifference, until she is the most affectionate and loving wife.

Inspiration for the musical *Kiss Me Kate.*

"Kiss me, Kate, we will be married o' Sunday." (Petruchico)

"This is a way to kill [a wife] with kindness." (Petruchio)

The Tempest

(Setting: an island)

Main characters:

Prospero, *former Duke of Milan;* Miranda, *his daughter;* Antonio, *Prospero's brother and usurper of his title;* Ariel, *a spirit serving Prospero;* Caliban, *a savage and deformed slave serving Prospero;* Ferdinand, *son of the King of Naples.*

Plot:

Prospero and Miranda live on an island, where he practices magic. He creates a tempest that brings the enemies who deposed him to the island; they are shipwrecked and separated. Miranda meets Ferdinand; they fall in love. Prospero uses his magical powers, and Ariel, to confound his guests and to defeat Caliban's plots against him. All the rivalries are ended; Prospero frees Ariel as he had long promised.

This was Shakespeare's last play.

"We are such stuff
As dreams are made on, and our little life
Is rounded with a sleep." (Prospero)

"O brave new world,
That has such people in't!" (Miranda)

Titus Andronicus

(Setting: Ancient Rome)

Main characters:

Titus Andronicus, *a Roman general;* Lavinia, *his daughter;* Tamora, *Queen of the Goths;* Aaron, *a Moor, her lover.*

Plot:

Titus lost 21 of his 25 sons in wars. He returns to Rome with his prisoners: Tamora and her three sons, one of whom is sacrificed as part of the burial of Titus' son. Revenge and more revenge ensues. This was Shakespeare's first tragedy and is renowned for its violence (Aaron chops off Titus' hand; Lavinia is raped and mutilated; Tamora's sons are killed and served to her in a pie).

Troilus and Cressida

(Setting: The Trojan War)

Main characters;

Troilus, *a Trojan prince;* Cressida, *daughter of Calchas;* Aeneas and Hector, *Troilus' brothers;* Diomedes, *a Greek warrior;* Calchas, *a Trojan priest.*

Plot:

In Troy, Troilus and Cressida fall in love; but Cressida, whose father, Calchas, defected to the Greeks, is exchanged for a Trojan prisoner. Troilus and Cressida exchange love tokens. During a truce, Troilus sees Cressida give his token to Diomedes. The truce ends; the war resumes, with Achilles killing Hector.

Twelfth Night

(Setting: Illyria)

Main characters:

Duke Orsino; Countess Olivia; Viola and Sebastian, *twins;* Sir Toby Belch, *Olivia's uncle;* Malvolio, *Olivia's steward;* Sir Andrew Aguecheek, *a suitor for Olivia.*

Plot:

Viola and Sebastian are shipwrecked and separated in Illyria; Viola dresses as a man (Cesario) and meets Olivia, who falls in love with "him." Viola, however, falls in love with the Duke, who is enamored of Olivia. In the end, Olivia is matched with Sebastian (who resembles his "twin," Cesario), and the Duke with Viola. "Twelfth Night" refers to Epiphany, the 12th night after Christmas; at country house revels the social order was reversed: lords waited on their stewards, etc. This was Shakespeare's last true comedy.

"If music be the food of love, play on: . . . " (Duke Orsino)

The Two Gentlemen of Verona

(Setting: Verona, Milan)

Main characters:

Valentine and Proteus, *the two gentlemen;* Silvia and Julia, *their respective girlfriends.*

Plot:

Two different styles of love: Proteus' inconstancy and Valentine's head-over-heels approach. After much travail, including Valentine's exile among outlaws, both couples are happily united.

"Who is Silvia? What is she
That all the Swains adore her?" (Thurio and Musician)

The Winter's Tale

(Setting: Sicily, Bohemia)

Main characters:

Leontes, *King of Sicily;* Hermione, *his wife;* Polixenes, *King of Bohemia, their friend;* Perdita, *their daughter;* Florizel, *Polixenes' son;* Antigonus, *a courtier to Leontes.*

Plot:

Leontes suspects Hermione and Polixenes of adultery; she and her infant apparently die in childbirth. Antigonus secretly raises Perdita in Bohemia; she meets Florizel and they fall in love. Polixenes, not knowing who she is, objects to the wedding. In the end, all are reconciled, and it is revealed that Hermione is still alive when she is presented to Leontes as a lifelike statue.

"A sad tale's best for winter." (Mamillius)

Exit, pursued by a bear. [famed stage direction]

Major Characters Appearing in More than One Play

Mark Antony (2): *Julius Caesar, Antony and Cleopatra*
Octavian (2): *Julius Caesar, Antony and Cleopatra*
Bolingbroke/Henry IV (3): *Richard II, Henry IV,* Parts I and II
Prince Hal/Henry V (3): *Henry IV,* Parts I and II; *Henry V*
Falstaff (3): *Henry IV,* Parts I and II; *Merry Wives of Windsor*
Edward IV (2): *Henry VI,* Part III; *Richard III*
Richard III (2): *Henry VI,* Part III; *Richard III*

Shakespeare on Film

As You Like It

1936: Laurence Olivier (Orlando)

Hamlet

1948: Laurence Olivier (Hamlet); Jean Simmons (Ophelia); won Best Picture and Best Actor (Olivier) Oscars
1969: Nicol Williamson (Hamlet); Marianne Faithfull (Ophelia); Anthony Hopkins (Claudius)
1991: Mel Gibson (Hamlet); Glenn Close (Gertrude); Alan Bates (Claudius)

Henry IV

1967: **The Chimes at Midnight,** Orson Welles (Falstaff)

Henry V

1945: Laurence Olivier (Henry V)
1989: Kenneth Branagh (Henry V)

Julius Caesar

1953: Louis Calhern (Caesar); Marlon Brando (Antony); James Mason (Brutus); John Gielgud (Cassius); Deborah Kerr (Portia); Greer Garson (Calpurnia)
1970: John Gielgud (Caesar); Jason Robards (Brutus); Charlton Heston (Antony); Richard Chamberlain (Octavius); Robert Vaughn (Casca); Diana Rigg (Portia)

King Lear

1970: Paul Scofield (Lear)
1983: Laurence Olivier (Lear); Diana Rigg, John Hurt (Fool)
(1985: Akira Kurosawa's *Ran* is based on *King Lear*)

Macbeth

1948: Orson Welles (Macbeth); Roddy MacDowell (Malcolm)
1960: Maurice Evans (Macbeth); Judith Evans (Lady Macbeth)
1971: Jon Finch (Macbeth); Annis Martin (Lady Macbeth); directed by Roman Polanski
(1957: Akira Kurosawa's *Throne of Blood* is based on *Macbeth*)

A Midsummer Night's Dream

1935: James Cagney (Bottom); Mickey Rooney (Puck); Dick Powell and Olivia de Havilland (Athenian lovers); Victor Jory (Oberon); Anita Loos (Titania)

Othello

1951: Orson Welles (Othello)
1965: Laurence Olivier (Othello); Maggie Smith (Desdemona)

Richard III

1955: Laurence Olivier (Richard); Claire Bloom (Queen Anne); Ralph Richardson (Buckingham); John Gielgud (Clarence); Cedric Hardwicke (Edward IV)

Romeo and Juliet

1936: Leslie Howard (Romeo); Norma Shearer (Juliet); John Barrymore (Mercutio); Basil Rathbone (Tybalt)
1954: Laurence Olivier (Romeo); Susan Shentall (Juliet)
1968: Leonard Whiting (Romeo); Olivia Hussey (Juliet); directed by Franco Zefferelli

The Taming of the Shrew

1967: Richard Burton (Petruchio); Elizabeth Taylor (Katherina)

Quiz 7:
SHAKESPEARE

Clues:

1. After Britain, more Shakespeare plays are set here than in any other country.
2. Ironically, Shakespeare's longest play contains the line: "Brevity is the soul of wit."
3. He, not Shylock, is the Merchant of Venice.
4. Not one of Shakespeare's "hot" plays, a cannon shot during it burned down the Globe Theater.
5. England had three kings named Richard, but this one never had a play by Shakespeare.
6. Alphabetically, the first Shakespeare play.
7. He said to her: "I am dying, Egypt, dying."
8. Both of these actors played Henry V on film.
9. Many an actor has been an "ass" in this comedy.
10. Huxley's *Brave New World* draws its title from this play.

Answers:

1. What is Italy?
2. What is *Hamlet?*
3. Who is Antonio?
4. What is *Henry VIII?*
5. Who is Richard I (the Lionheart)?
6. What is *All's Well That Ends Well?*
7. Who are Antony and Cleopatra?
8. Who are Laurence Olivier and Kenneth Branagh?
9. What is *A Midsummer Night's Dream?*
10. What is *The Tempest?*

CHAPTER 8

American Literature

As long as we're discussing literature, let's turn to American Lit. Who wrote the poems that became the musical *Cats*? Which book "started the Civil War," according to Lincoln? Which emigré author was also a famous lepidopterist? This topic, which shows up on **Jeopardy!** with some regularity, gives a lot of contestants trouble. Many of the great American works have been filmed as well, so along with the author, you'll find the stars of the film version.

Dramatists

Edward Albee: *Who's Afraid of Virginia Woolf?* (Elizabeth Taylor with a Best Actress Oscar; Richard Burton; Sandy Dennis, Best Supporting Actress); *Tiny Alice; A Delicate Balance.*

T. S. Eliot: *Murder in the Cathedral* (about Henry II and the murder of Thomas à Becket).

Lillian Hellman: *The Children's Hour* (Audrey Hepburn, Shirley MacLaine, James Garner); *The Little Foxes* (Bette Davis); *Watch on* *the Rhine* (Bette Davis, Paul Lukas with an Oscar as Best Actor); *Toys in the Attic* (Dean Martin, Geraldine Page, Wendy Hiller); *Another Part of the Forest* (Frederic March, Ann Blyth). (Hellman's lover was mystery writer Dashiell Hammett.)

Lorraine Hansberry: *A Raisin in the Sun* (Sidney Poitier, Ruby Dee, Louis Gossett).

William Inge: *Come Back, Little Sheba* (Shirley Booth with an Oscar as Best Actress, Burt Lancaster); *Bus Stop* (Marilyn Monroe); *Picnic* (William Holden, Kim Novak).

Arthur Miller: *Death of a Salesman* (Frederic March; two TV versions: Lee J. Cobb, Dustin Hoffman); *The Crucible* (a McCarthy-era parable set in Puritan New England); *After the Fall* (about Miller's wife, Marilyn Monroe); *All My Sons* (Edward G. Robinson, Burt Lancaster); *A View from the Bridge* (Raf Vallone, Maureen Stapleton); *The Price.*

Clifford Odets: *Golden Boy* (Barbara Stanwyck, William Holden); *Waiting for Lefty; The Country Girl* (Bing Crosby, Grace Kelly—won Best Actress).

Eugene O'Neill: *Mourning Becomes Electra* (Rosalind Russell, Michael Redgrave, Raymond Massey, Kirk Douglas); *Anna Christie* (Greta Garbo); *Strange Interlude* (Norma Shearer, Clark Gable); *Desire Under the Elms* (Sophia Loren, Anthony Perkins, Burl Ives); *The Hairy Ape* (William Bendix, Susan Hayward); *The Emperor Jones* (Paul Robeson); *The Iceman Cometh* (Lee Marvin, Frederic March; note that Jason Robards is most often associated with this play); *A Long Day's Journey Into Night* (Katharine Hepburn, Jason Robards); *Marco Millions* (about Marco Polo). O'Neill won the Nobel Prize for Literature, 1936, the only U.S. playwright to do so.

Sam Shepard: *Fool for Love* (Sam Shepard, Kim Basinger); *True West; A Lie of the Mind; Buried Child.*

Neil ("Doc") Simon: *Barefoot in the Park* (Robert Redford, Jane Fonda); *Plaza Suite* (Walter Matthau, Maureen Stapleton); *The Odd Couple* (Walter Matthau, Jack Lemmon); *Last of the Red Hot Lovers*

(Alan Arkin, Sally Kellerman); *Prisoner of Second Avenue* (Jack Lemmon, Anne Bancroft); *The Sunshine Boys* (Walter Matthau, George Burns, with a Best Supporting Actor Oscar); *California Suite* (Maggie Smith, Best Supporting Actress Oscar); his autobiographical trilogy—*Brighton Beach Memoirs, Biloxi Blues, Broadway Bound.* Pulitzer Prize for Drama, 1990.

Booth Tarkington: *Penrod; The Magnificent Ambersons* (directed by Orson Welles, with Joseph Cotten, Agnes Moorehead).

Thornton Wilder: *Our Town* (William Holden); *The Matchmaker* (the basis of the musical *Hello, Dolly*); *The Skin of Our Teeth.*

Tennessee Williams: *The Glass Menagerie* (Jane Wyman, Kirk Douglas; second version: directed by Paul Newman, starring Joanne Woodward); *A Streetcar Named Desire* (Marlon Brando, Vivien Leigh, Kim Hunter, Karl Malden, with Oscars for all but Brando); *Cat on a Hot Tin Roof* (Elizabeth Taylor, Paul Newman, Burl Ives); *Sweet Bird of Youth* (Geraldine Page, Paul Newman, Ed Begley with a Best Supporting Actor Oscar); *Night of the Iguana* (Deborah Kerr, Richard Burton); *Summer and Smoke* (Geraldine Page, Laurence Harvey); *The Milk Train Doesn't Stop Here Anymore.*

Poets and Authors

James Baldwin: *Go Tell It on the Mountain; If Beale Street Could Talk.*

Pearl S. Buck: *The Good Earth* (Luise Rainer, Best Actress, 1937). Buck won the Nobel Prize for Literature, 1938.

Saul Bellow: *Herzog; The Adventures of Augie March; Henderson the Rain King; Mr. Sammler's Planet.* Bellow won the Nobel Prize for Literature, 1976.

Willa Cather: *My Antonia; O, Pioneers; Death Comes for the Archbishop.*

Raymond Chandler: mystery writer, creator of Philip Marlowe; *The Big Sleep* (Humphrey Bogart, Lauren Bacall); *Farewell My Lovely* (Robert Mitchum); *The High Window; The Lady in the Lake* (Robert

Montgomery); *The Long Goodbye* (Elliott Gould). (Paul Newman and James Garner have also portrayed Marlowe.)

Samuel Clemens: better known as Mark Twain; *The Celebrated Jumping Frog of Calaveras County; The Innocents Abroad; Roughing It; The Gilded Age; The Adventures of Tom Sawyer; The Prince and the Pauper; Life on the Mississippi; The Adventures of Huckleberry Finn; A Connecticut Yankee in King Arthur's Court* (Bing Crosby); *The Tragedy of Puddin' Head Wilson.*

James Fenimore Cooper: *The Last of the Mohicans* (Randolph Scott); *The Pathfinder; The Deerslayer; The Pioneers* (all known collectively as The Leatherstocking Tales).

Stephen Crane: *The Red Badge of Courage* (Audie Murphy).

Emily Dickinson: poet; "I Heard a Fly Buzz"; "Because I Could Not Stop for Death."

John Dos Passos: *USA* trilogy (*The 42nd Parallel; 1919; The Big Money*); *The Three Soldiers; Manhattan Transfer.*

Theodore Dreiser: *Sister Carrie; An American Tragedy.*

T. S. Eliot: *The Love Song of J. Alfred Prufrock; The Waste Land; Old Possum's Book of Practical Cats* (inspiration for the musical *Cats*).

James Farrell: the *Studs Lonigan* trilogy.

William Faulkner: *Sartoris; The Sound and the Fury; As I Lay Dying; Light in August; Absalom, Absalom; Intruder in the Dust; The Reivers* (Steve McQueen). Won Nobel Prize for Literature, 1949. Made famous the fictional Yoknapatawpha County, Mississippi.

F. Scott Fitzgerald: *The Great Gatsby* (Robert Redford); *This Side of Paradise; Tender Is the Night; The Beautiful and the Damned; The Last Tycoon* (Robert De Niro).

Robert Frost: poet; "Stopping by Woods on a Snowy Evening," "Mending Wall," "The Road Not Taken," etc.

Erle Stanley Gardner: mystery writer, creator of Perry Mason.

Allen Ginsberg: the "Beat" poet; *Howl; Kaddish.*

Zane Grey: western novels, including *Riders of the Purple Sage.*

Dashiell Hammett: mystery writer; *The Glass Key; The Thin Man* (became an entire film series starring William Powell and Myrna Loy as Nick and Nora Charles, with their dog Asta); *The Maltese Falcon* (Humphrey Bogart as Sam Spade).

Joel Chandler Harris: the Uncle Remus stories (*Uncle Remus and Br'er Rabbit, The Tar-Baby,* etc.).

Bret Harte: western stories, including *The Luck of Roaring Camp, The Outcasts of Poker Flats.*

Nathaniel Hawthorne: *The Scarlet Letter; The House of the Seven Gables* (Vincent Price); *Twice Told Tales; Fanshawe.*

Lillian Hellman: *Pentimento* (basis for *Julia,* Vanessa Redgrave, Best Actress; Jason Robards, Best Supporting Actor).

Ernest Hemingway: *The Sun Also Rises* (Tyrone Power, Errol Flynn, Ava Gardner); *A Farewell to Arms* (Gary Cooper, Helen Hayes); *Death in the Afternoon* (about bull fighting); *To Have and Have Not* (Humphrey Bogart, Lauren Bacall); *For Whom the Bell Tolls* (Gary Cooper, Ingrid Bergman, Katina Paxinou with Best Supporting Actress Oscar, 1943); *The Snows of Kilimanjaro* (Gregory Peck, Susan Hayward, Ava Gardner); *Across the River and Into the Trees; The Old Man and the Sea* (Spencer Tracy). Hemingway won the Nobel Prize for Literature, 1954.

Washington Irving: *The Legend of Sleepy Hollow; Rip Van Winkle; The Alhambra; A History of New York by Diedrich Knickerbocker.*

Henry James: *The American; The Europeans; Daisy Miller* (Cybill Shepherd); *Washington Square; The Portrait of a Lady; The Turn of the Screw; The Bostonians* (Vanessa Redgrave, Christopher Reeve); *The Golden Bowl.*

Sinclair Lewis: *Main Street; Babbitt; Arrowsmith; Elmer Gantry* (Burt Lancaster, Best Actor Oscar; Shirley Jones, Best Supporting Actress Oscar, 1960); *Dodsworth.* Refused Pulitzer Prize, 1926, for *Arrowsmith;* won Nobel Prize for Literature, 1930.

Jack London: *White Fang* (Klaus Maria Brandauer); *The Seawolf* (Edward G. Robinson); *The Call of the Wild* (Clark Gable).

Henry Wadsworth Longfellow: *Psalm of Life; The Wreck of the Hesperus; Evangeline; The Song of Hiawatha.*

Jack Kerouac: gave the "Beat Generation" their name; *On the Road; The Dharma Bums.*

Norman Mailer: *The Naked and the Dead; The Armies of the Night; Ancient Evenings; The Deer Park; The Executioner's Song.*

Edgar Lee Masters: *Spoon River Anthology.*

Herman Melville: *Moby Dick* (Gregory Peck); *Typee; Omoo; Billy Budd* (made into an opera by Benjamin Britten); *White Jacket; Bartleby the Scrivener.*

H. L. Mencken: *The American Language.*

Margaret Mitchell: *Gone with the Wind* (Vivien Leigh, Best Actress Oscar; Hattie McDaniel, Best Supporting Actress Oscar—first black winner; Best Picture Oscar, 1939).

Vladimir Nabokov: *Lolita* (James Mason); *Ada;* was also a noted butterfly collector.

Frank Norris: *The Octopus; McTeague.*

John O'Hara: *Butterfield 8* (Elizabeth Taylor, Best Actress Oscar, 1960); *Appointment in Samarra; Pal Joey* (Frank Sinatra, Kim Novak).

Edgar Allan Poe: "The Raven"; *The Gold Bug; The Fall of the House of Usher; Annabel Lee; The Tell-tale Heart; The Pit and the Pendulum* (Vincent Price); *The Masque of the Red Death.*

Ezra Pound: *The Pisan Cantos.*

Ellery Queen: mystery writer, actually the pen name for Frederic Dannay and Manfred Lee.

Ayn Rand: *Atlas Shrugged; The Fountainhead* (Gary Cooper; Patricia Neal).

Carl Sandburg: *Chicago Poems; Smoke and Steel;* biography of Lincoln.

John Steinbeck: *The Grapes of Wrath* (Henry Fonda; Jane Darwell, Best Supporting Actress Oscar; Best Director, John Ford, 1940); *Of Mice and Men* (Burgess Meredith, Lon Chaney); *The Red Pony* (Robert Mitchum, Myrna Loy); *The Pearl; Cannery Row* (Debra Winger, Nick Nolte); *Tortilla Flat* (Spencer Tracy, John Garfield, Hedy Lamar); *East of Eden* (Jo Van Fleet, Best Supporting Actress Oscar, 1955); *The Winter of Our Discontent; Travels with Charley.* Won the Nobel Prize for Literature, 1962.

Harriet Beecher Stowe: *Uncle Tom's Cabin* ("the book that started the Civil War," according to Abraham Lincoln).

Booth Tarkington: *Seventeen; Alice Adams.*

Henry David Thoreau: *Walden; The Maine Woods; A Week on the Concord and Merrimack Rivers.*

Robert Penn Warren: *All the King's Men* (Broderick Crawford, Best Actor Oscar; Mercedes McCambridge, Best Supporting Actress Oscar; Best Picture, 1949; the story is based on the life of Louisiana's Huey Long).

Nathaniel West: *The Day of the Locust* (Donald Sutherland); *Miss Lonelyhearts.* (West was killed in a car crash on his way to F. Scott Fitzgerald's funeral.)

Edith Wharton: *The House of Mirth; The Age of Innocence; Ethan Frome.*

Walt(er) Whitman: *Leaves of Grass.*

Thornton Wilder: *The Bridge of San Luis Rey.*

Thomas Wolfe: *Look Homeward, Angel; You Can't Go Home Again; Of Time and the River.*

Richard Wright: *Native Son.*

Quiz 8:
AMERICAN LITERATURE

Clues:

1. The Joad family traveled west in this book.
2. This play put Grover's Corners on the map.
3. He refused a Pulitzer but accepted a Nobel.
4. This macabre writer was once enrolled at West Point.
5. Faulkner's fictional Mississippi county.
6. This novel is named for the Indian brave Uncas.
7. Only U.S. playwright to win a Nobel Prize.
8. The "Scarlet Letter" stood for this.
9. Frederic Dannay and Manfred Lee were both this "mystery man."
10. He gave the "Beat Generation" their name.

Answers:

1. What is *The Grapes of Wrath?*
2. What is *Our Town?*
3. Who is Sinclair Lewis?
4. Who is Edgar Allan Poe?
5. What is Yoknapatawpha?
6. What is *The Last of the Mohicans?*
7. Who is Eugene O'Neill?
8. What is "A" for adultery?
9. Who is Ellery Queen?
10. Who is Jack Kerouac?

C H A P T E R 9

English Lit . . . and Others

Before Americans put pen to paper, indeed, before anyone even knew America was out there, people were writing. **Jeopardy!** emphasizes English Literature, as we have. But there are some famous writers in other languages you ought to know. (Once again, we've included the actors or actresses who appeared in the film versions.)

English Literature

14th Century

Geoffrey Chaucer: *Canterbury Tales* (the first work in the English vernacular).

15th Century

Sir Thomas Malory: *Le Morte d'Arthur* (about King Arthur).

Sir Thomas More: *Utopia.* (More is the subject of *A Man for All Seasons*; Paul Scofield won a Best Actor Oscar, 1966.)

16th Century

Edmund Spenser: *The Faerie Queene.*

Francis Bacon: *The Advancement of Learning.*

Christopher Marlowe: playwright; *Dr. Faustus; Tamburlaine the Great.*

John Donne: poems.

Ben Jonson: *Volpone: or the Foxe.*

Thomas Hobbes: *Leviathan.*

Izaak Walton: *The Compleat Angler.*

17th Century

John Bunyan: *The Pilgrim's Progress.*

William Congreve: playwright; *The Way of the World.*

Daniel Defoe: *The Life and Adventures of Robinson Crusoe* (based on the adventures of Alexander Selkirk); *Moll Flanders* (Kim Novak).

John Locke: *Essay Concerning Human Understanding.*

John Milton: blind poet; *Paradise Lost; Samson Agonistes.*

Sir Isaac Newton: *Principia Mathematica; Philosophiae Naturalis; Opticks.*

Samuel Pepys: Diary.

Alexander Pope: "The Rape of the Lock."

Jonathan Swift: *Gulliver's Travels.*

18th Century

William Blake: *Songs of Innocence; Songs of Experience.*

James Boswell: *Life of Johnson.*

Robert Burns: the great Scots poet; "Tam O'Shanter"; "Auld Lang Syne."

Thomas De Quincey: *Confessions of an Opium Eater.*

Henry Fielding: *The History of Tom Jones* (Albert Finney; Best Picture, Best Director, 1963).

Edward Gibbon: *A History of the Decline and Fall of the Roman Empire.*

Oliver Goldsmith: *The Vicar of Wakefield; She Stoops to Conquer.*

Thomas Gray: "Elegy Written in a Country Churchyard."

Thomas Macaulay: *Lays of Ancient Rome.*

Richard Brinsley Sheridan: playwright; *The School for Scandal; The Rivals.*

Adam Smith: *The Wealth of Nations.*

Laurence Sterne: *Tristram Shandy.*

19th Century

Jane Austen: *Pride and Prejudice* (Laurence Olivier, Greer Garson); *Sense and Sensibility; Emma; Mansfield Park; Northanger Abbey.*

Sir James Barrie: *Peter Pan; The Admirable Crichton.*

Charlotte Bronte: *Jane Eyre* (Joan Fontaine, Orson Welles).

19th Century

Emily Bronte: *Wuthering Heights* (Laurence Olivier, Merle Oberon).

Elizabeth Barrett Browning: poems; *Aurora Leigh.*

George Gordon Lord Byron: *Don Juan; Childe Harold.*

Lewis Carroll: the pen name of Rev. Charles Dodgson; *Alice's Adventures in Wonderland; Through the Looking Glass.*

Samuel Taylor Coleridge: "The Rime of the Ancient Mariner"; "Kubla Khan."

Wilkie Collins: *The Moonstone* (considered to be one of the first modern mystery novels); *The Woman in White.*

Joseph Conrad: Polish-born; *Lord Jim* (Peter O'Toole); *The Nigger of the 'Narcissus'; Nostromo; Heart of Darkness* (basis of Coppola's *Apocalypse Now,* starring Marlon Brando).

Charles Darwin: *On the Origin of Species.*

Charles Dickens: *Sketches by Boz; The Pickwick Club; Oliver Twist* (Alec Guinness, Robert Newton); *Nicholas Nickleby; The Old Curiosity Shop; A Christmas Carol; David Copperfield* (W.C. Fields); *Bleak House; Hard Times; Great Expectations* (Alec Guinness, John Mills); *Our Mutual Friend; The Mystery of Edwin Drood.*

Sir Arthur Conan Doyle: *The Adventures of Sherlock Holmes* (Basil Rathbone as Holmes, Nigel Bruce as Watson); *The White Company.*

George Eliot: the pen name of Mary Ann (or Marian) Evans; *Adam Bede; The Mill on the Floss; Silas Marner; Middlemarch.*

John Galsworthy: *The Forsyte Saga*; Nobel Prize winner.

Sir William Schwenck Gilbert: lyricist, collaborated with composer Sir Arthur Sullivan in many operettas: *The Mikado; H.M.S. Pinafore; The Pirates of Penzance; The Gondoliers.*

Thomas Hardy: *Tess of the D'Urbervilles* (Nastassia Kinski); *Far from the Madding Crowd* (Julie Christie); *The Return of the Native; The Mayor of Casterbridge; Jude the Obscure.*

A(lfred) E(dward) Housman: *A Shropshire Lad.*

John Keats: "Endymion"; "Ode on a Grecian Urn"; "Ode to a Nightingale"; "La Belle Dame Sans Merci."

Rudyard Kipling: *The Jungle Book* (Sabu); *Just So Stories; Kim* (Errol Flynn; remake with Peter O'Toole); *Captains Courageous* (Spencer Tracy, Best Actor Oscar; Freddie Bartholomew); *The Man Who Would Be King* (Sean Connery, Michael Caine); Nobel Prize winner.

John Stuart Mill: *On Liberty.*

Sir Walter Scott: *Ivanhoe* (Robert Taylor, Elizabeth Taylor); *Waverley; Rob Roy.*

George Bernard Shaw: playwright, began as a music critic; *Mrs. Warren's Profession; Arms and the Man; Candida; The Devil's Disciple; Caesar and Cleopatra; Man and Superman; Major Barbara; Androcles and the Lion; St. Joan; Pygmalion* (basis of the musical *My Fair Lady*); Nobel Prize winner.

Mary Shelley: *Frankenstein, or The New Prometheus* (Boris Karloff as the monster, Colin Clive as Dr. Frankenstein).

Percy Bysshe Shelley: "Prometheus Unbound"; "Adonais" (about Keats); "To a Skylark."

Robert Louis Stevenson: *Treasure Island* (Wallace Beery, Jackie Cooper; in a second version, Robert Newton); *The Strange Case of Dr. Jekyll and Mr. Hyde* (Frederic March, Best Actor Oscar, 1931–32); *Kidnapped; Master of Ballantrae; A Child's Garden of Verses.*

Bram Stoker: *Dracula* (Bela Lugosi).

Alfred Lord Tennyson: "Charge of the Light Brigade"; "Idylls of the King."

William Makepeace Thackeray: *Vanity Fair.*

Anthony Trollope: *Barchester Towers* (one of six Barsetshire novels); also the *Palliser* novels.

Oscar Wilde: *The Picture of Dorian Gray* (Hurd Hatfield, George Sanders); *The Importance of Being Ernest* (Michael Redgrave); *Lady Windermere's Fan.*

20th Century

Kingsley Amis: *Lucky Jim.*

Agatha Christie: mystery writer, creator of Hercule Poirot; *Murder on the Orient Express* (Albert Finney; Lauren Bacall; Ingrid Bergman, Best Supporting Actress Oscar, 1974); *Death on the Nile* (Peter Ustinov); *The Mousetrap* (the longest-running play in Britain).

Noel Coward: *Blithe Spirit* (Rex Harrison, Constance Cummings).

Ian Fleming: creator of James Bond (portrayed by Sean Connery, George Lazenby, Roger Moore and Timothy Dalton).

Ford Madox Ford: *The Good Soldier.*

E(dward) M(organ) Forster: *A Room with a View* (Helena Bonham-Carter, Denholm Elliott); *A Passage to India* (Peggy Ashcroft); *Howard's End*; *Maurice.*

Kenneth Grahame: *The Wind in the Willows.*

Graham Greene: *Our Man in Havana* (Alec Guinness); *The Power and the Glory* (Spencer Tracy); *The Third Man* (Joseph Cotten, Orson Welles).

Aldous Huxley: *Brave New World.*

Christopher Isherwood: *Goodbye to Berlin* (basis of the musical *Cabaret* starring Joel Grey and Liza Minnelli).

D(avid) H(erbert) Lawrence: *Sons and Lovers* (Trevor Howard, Dean Stockwell); *Lady Chatterley's Lover*; *Women in Love* (Glenda Jackson).

Doris Lessing: *The Golden Notebooks.*

(William) Somerset Maugham: *Of Human Bondage* (Bette Davis, Leslie Howard; in the remake, Laurence Harvey, Kim Novak); *The Moon and Sixpence; The Razor's Edge* (Tyrone Power, Gene Tierney; remade by Bill Murray).

A(lan) A(lexander) Milne: *Winnie the Pooh; The House at Pooh Corner.*

George Orwell: pen name of Eric Blair; *1984* (Edmund O'Brien; in the remake, John Hurt); *Animal Farm.*

Dorothy Sayers: mystery writer, creator of Lord Peter Wimsey.

Dylan Thomas: *Under Milk Wood* (drama); poetry including "Do Not Go Gentle into That Good Night."

J(ohn) R(onald) R(euel) Tolkien: *The Hobbit; The Lord of the Rings* trilogy.

Evelyn Waugh: *Scoop; Brideshead Revisited.*

H(erbert) G(eorge) Wells: *The Invisible Man* (Claude Rains); *The War of the Worlds* (Gene Barry); *The Shape of Things to Come* (Raymond Massey, Ralph Richardson).

P(elham) G(renville) Wodehouse: the Bertie Wooster and Jeeves novels.

Virginia Woolf: *Mrs. Dalloway*; *Jacob's Room*; *To the Lighthouse*; *A Room of One's Own.*

Non-English Literature

Argentina

Jorge Luis Borges: *The Labyrinth.*

Austria

Franz Kafka: *The Trial; The Castle; Metamorphosis* (Kafka was born and raised in Prague, now Czechoslovakia, but then part of Austria-Hungary).

Colombia

Gabriel Garcia Marquez: *One Hundred Years of Solitude.*

Denmark

Hans Christian Andersen: various fairy tales, including *The Emperor's New Clothes; The Ugly Duckling; The Princess and the Pea.*

Isak Dinesen: pen name of Karen Blixen; *Out of Africa* (portrayed by Meryl Streep, with Robert Redford).

France

Honore de Balzac: *The Human Comedy.*

Albert Camus: *The Plague; The Stranger*; Nobel Prize winner.

Colette: *Cheri; Gigi* (Leslie Caron, Maurice Chevalier, Louis Jourdan; Best Director Oscar, Vincente Minnelli; Best Picture Oscar, 1958).

Alexandre Dumas (father): *The Three Musketeers; The Man in the Iron Mask; The Count of Monte Cristo.*

Alexandre Dumas (son): *The Lady of the Camelias* (also known as *Camille;* Greta Garbo and Robert Taylor).

Gustave Flaubert: *Madame Bovary.*

Victor Hugo: *Les Miserables; The Hunchback of Notre Dame.*

Eugene Ionesco: *The Bald Soprano* (but born in Romania).

Guy de Maupassant: short story writer.

Moliere: pen name of Jean Baptiste Poquelin; *Tartuffe; The Misanthrope.*

Marcel Proust: *Remembrance of Things Past.*

Francois Rabelais: *Gargantua; Pantagruel.*

Jean Racine: *Phedre.*

Arthur Rimbaud: *Illuminations; A Season in Hell.*

Edmund Rostand: *Cyrano de Bergerac* (Jose Ferrer won Best Actor Oscar; Gerard Depardieu also portrayed him).

Antoine de Saint-Exupery: *The Little Prince.*

Jean-Paul Sartre: *The Age of Reason; Nausea; No Exit*; refused Nobel Prize.

Stendhal: pen name of Henri Beyle; *The Red and the Black; The Charterhouse of Parma.*

Jules Verne: a founder of science fiction; *20,000 Leagues Under the Sea; Around the World in 80 Days* (David Niven; Shirley MacLaine; Best Picture, 1956).

Voltaire: pseudonym of Francois-Marie Arouet; *Candide.*

Emile Zola: *Nana; I Accuse* (article written in defense of Major Dreyfus); Paul Muni portrayed Zola in "The Life of Emile Zola"; won Best Picture and Best Supporting Actor, Joseph Schildkraut, 1937.

Germany

Bertolt Brecht: *The Threepenny Opera* (source of "Mack the Knife"); *Mother Courage.*

Johann von Goethe: *Faust.*

Gunter Grass: *The Tin Drum.*

Hermann Hesse: *Steppenwolf; Siddhartha;* Nobel Prize winner.

Thomas Mann: *Death in Venice* (Dirk Bogarde); *The Magic Mountain*; Nobel Prize winner.

Erich Maria Remarque: *All Quiet on the Western Front* (Best Picture Oscar, 1929–30).

Friederich von Schiller: *William Tell.*

Ireland

Samuel Beckett: *Waiting for Godot*; Nobel Prize Winner.

Brendan Behan: *Borstal Boy* (a "borstal" is a reform school).

James Joyce: *Ulysses; Finnegans Wake; Portrait of the Artist as a Young Man.*

Sean O'Casey: *Juno and the Paycock; The Plough and the Stars.*

John Millington Synge: *The Playboy of the Western World.*

Italy

Dante Alighieri: *The Divine Comedy.*

Niccolo Machiavelli: *The Prince.*

Petrarch: *Sonnets.*

Luigi Pirandello: *Six Characters in Search of an Author*; Nobel Prize winner.

Norway

Henrik Ibsen: *Ghosts; Hedda Gabler; A Doll's House* (Jane Fonda); *The Wild Duck; An Enemy of the People* (Steve McQueen).

Russia

Anton Chekhov: playwright; *The Seagull; The Cherry Orchard; Uncle Vanya; The Three Sisters.*

Fyodor Dostoyevsky: *The Idiot; The Brothers Karamazov; Crime and Punishment; The Possessed.*

Nikolai Gogol: *Dead Souls; The Inspector General.*

Maxim Gorky: *The Lower Depths.*

Boris Pasternak: *Dr. Zhivago*; refused Nobel Prize under orders from Soviet government; Omar Sharif and Julie Christie in the film version.

Alexander Pushkin: poet; *The Bronze Horseman; Eugene Onegin; Boris Godunov.*

Mikhail Sholokov: *And Quiet Flows the Don; The Don Flows Home to the Sea*; Nobel Prize winner.

Aleksandr Solzhenitsyn: *A Day in the Life of Ivan Denisovich; The Gulag Archipelago; First Circle; Cancer Ward*; Nobel Prize winner.

Count Leo Tolstoy: *War and Peace* (Henry Fonda, Audrey Hepburn, Mel Ferrer); *Anna Karenina* (Vivien Leigh, Basil Rathbone).

Ivan Turgenev: *A Month in the Country; Fathers and Sons.*

Spain

Miguel de Cervantes Saavedra: *Don Quixote* (basis of the musical *Man of La Mancha*); Cervantes died April 23, 1616, the same day as Shakespeare.

Sweden

August Strindberg: *Miss Julie.*

Quiz 9A: ENGLISH LITERATURE

Clues:

1. He is the title character in Tennyson's *Idylls of the King.*
2. This 19th-century Prime Minister was also a successful novelist.
3. Mary Ann Evans' pen name.
4. This satire includes a debate on the proper end to crack open eggs.
5. This poem is set in Xanadu.
6. "Prometheus" figures in the title of works by this literary couple.
7. As "Boz," he got paid by the word.
8. Dorothy Sayers' noble detective.
9. It's the longest-running play in British history.
10. Joseph Conrad's native tongue before he began writing in English.

Answers:

1. Who is King Arthur?
2. Who is Benjamin Disraeli?
3. Who is George Eliot?
4. What is *Gulliver's Travels*?
5. What is Coleridge's *Kubla Khan*?
6. Who are Mary and Percy Shelley?
7. Who is Charles Dickens?
8. Who is Lord Peter Wimsey?
9. What is Agatha Christie's *The Mousetrap*?
10. What is Polish?

Quiz 9B: FOREIGN LITERATURE

Clues:

1. Francois-Marie Arouet's pen name.
2. This author offers *No Exit.*
3. "Nasal sensitivity" is a key to this character.
4. Ibsen play that ends with Nora slamming a door.
5. The Soviet government allowed publication of his works in 1990.
6. An Italian treatise on deviousness in governing.
7. Creator of "Mack the Knife."
8. Zola's ringing defense of Major Dreyfus.
9. He left us waiting for Godot.
10. This character literally tilted at windmills.

Answers:

1. Who is Voltaire?
2. Who is Jean-Paul Sartre?
3. Who is Cyrano de Bergerac?
4. What is *A Doll's House*?
5. Who is Aleksandr Solzhenitsyn?
6. What is Machiavelli's *The Prince*?
7. Who is Bertolt Brecht (*The Threepenny Opera*?)
8. What is *I Accuse*?
9. Who is Samuel Beckett?
10. Who is Don Quixote?

CHAPTER 10

Science

Chemistry

This can be a really tough category. After all, there are more than 100 chemical elements, plus their symbols, some of which are predictable and others of which are just tricky. But beyond that, there are the various interesting ways in which the elements can be grouped, which is what we've given you here.

Periodic Table

The Periodic Table was devised by Dmitri Mendeleyev (Element 101, Md: Mendelevium), who first noticed the repetitive nature of groups of elements. We've listed them alphabetically and noted the numbers of the first ten.

Ac	actinium	Ar	argon	B	boron (5)
Al	aluminum*	As	arsenic	Ba	barium
Ag	silver	At	astatine	Be	beryllium (4)
Am	americium	Au	gold	Bi	bismuth

*In Britain, "Aluminum" is spelled "Aluminium."

Bk berkelium
Br bromine
C carbon (6)
Ca calcium
Cd cadmium
Ce cerium
Cf californium
Cl chlorine
Cm curium
Co cobalt
Cr chromium
Cs cesium
Cu copper
Dy dysprosium
Er erbium
Es einsteinium
Eu europium
F fluorine (9)
Fe iron
Fm fermium
Fr francium
Ga gallium
Gd gadolinium
Ge germanium
H hydrogen (1)
Ha hahnium
He helium (2)
Hf hafnium
Hg mercury
Ho holmium
I iodine
In indium
Ir iridium
K potassium
Kr krypton
La lanthanum
Li lithium (3)
Lr lawrencium
Lu lutetium
Md medelevium
Mg magnesium
Mn manganese
Mo molybdenum
N nitrogen (7)
Na sodium
Nb niobium
Nd neodymium
Ne neon (10)
Ni nickel
No nobelium
Np neptunium
O oxygen (8)
Os osmium
P phosphorus
Pa protactinium
Pb lead
Pd palladium
Pm promethium
Po polonium
Pr praseodymium
Pt platinum
Pu plutonium
Ra radium
Rb rubidium
Re rhenium
Rf rutherfordium
Rh rhodium
Rn radon
Ru ruthenium
S sulfur
Sb antimony
Sc scandium
Se selenium
Si silicon
Sm samarium
Sn tin
Sr strontium
Ta tantalum
Tb terbium
Tc technetium
Te tellurium
Th thorium
Ti titanium
Tl thallium
Tm thulium
U uranium
V vanadium
W tungsten
Xe xenon
Y yttrium
Yb ytterbium
Zn zinc
Zr zirconium

(Note: no elements or their symbols begin with J or Q.)

Lightest Element

Hydrogen

Elements with Unusual Symbols

Antimony: Sb (Latin: stibnum)
Gold: Au (Latin: aurium)
Iron: Fe (Latin: ferrium)
Lead: Pb (Latin: plumbum)
Mercury: Hg (Latin: hydragyrus)
Potassium: K (Latin: kalium)
Silver: Ag (Latin: argentum)
Sodium: Na (Latin: natrium)
Tin: Sn (Latin: stannum)
Tungsten: W (wolfram)

Halogens

Astatine
Bromine
Chlorine
Fluorine
Iodine

Noble Gases

Argon
Helium
Krypton
Neon
Xenon

Elements Named for People

Curium: Marie and Pierre Curie, Franco-Polish scientist and her husband, discoverers of radium
Einsteinium: Albert Einstein
Fermium: Enrico Fermi, Italo-American physicist
Gadolinium: Johan Gadolin, Finnish chemist
Hahnium (alternately called unnilpentium): Otto Hahn, co-discoverer of nuclear fission
Lawrencium: Ernest O. Lawrence, physicist
Mendelevium: Dmitri Mendeleyev, creator of the Periodic Table

Nobelium: Alfred Nobel, inventor of dynamite, founder of the Nobel prizes
Rutherfordium (unnilquadium): Ernest Rutherford, the British atomic physicist
Samarium: C. M. Samarski, Russian engineer

Elements Named for Places

Americium: America
Californium: California
Copper: Cyprus
Erbium, Terbium, Ytterbium: all named for Ytterby, Sweden
Europium: Europe
Francium: France
Germanium: Germany
Hafnium: Copenhagen
Holmium: Stockholm
Lutetium: Paris (its Roman name was Lutetia)
Magnesium: Magnesia (region in Greece)
Polonium: Poland
Rhenium: Rhine River
Ruthenium: Ruthenia (part of the Ukraine)
Scandium: Scandinavia
Strontium: Strontia (a village in Scotland)
Thulium: Thule (the north)

Elements Named for Ancient Gods and the Planets

Mercury
Neptunium
Promethium (Prometheus)
Plutonium
Selenium (for Selene, the Moon personified)
Titanium (the Titans)
Tantalum (for mythical figure Tantalus condemned to Hades)
Uranium

Quiz 10A: ELEMENTS

Clues:

1. In 1964, bumper stickers reading "Au H_2O" supported him.
2. It's a noble gas, not a super-hero's nemesis.
3. The only couple to have an element named for them.
4. Your plumber knows, this element's symbol is "Pb."
5. Alphabetically, the last element.
6. No elements or symbols begin with these letters.
7. Creator of the Periodic Table.
8. The only river honored with an element.
9. The symbol for antimony.
10. Three elements are named for the town of Ytterby in this country.

Answers:

1. Who is Barry Goldwater (Au = Gold; H_2O = water)?
2. What is krypton?
3. Who are Marie and Pierre Curie?
4. What is lead?
5. What is zirconium?
6. What are J and Q?
7. Who is Dmitri Mendeleyev?
8. What is the Rhine?
9. What is Sb?
10. What is Sweden?

Common Knowledge

Four Forces of Nature

Gravity, Electromagnetic Force, Nuclear Strong Force, Nuclear Weak Force

Measurement Scales

Beaufort: relative force of wind
Mohs': hardness of various minerals; talc is softest, diamonds are hardest
Richter: strength of earthquakes (this scale is logarithmic; i.e., a quake registering "7" is 10 times stronger than a quake registering "6")

Composition of Air

78% nitrogen
21% oxygen
1% argon

Biology

Carbohydrates: compounds such as sugars, starch and cellulose that provide energy for living organisms.

Carbon Cycle: process by which carbon is taken into plants through photosynthesis, consumed by animals or by other plants, and returned to the environment through respiration and decay.

Cells: the fundamental units of plants and animals, consisting of a nucleus and cytoplasm surrounded by a non-living wall.

Chromosomes: rod-like structures, made up of DNA, which contain genes; female sex chromosomes are XX, male are XY.

Cytology: study of the interior of cells.

DNA: double-helix shaped molecule that forms the genetic material of all organisms. In full, deoxyribonucleic acid.

Ecology: study of the interaction of organisms with each other and with their environment.

Enzyme: proteins that act as catalysts in biological functions.

Histology: study of the cellular structure of organisms.

Mitochondria: tiny organisms that live within cells, carrying out the process of converting glucose into energy usable by cells.

Mitosis: the process of growth via cell division.

Osmosis: absorption of substances though cell walls.

Protein: substances comprised of amino acids, which perform numerous functions in cell structure and operation.

Botany

If you're a plant lover, this is a snap; if not, you're not likely to learn many flowers and trees now. Also, it doesn't come up that often. However, there are some facts that do "pop up" from time to time.

Angiosperms: flowering plants.

Annual: a plant that germinates, grows, flowers and dies in a single year.

Biennial: a plant that germinates and grows one year, and flowers and dies the following year.

Fruit: the blossom or flower of a plant; the ripened ovary of a flower. This term includes many items usually thought of as vegetables or flowers.

Gymnosperm: non-flowering plants (trees and shrubs with uncovered seeds).

Perennial: a plant that lives for many years.

Photosynthesis: process by which plants use light to convert carbon dioxide into carbohydrates.

Vegetable: the leaf, stalk or root of a plant.

- Flowers usually contain a *stamen* (male reproductive organ) and a *pistil* (female organ). The tip of the stamen, which produces pollen, is called the *anther*.
- Plants have *phloem,* the vascular tissue that carries fluids, and *xylem,* the woody tissue that provides structure.
- Trees come in two types: *evergreen,* which keep their leaves; and *deciduous,* which shed their leaves. Human baby teeth are also called "deciduous," because we shed them.
- "Wood" is famous in **Jeopardy!** annals as one of the least successful categories ever. Unless this comes back from **Jeopardy!**-oblivion, you probably don't need to know much else about plants. We don't!

Quiz 10B: SCIENCE

Clues:

1. Surprisingly, a tomato is classified as this.
2. The scale that measures wind force.
3. The female reproductive organ in plants.
4. It's the main component of air.
5. He is credited with "discovering" gravity.
6. If your chromosomes are XY, this is your sex.
7. Pollen is produced here.
8. This type of seed-bearing plant never flowers.
9. It's the softest mineral.
10. This provides plants with their structure.

Answers:

1. What is a fruit?
2. What is the Beaufort scale?
3. What is the pistil?
4. What is nitrogen?
5. Who is Sir Isaac Newton?
6. What is male?
7. What is the anther?
8. What is a gymnosperm?
9. What is talc?
10. What is xylem?

CHAPTER 11

Pop Music: Rock and Country & Western

Rock and Roll

"Rock and roll is here to stay, it will never die," as Danny and the Juniors sang in 1958. This can be a tough category, as most people stop listening to current pop music some time around the age of 20. You may not need to remember "Who Put the Bomp in the Bomp, Bomp, Bomp" (Barry Mann, 1961) but **Jeopardy!** does expect you to know these "records of record." And remember, *any* music category is a likely place for the often dreaded "Audio Daily Double." Finally, if they should ask, the term "rock and roll" was coined by Alan Freed, a 1950s disc jockey.

Longest stay at No. 1

Elvis Presley, "Don't Be Cruel/Hound Dog" (11 weeks)

Second longest No. 1, male

Guy Mitchell, "Singing the Blues" (10 weeks)

THE ALL-TIME RECORD HOLDERS

	Male Singer	Female Singer	Male Group	Female Group
Most Top 40 Hits	Elvis Presley*	Aretha Franklin	Beatles	Supremes
Most No. 1 Records	Elvis Presley	Whitney Houston	Beatles*	Supremes
Most Top 10 Records	Elvis Presley*	Aretha Franklin	Beatles	Supremes

* Overall leader in that category.

Longest No. 1, female (tie)

Debby Boone, "You Light Up My Life" (10 weeks)
Olivia Newton-John, "Physical" (10 weeks)

Only song to hit No. 1 on two separate runs

Chubby Checker, "The Twist" (September 1960, January 1962)

Only No. 1 song re-recorded by same artist to re-enter Top 10

Neil Sedaka, "Breaking Up Is Hard to Do" (No. 1, 1962; No. 8, 1975)

First group to have three consecutive No. 1 hits

The Four Seasons ("Sherry"; "Big Girls Don't Cry"; "Walk Like a Man")

Foreigners at No. 1

Domenico Modugno, "Volare," Italian origin ("*Nel Blu Dipinto di Blu*")
Kyu Sakamoto, "Sukiyaki," Japanese
A-ha, "Take on Me," Norwegian
Paul Mauriat, "Love Is Blue," French

Artists with back-to-back No. 1 hits

Elvis Presley, "Don't Be Cruel/Hound Dog," followed by "Love Me Tender"
Beatles, "I Want to Hold Your Hand," followed by "She Loves You"

Other Elvis data:

First No. 1: "Heartbreak Hotel"
His favorite among his hits: "It's Now or Never"
His favorite Elvis film: *King Creole*

Other Beatles data:

Longest run at No. 1: "Hey Jude," 9 weeks
In 1964 the Beatles had all Top 5 songs
"Yesterday" is actually a Paul McCartney solo; it is also the most "covered" (i.e., recorded by other artists) song of all time
1st Beatles solo at No. 1: George Harrison, "My Sweet Lord"
Most Beatles solos at No. 1: Ringo Starr (2)
Paul McCartney holds the record for the most No. 1 songs written (31), followed by John Lennon (25)

Two different No. 1 hits with the same song

"Go Away Little Girl": Steve Lawrence, Donny Osmond
"The Loco-Motion": Little Eva, Grand Funk
"Please, Mr. Postman": Marvellettes, The Carpenters
"Venus": Shocking Blue, Bananarama
"Lean on Me": Bill Withers, Club Nouveau
"You Keep Me Hangin' On": Supremes, Kim Wilde

Longest span between Top 10 hits

Frank Sinatra (8 yrs, 1958–66)

Oldest No. 1 artist

Louis Armstrong, "Hello Dolly" (64 yrs. old)

Youngest No. 1 artist

Stevie Wonder, "Fingertips" (13 yrs. old)

First live album at No. 1

Beach Boys, "Beach Boys Concert"

Album that stayed No. 1 for longest

Monkees, "Pleasant Valley Sunday"

Album on top charts longest

Pink Floyd, "Dark Side of the Moon" (570 weeks)

No. 1 groups with foreign capitals for names

Berlin
Kingston Trio

Artists with No. 1 hits as solo *and* as member of a duo or group

Peter Cetera
Phil Collins
Michael Jackson
Elton John
Paul McCartney
Diana Ross
Lionel Ritchie

Duos with most Top 10 hits (15 each)

Everly Brothers
Hall & Oates

Only artist to win Grammy for Best Album, Best Record, Best Song and Best Vocal Performance in same year

Carole King

Female artist, 10 Top 10 hits

Brenda Lee
Madonna

Only Female with No. 1 album yielding three No. 1 hits

Whitney Houston ("Greatest Love of All")

Most chart hits without ever having No. 1

James Brown
Fats Domino

First instrumental No. 1

"Autumn Leaves," Roger Williams

Most successful instrumental

"Theme from a Summer Place," Percy Faith

Shortest No. 1

"Stay," Maurice Williams and the Zodiacs (1 min, 37 sec)

Longest No. 1

"Hey Jude," The Beatles (7 min, 11 sec)

Only father-daughter duet at No. 1

Frank and Nancy Sinatra, "Something Stupid"

Fathers and daughters who had separate No. 1 hits

Pat and Debby Boone
Frank and Nancy Sinatra

Mother and son who had separate No. 1 hits

Shirley Jones and Shaun Cassidy

Winner of the most pop Grammys and Oscars

Henry Mancini (20 Grammys, 4 Oscars)

Posthumous No. 1 hits

Otis Redding, "Sitting on the Dock of the Bay"
Janis Joplin, "Me and Bobby McGee"

TV themes that were No. 1

"Miami Vice," by Jan Hammer
"Rise," by Herb Alpert (from "General Hospital")
"SWAT," by Rhythm Heritage
"Welcome Back," by John Sebastian (from "Welcome Back, Kotter")

Most No. 1 hits from a single movie: *Saturday Night Live* (4)

Country & Western

You may love it, or you may hate it, but you can't ignore it if you want to succeed on **Jeopardy!** At least learn the nicknames of some of the C&W legends, along with some of their best-known hits.

Roy Acuff (The King of Country Music): "Wabash Cannonball"; "Great Speckled Bird."

Johnny Cash (The Man in Black): "I Walk the Line"; "Folsom Prison Blues"; "A Boy Named Sue"; along with Jerry Lee Lewis, Carl Perkins and Elvis Presley, was one of the original "Rockabillies."

Patsy Cline: "I Fall to Pieces," "Crazy" (written by Willie Nelson); died in a plane crash, 1963; portrayed by Jessica Lange in *Sweet Dreams,* and by Beverly D'Angelo in *Coal Miner's Daughter*.

Merle Haggard (Okie from Muskogee): along with Buck Owens, a pioneer of the "Bakersfield" (California) sound.

George Jones (The Possum): "He Stopped Loving Her Today"; "The Race is On."

Jerry Lee Lewis (The Killer): "Great Balls of Fire"; "Whole Lotta Shakin' "; portrayed by Dennis Quaid in *Great Balls of Fire* (1989).

Loretta Lynn (Coal Miner's Daughter): "Honky Tonk Girl"; "The Pill"; portrayed by Sissy Spacek in *Coal Miner's Daughter,* which won her a Best Actress Oscar; Loretta's sister is Crystal Gayle.

Bill Monroe (Father of Bluegrass): "Blue Moon of Kentucky."

Willie Nelson: "On the Road Again"; "Blue Eyes Crying in the Rain"; with Waylon Jennings, one of the C&W "Outlaws" based in Austin, Texas.

Minnie Pearl (real name Sarah Ophelia Colley Cannon: Grand Ole Opry comedienne; her trademark is her greeting: "How-dee!"

Charley Pride: first major black Country star; "Kiss an Angel Good Mornin' "; "Is Anybody Goin' to San Antone?"

Jimmie Rodgers (The Singing Brakeman; The Father of Country Music): "Blue Yodel."

Ernest Tubb (The Texas Troubadour): "Walking the Floor Over You."

Hank Williams: "Cold, Cold Heart"; "Your Cheatin' Heart"; portrayed by George Hamilton in *Your Cheatin' Heart*.

Bob Wills (The Father of Western Swing): "San Antonio Rose"; his back-up band was The Texas Playboys.

Tammy Wynette: "Stand By Your Man"; "D-I-V-O-R-C-E"; Tammy was formerly married to George Jones.

Quiz 11:
POP MUSIC

Clues:

1. He was "the Father of Country Music."
2. Little Eva and Grand Funk both chugged to No. 1 with this song.
3. More than a meal, the only Japanese song to hit No. 1 on U.S. Pop charts.
4. Set in Louisiana, it's Elvis' favorite Elvis film.
5. He ended up "Walking the Floor Over You."
6. At one point in 1964, they had all top five songs on the charts.
7. This leader of C&W's "Outlaw" sound has run afoul of the IRS.
8. They didn't play all their own instruments, but they had the longest stay at No. 1 for an album.
9. Singer immortalized in *Sweet Dreams.*
10. Sarah Ophelia Cannon's stage name.

Answers:

1. Who was Jimmie Rodgers?
2. What is "Loco-Motion"?
3. What is "Sukiyaki"?
4. What is *King Creole*?
5. Who is Ernest Tubb?
6. Who are the Beatles?
7. Who is Willie Nelson?
8. Who are the Monkees?
9. Who is Patsy Cline?
10. Who is Minnie Pearl?

CHAPTER 12

Television

When it comes to television, **Jeopardy!** players seem to come in two categories. First, there are those who seem to have seen every show ever run in the history of TV. And then there are those who say they *never* watch TV except for the news, public television and, of course, **Jeopardy!** Well, no matter which group you fall in, you have to know something about television. Maybe not *every* show that's ever been on, but there are some essential facts.

TV Show Locales

Some of these places are real, others are fictional but famous, such as the Goldbergs' address. Can you identify the TV residents of Cabot's Cove, Maine? Mayberry, North Carolina? Taratupta?

"Alice":	Phoenix
"All in the Family":	704 Hauser Street, Queens, N.Y.
"Amen":	First Community Church of Philadelphia

"Andy Griffith":	Mayberry, North Carolina
"Bob Newhart Show":	Chicago
"Cheers":	Boston
"Father Knows Best":	Springfield
"Frank's Place":	Chez Louisiane, New Orleans
"Happy Days":	Milwaukee
"Gimme a Break":	Glen Lawn, California
"The Goldbergs":	Apt. 3B, 1330 E. Tremont Avenue, The Bronx
"Green Acres":	Hooterville
"Laverne and Shirley":	Milwaukee
"Mama":	Steiner Street, San Francisco
"Mary Hartman, Mary Hartman":	Fernwood, Ohio
"Mary Tyler Moore Show":	WJM-TV, Minneapolis, Minnesota
"Maude":	Tuckahoe, N.Y.
"McHale's Navy":	Taratupta, Voltafiore
"Mork and Mindy":	Boulder, Colorado
"The Munsters":	1313 Mockingbird Lane, Mockingbird Heights
"Murder, She Wrote":	Cabot Cove, Maine
"Newhart":	Stratford Inn, Norwich, Vermont
"One Day at a Time":	Indianapolis, Indiana
"Petticoat Junction":	Hooterville
"The Simpsons":	Springfield
"Spenser for Hire":	Boston

TV Doctors

TV loves doctor shows, and most doctors work in hospitals, largely because a hospital provides more plot possibilities. A few, like Marcus Welby, have survived in private practice. Which doctors would you expect to see at Blair General Hospital? Los Angeles University Medical Center?

"Ben Casey":	County General Hospital (Vince Edwards, Sam Jaffe)

"Dr. Kildare":	Blair General Hospital (Richard Chamberlain, Raymond Massey)
"Emergency":	Rampart Hospital, Los Angeles (Robert Fuller, Julie London)
"Marcus Welby, M.D.":	Santa Monica, California (Robert Young, James Brolin)
"Medical Center":	University Medical Center, Los Angeles (Chad Everett, James Daly). This is the longest-running medical show.
"St. Elsewhere":	St. Eligius Hospital, Boston (Ed Flanders, William Daniels)
"Trapper John, M.D.":	San Francisco Memorial Hospital (Pernell Roberts, Gregory Harrison)

TV Westerns

What could be more American than the Western? TV historians say the golden age of TV Westerns was in the late 1950s, when this genre dominated the airwaves, but the Western has always been a staple of TV land. Here are some of the classics. Saddle up! Which cowboys rode the range in these locales: The Ponderosa? The Big Valley? The High Chaparral? Cimarron City?

"Adventures of Rin Tin Tin": The star was Rin Tin Tin, a German shepherd, based with a cavalry unit at Ft. Apache.

"Adventures of Wild Bill Hickok": Starring Guy Madison, one of several shows very broadly based on real characters of the west.

"Annie Oakley": The real Annie Oakley was a sharpshooter in Buffalo Bill's traveling western show; TV's version lived near the town of Diablo with her brother.

"Bat Masterson": Another real-life character, renowned as a dude (cane and derby hat), played by Gene Barry.

"Big Valley": The matriarchal counterpart to Bonanza. Barbara Stanwyck headed the Barkley clan on their San Joaquin Valley ranch. Lee Majors and Linda Evans also starred.

"Bonanza": One of the classics. The Cartwright men—father Ben (Lorne Greene), sons Adam, Hoss and Little Joe (Pernell Roberts, Dan Blocker, Michael Landon) on their huge ranch, the Ponderosa, near Virginia City, Nevada.

"Broken Arrow": One of the few to have an Indian hero, the Apache chief Cochise, played by Michael Ansara.

"Cimarron City": George Montgomery as marshal of the Oklahoma town.

"The Cisco Kid": The "Robin Hood of the West," one of the few Hispanic heroes (Zorro was another); played by Duncan Rinaldo, with Leo Carillo as his sidekick Pancho. The Cisco Kid was actually a character in an O. Henry story.

"Custer": Wayne Maunder as Custer, in his days at Ft. Hays, Kansas, before his fatal encounter at Little Big Horn.

"Daniel Boone": Fess Parker, who initially gained fame portraying Davy Crockett, played the Kentucky woodsman. Ed Ames played his Indian sidekick, Mingo.

"Death Valley Days": Another classic, a different story and actors each week, introduced by the Old Ranger, who was later succeeded by Ronald Reagan.

"The Deputy": Henry Fonda in a rare TV series role, at Silver City, Arizona Territory.

"The Gene Autry Show": The Singing Cowboy in his own show.

"Gunsmoke": The most successful TV western. James Arness played Marshal Matt Dillon in Dodge City for 20 years; with Milburn Stone as Doc, Amanda Blake as Miss Kitty, Dennis Weaver as Chester.

"Have Gun, Will Travel": Richard Boone as the "gun for hire" Paladin.

"The High Chaparral": A "Bonanza" clone; the sprawling Cannon family in the Arizona Territory.

"Hopalong Cassidy": An early classic. William Boyd as "Hoppy," with his horse Topper.

"Kung Fu": Not entirely a Western, but set in the West as Kwai Chung Caine (David Carradine) searches for his father.

"The Lawman": John Russell as Marshal Dan Troop in Laramie.

"The Life and Legend of Wyatt Earp": Another real-life character; Hugh O'Brien portraying the marshal with the long-barrelled .45.

"The Lone Ranger": Clayton Moore (and John Hart also) atop Silver, with Jay Silverheels as Tonto (atop Scout), shouting "Hi, ho Silver away," to the strains of Rossini's "William Tell Overture."

"Maverick": One of the few tongue-in-cheek Westerns, with James Garner as Bret Maverick, Jack Kelly as Bart, and Roger Moore (later James Bond) occasionally as Cousin Beauregard, all good-natured scoundrels and gamblers.

"Rawhide": Years of cattle drives, headed by Gil Favor (Eric Fleming), accompanied by Rowdy Yates (Clint Eastwood).

"The Rifleman": Chuck Connors as Lucas McCain in North Fork, New Mexico, with the fast-repeating rifle.

"Roy Rogers": Another singing cowboy, Roy (atop Trigger), sang "Happy Trails" with wife Dale Evans (atop Buttermilk) at the end of every show. There was also sidekick Pat Brady and his cantankerous jeep Nellybelle, and Bullet, the dog.

"Sky King": The flying cowboy, played by Kirby Grant, aloft in his Cessna, "The Songbird," along with his niece Penny and nephew Clipper.

"The Tall Man": The title referred to Marshal Pat Garrett (Barry

Sullivan), but the plots bore little relationship to his life or his friend and later victim, Billy the Kid (Clu Gulager).

"The Virginian": The first 90-minute show. The title comes from Owen Wister's novel, but the goings-on on Shiloh Ranch, Wyoming bore no relationship to the novel's plot. James Drury in the title role.

"Wagon Train": Another classic, as Ward Bond led travelers from St. Joseph, Missouri to California, with different stories and guest stars each week.

"Wanted: Dead or Alive": Steve McQueen as bounty hunter Josh Randall, with his sawed-off shotgun.

"Zorro": another Hispanic hero (see "Cisco Kid"), Guy Williams led the double life as feckless Don Diego and brave Zorro, atop Diablo.

TV Detectives and Police

Crime shows of various ilks are another TV staple, offering numerous plot opportunities, as well as a bit of gunplay and some violence. What's your P.I.I.Q? Can you name three detective shows sets in Hawaii? How about two working out of Boston?

"Adam-12": Officers Malloy and Reed with the Los Angeles Police Department, played by Martin Milner and Kent McCord.

"Archer": Ross McDonald's detective, portrayed by Brian Keith.

"Banacek": George Peppard solving unsolvable crimes, out of Boston.

"Baretta": Robert Blake (and his pet cockatoo) won a cult following in this police show.

"Barnaby Jones": Buddy Ebsen as the L.A. detective.

"Bourbon Street Beat": Andrew Duggan and Richard Long as detectives based in New Orleans.

"Cagney and Lacey": One of the most successful cop shows, with Sharon Gless (Cagney) and Tyne Daley (Lacey).

"Cannon": William Conrad (the radio voice of the Lone Ranger) as the rotund detective.

"Charlie's Angels": An immensely popular show, with many male viewers watching for the "jiggles." Over the years there were six different Angels: Sabrina (Kate Jackson); Jill (Farrah Fawcett-Majors); Kelly (Jaclyn Smith); Kris (Cheryl Ladd); Tiffany (Shelly Hack); Julie (Tanya Roberts). John Forsythe provided the voice of the unseen Charlie.

"CHiPs": The title acronym stood for California Highway Patrol; starring Erik Estrada.

"Columbo": Peter Falk as the apparently bumbling but always dogged homicide lieutenant. This show turned the plot tables around, showing the murder first and then watching Columbo solve it; the suspense was in the solution, not in "who done it."

"Dragnet": An early classic, with Jack Webb as Sgt. Joe Friday, asking for "Just the facts, ma'am." The show was revived in the 1960s, with Harry Morgan joining Webb.

"The F.B.I.": Efrem Zimbalist, Jr., as Inspector Lewis Erskine. Based on real cases, though "the names have been changed to protect the innocent."

"Hawaii Five-O": Jack Lord as Steve McGarrett, always telling James MacArthur, "Book 'em, Danno."

"Hawaiian Eye": A "Sunset Strip" clone, set in Hawaii.

"Highway Patrol": Broderick Crawford in charge, with all that memorable radio patter, "Ten-four, ten-four."

"Hill Street Blues": One of the most acclaimed cop shows, with Captain Frank Furillo (Daniel Travanti) heading the besieged precinct.

"Honey West": Anne Francis starred as one of TV's few female detectives.

"Hunter": Footballer Fred Dryer as police detective Hunter.

"Ironside": Raymond Burr, formerly Perry Mason, solved crimes in San Francisco from a wheelchair.

"Kojak": Telly Savalas as N.Y.P.D. Lt. Theo Kojak, with his trademark lollipop.

"M Squad": An early cop show with a gritty feel in Chicago, starring Lee Marvin.

"Magnum, P.I.": Tom Selleck in one of the most successful detective shows, set in Hawaii.

"Mannix": Mike Connors, in another successful detective show, set in L.A.

"McCloud": Dennis Weaver as the cowboy cop from Taos, New Mexico, on extended detail to the N.Y.P.D.

"McMillan and Wife": San Francisco police commissioner Stewart McMillan (Rock Hudson) and his wife Sally (Susan Saint James) solving various crimes.

"Miami Vice": Detectives James "Sonny" Crockett (Don Johnson) and Ricardo Tubbs (Philip Michael Thomas) fight drug dealers and other felons to a rock beat, under the command of Lt. Martin Castillo (Edward James Olmos).

"Mike Hammer": Mickey Spillane's detective has had two incarnations: Darren McGavin and Stacy Keach.

"The Mod Squad": Michael Cole, Clarence Williams III and Peggy Lipton as hippie cops, "one white, one black, one blonde."

"Murder, She Wrote": Mystery writer Jessica Fletcher (Angela Lansbury) solves murders from Cabot Cove, Maine.

"The Naked City": An early TV classic, always opening with, "There are eight million stories in the Naked City."

"Peter Gunn": Craig Stevens as the suave detective.

"Police Woman": Angie Dickinson in another rare female lead.

"Quincy, M.E.": Jack Klugman as the L.A. county coroner; "M.E." stands for "medical examiner."

"Remington Steele": Stephanie Zimbalist (Efrem's daughter) created the detective agency; Pierce Brosnan claimed to be Remington.

"The Rockford Files": James Garner as Jim Rockford, working out of his trailer on the beach.

"S.W.A.T.": Steve Forrest led the Special Weapons and Tactics group.

"77 Sunset Strip": Efrem Zimbalist, Jr., starred in this successful and often copied detective series.

"Spenser: For Hire": Robert Urich as the Boston-based detective created by Robert B. Parker.

"Starsky and Hutch": Paul Michael Glaser and David Soul as the cop leads.

"The Streets of San Francisco": Karl Malden teamed up with Michael Douglas.

"T. J. Hooker": William Shatner, forsaking "Star Trek," played the title police sergeant.

"The Untouchables": Robert Stack as Eliot Ness, fighting the Capone mob and others, with Walter Winchell narrating.

TV Teachers and Schools

For all of the conflict between TV and education, there have been an awful lot of shows about schools, and quite a few using the same school names.

"Facts of Life": Eastland School.

"Happy Days": Jefferson High, Milwaukee.

"Head of the Class": Monroe High, New York City, with Howard Hesseman as Charlie Moore.

"Lucas Tanner": Harry S. [sic] Truman High, Webster Grove, Missouri, with David Hartman in the lead role.

"Mr. Novak": Jefferson High, Los Angeles, with James Franciscus in the lead role.

"Mr. Peepers": Jefferson High, Jefferson City, with Wally Cox as Robinson Peepers.

"Our Miss Brooks": Madison High, with Eve Arden as Connie Brooks.

"Room 222": Whitman High, with Lloyd Haynes starring as Pete Dixon.

"Welcome Back, Kotter": Buchanan High, Brooklyn, with Gabe Kaplan as Gabe Kotter, teacher of the "Sweathogs," and John Travolta as Vinnie Barbarino.

"The White Shadow": Carver High, Los Angeles, with Ken Howard as Ken Reeves, late of the Chicago Bulls.

"The Wonder Years": John F. Kennedy Junior High.

Quiz 12: TELEVISION

Clues:

1. TV's two western Hispanic heroes.
2. These two spin-offs from "The Mary Tyler Moore Show" had one-word titles.
3. "Petticoat Junction" shared its locale with this "hick comedy."
4. This nitwit Marine came from Andy Griffith's Mayberry, N.C.
5. Darren McGavin and Stacy Keach both played this detective.
6. Robert Stack played him on TV, Kevin Costner on film.
7. "Happy Days," "Mr. Novak" and "Mr. Peepers" were all set in high schools named after this president.
8. John Sebastian's theme song for this show went to No. 1.
9. He preceded Tom Brokaw as NBC News' anchor.
10. UHF channels include these numbers.

Answers:

1. Who are the Cisco Kid and Zorro?
2. What are Rhoda and Phyllis?
3. What is Green Acres (Hooterville)?
4. Who is Gomer Pyle?
5. Who is Mike Hammer?
6. Who is Eliot Ness?
7. Who is Jefferson?
8. What is "Welcome Back, Kotter?"
9. Who is John Chancellor?
10. What is 14–83?

CHAPTER 13

Sports

This is not a category that shows up very frequently on **Jeopardy!**, and when it does, it's often phrased so that even the least interested, non-sports fan has a shot at the answer. Quite simply, if you want to get into a tough sports trivia contest, **Jeopardy!** is not for you; go to a bar.

The Professional Teams

PROFESSIONAL SPORTS TEAMS BY CITY

City	Baseball	Football	Basketball	Hockey
Atlanta	Braves	Falcons	Hawks	—
Baltimore	Orioles	—	—	—
Boston	Red Sox	—	Celtics	Bruins
Buffalo	—	Bills	—	Sabres
Calgary	—	(Stampeders)	—	Flames

City	Baseball	Football	Basketball	Hockey
California	Angels	—	—	—
Charlotte	—	—	Hornets	—
Chicago	Cubs, White Sox	Bears	Bulls	Blackhawks
Cincinnati	Reds	Bengals	—	—
Cleveland	Indians	Browns	—	—
Dallas	—	Cowboys	Mavericks	—
Denver	Rockies	Broncos	Nuggets	—
Detroit	Tigers	Lions	Pistons	Red Wings
Edmonton	—	(Eskimos)	—	Oilers
Green Bay	—	Packers	—	—
Hartford	—	—	—	Whalers
Houston	Astros	Oilers	Rockets	—
Indianapolis	—	Colts	Pacers	—
Kansas City	Royals	Chiefs	—	—
Los Angeles	Dodgers	Rams, Raiders	Clippers, Lakers	Kings
Milwaukee	Brewers	—	Bucks	—
Miami	Marlins	Dolphins	Heat	—
Minnesota	Twins	Vikings	Timberwolves	North Stars
Montreal	Expos	(Alouettes)	—	Canadiens
New England	—	Patriots	—	—
New Jersey	—	—	Nets	Devils
New Orleans	—	Saints	—	—
New York	Mets, Yankees	Giants, Jets	Knicks	Islanders, Rangers
Oakland	Athletics	—	Golden State Warriors	—
Orlando	—	—	Magic	—
Philadelphia	Phillies	Eagles	76ers	Flyers
Phoenix	—	Cardinals	Suns	—
Pittsburgh	Pirates	Steelers	—	Penguins
Portland	—	—	Trailblazers	—
Quebec	—	—	—	Nordiques
Sacramento	—	—	Kings	—

City	Baseball	Football	Basketball	Hockey
St. Louis	Cardinals	—	—	Blues
San Antonio	—	—	Spurs	—
San Diego	Padres	Chargers	—	—
San Francisco	Giants	49ers	—	—
San Jose	—	—	—	Sharks
Seattle	Mariners	Seahawks	Supersonics	—
Tampa Bay	—	Buccaneers	—	—
Texas	Rangers	—	—	—
Toronto	Blue Jays	(Argonauts)	—	Maple Leafs
Utah	—	—	Jazz	—
Vancouver	—	—	—	Canucks
Washington	—	Redskins	Bullets	Capitols
Winnipeg	—	(Blue Bombers)	—	Jets

Note: Football teams with names in parentheses are part of the *Canadian* Football League, not the U.S.-based National Football League.

Cities with one baseball team in each league

New York: Mets (National), Yankees (American)
Chicago: Cubs (National), White Sox (American)

Most baseball teams in one state

California (5)

States with one baseball team in each league

Texas: Astros (National), Rangers (American)
Ohio: Reds (National), Indians (American)
Missouri: Cardinals (National), Royals (American)

States with more than one baseball team in same league

California: Dodgers, Giants, Padres (National); A's, Angels (American) Pennsylvania: Phillies, Pirates (National)

Teams on the Move

Many of the teams listed above once played somewhere else. Here's an itinerary of where they've been, chronologically for those who have moved more than once:

Atlanta Braves: from Boston, Milwaukee
Baltimore Orioles: formerly the St. Louis Browns
Indianapolis Colts: from Baltimore
L.A. Dodgers: from Brooklyn
L.A. Lakers: from Minnesota
L.A. Raiders: from Oakland
Milwaukee Brewers: formerly the Seattle Pilots
Minnesota Twins: formerly the Washington Senators
Oakland Athletics: from Philadelphia, Kansas City
Phoenix Cardinals: from St. Louis
San Francisco Giants (baseball): from New York
Texas Rangers: formerly the Washington Senators
Utah Jazz: from New Orleans
Washington Bullets: from Baltimore

Team Nicknames

Readers of the sports pages know that many teams have nicknames, often given them by headline writers. Many of them fall to more than one team. Here are some of them:

Athletics:	A's
Cardinals:	Cards, Redbirds
Capitols:	Caps
Celtics:	Irish
Dodgers:	Bums
Falcons:	Birds
Indians:	The Tribe
Orioles:	Birds
Packers:	The Pack
Patriots:	Pats
Pirates:	Bucs (for Buccaneers)
Redskins:	'Skins
Red Sox:	Bosox
Reds:	Redlegs

Tigers:	Bengals
White Sox:	Chisox
Yankees:	Bronx Bombers

Professional Sports Leagues and Their Divisions

Major League Baseball

NATIONAL LEAGUE
Eastern Division
Western Division

AMERICAN LEAGUE
Eastern Division
Western Division

National Football League

NATIONAL FOOTBALL CONFERENCE
East Division
Central Division
West Division

AMERICAN FOOTBALL CONFERENCE
East Division
Central Division
West Division

National Hockey League

WALES CONFERENCE
Patrick Division
Adams Division

CAMPBELL CONFERENCE
Norris Division
Smythe Division

National Basketball Association

EASTERN CONFERENCE
Atlantic Division
Central Division

WESTERN CONFERENCE
Midwest Division
Pacific Division

Stadiums

Baseball

Atlanta Braves:	Atlanta-Fulton County Stadium
Baltimore Orioles:	Memorial Stadium
Boston Red Sox:	Fenway Park (smallest baseball stadium)
California Angels:	Anaheim Stadium
Chicago Cubs:	Wrigley Field
Chicago White Sox:	New Comiskey Park
Cincinnati Reds:	Riverfront Stadium
Cleveland Indians:	Cleveland Stadium (largest baseball stadium)
Detroit Tigers:	Tiger Stadium
Houston Astros:	Astrodome
Kansas City Royals:	Royals Stadium
Los Angeles Dodgers:	Dodger Stadium
Milwaukee Brewers:	Milwaukee County Stadium
Minnesota Twins:	Hubert H. Humphrey Metrodome
Montreal Expos:	Olympic Stadium
New York Mets:	Shea Stadium
New York Yankees:	Yankee Stadium
Oakland A's:	Oakland Coliseum
Philadelphia Phillies:	Veterans Stadium
Pittsburgh Pirates:	Three Rivers Stadium
St. Louis Cardinals:	Busch Stadium
San Diego Padres:	Jack Murphy Stadium
San Francisco Giants:	Candlestick Park
Seattle Mariners:	Kingdome
Texas Rangers:	Arlington Stadium
Toronto Blue Jays:	Skydome

Football

Atlanta Falcons:	Atlanta-Fulton County Stadium
Buffalo Bills:	Rich Stadium
Chicago Bears:	Soldier Field
Cincinnati Bengals:	Riverfront Stadium
Cleveland Browns:	Municipal Stadium
Dallas Cowboys:	Texas Stadium
Denver Broncos:	Mile High Stadium
Detroit Lions:	Pontiac Silverdome
Green Bay Packers:	Lambeau Field
Houston Oilers:	Astrodome (smallest football stadium)
Indianapolis Colts:	Hoosier Dome
Kansas City Chiefs:	Arrowhead Stadium
Los Angeles Raiders:	Memorial Coliseum (largest football stadium)
Los Angeles Rams:	Anaheim Stadium
Miami Dolphins:	Joe Robbie Stadium
Minnesota Vikings:	Hubert H. Humphrey Metrodome
New England Patriots:	Sullivan Stadium (Foxboro, Mass.)
New Orleans Saints:	Louisiana Superdome (largest domed stadium)
New York Giants:	Giants Stadium (E. Rutherford, N.J.)
New York Jets:	Giants Stadium (E. Rutherford, N.J.)
Philadelphia Eagles:	Veterans Stadium
Phoenix Cardinals:	Sun Devil Stadium
Pittsburgh Steelers:	Three Rivers Stadium
San Diego Chargers:	Jack Murphy Stadium
San Francisco 49ers:	Candlestick Park
Seattle Seahawks:	Kingdome
Tampa Bay Buccaneers:	Tampa Stadium
Washington Redskins:	Robert F. Kennedy Stadium

College Football

Conferences

Atlantic Coast
Big 8
Big 10
Big West
Ivy League
Mid-America
Pac 10 (formerly Pac 8)
Southeast
Southern
Southwest
Western Athletic

College Team Nicknames

Air Force:	Falcons
Alabama:	Crimson Tide
Arizona State:	Sun Devils
Arkansas:	Razorbacks
Auburn:	Tigers
Baylor:	Bears
Boston College:	Eagles
Brigham Young:	Cougars
Clemson:	Tigers
Colorado:	Buffalos
Cornell:	Big Red
Dartmouth:	Big Green
Delaware:	Blue Hens
Florida:	Gators
Florida State:	Seminoles
Georgetown:	Hoyas
Georgia:	Bulldogs
Georgia Tech:	Yellow Jackets
Harvard:	Crimson
Hawaii:	Rainbows
Idaho:	Vandals
Illinois:	Fighting Illini

Indiana:	Hoosiers
Iowa:	Hawkeyes
Iowa State:	Cyclones
Kansas:	Jayhawks
Kentucky:	Wildcats
Louisiana State:	Fighting Tigers
Louisville:	Cardinals
Maryland:	Terrapins, Terps (a turtle)
Miami:	Hurricanes
Michigan:	Wolverines
Michigan State:	Spartans
Minnesota:	Golden Gophers
Mississippi:	Rebels, Ole Miss
Nebraska:	Cornhuskers
New Mexico:	Lobos (Spanish for "Wolves")
North Carolina:	Tar Heels
North Carolina State:	Wolfpack
Northwestern:	Wildcats
Notre Dame:	Fighting Irish
Ohio State:	Buckeyes
Oklahoma:	Sooners
Oregon:	Ducks
Oregon State:	Beavers
U. of Pennsylvania (Penn):	Quakers
Penn State:	Nittany Lions
Pittsburgh:	Panthers
Princeton:	Tigers
Purdue:	Boilermakers
Rice:	Owls
South Carolina:	Gamecocks
Southern Methodist:	Mustangs
S.W. Louisiana:	Ragin' Cajuns
Stanford:	Cardinal (note no "s" at the end of Cardinal)
Syracuse:	Orangemen
Temple:	Owls
Tennessee:	Volunteers
Texas:	Longhorns
Texas A & M:	Aggies (for Agriculture, the "A" in A & M)

Texas Christian:	Horned Frogs
Tulane:	Green Wave
U.C.L.A.:	Bruins
U.S.C. (Southern California):	Trojans
Vanderbilt:	Commodores (after founder, "Commodore" Vanderbilt)
Virginia:	Cavaliers
Wake Forest:	Demon Deacons
Washington:	Huskies
West Virginia:	Mountaineers
Wisconsin:	Badgers
Wyoming:	Cowboys
Yale:	Bulldogs, Elis

Bowl Games

All-American Bowl, Birmingham, Alabama
Aloha Bowl, Honolulu, Hawaii
Bluebonnet Bowl, Houston, Texas
Citrus Bowl, Orlando, Florida
Cotton Bowl, Dallas, Texas
Fiesta Bowl, Tempe, Arizona
Freedom Bowl, Anaheim, California
Gator Bowl, Jacksonville, Florida
Hall of Fame Bowl, Tampa, Florida
Holiday Bowl, San Diego, California
Hula Bowl, Honolulu, Hawaii
Independence Bowl, Shreveport, Louisiana
Liberty Bowl, Memphis, Tennessee
Orange Bowl, Miami, Florida
Peach Bowl, Atlanta, Georgia
Rose Bowl, Pasadena, California (the oldest bowl game)
Sugar Bowl, New Orleans, Louisiana
Sun Bowl, El Paso, Texas

The Record Book

Baseball Records

Batting

Highest Career Batting Average:	Ty Cobb, .366
Highest Batting Average, Season:	Rogers Hornsby, .424
Most Consecutive Games:	Lou Gehrig, 2130
Most Games, Career:	Pete Rose, 3562
Most Home Runs, Career:	Henry Aaron, 755
Most Home Runs, Season:	Babe Ruth, 60 in 154 games Roger Maris, 61 in 162 games
Most RBIs, Career:	Henry Aaron, 2297
Most Runs Scored, Career:	Ty Cobb, 2245
Most Hits, Career:	Pete Rose, 4256
Most Hits, Season:	George Sisler, 257
Most Consecutive Games, Batted Safely:	Joe DiMaggio, 56
Most At Bats, Career:	Henry Aaron, 12,364
Most Grand Slams, Career:	Lou Gehrig, 23
Most Grand Slams, Season:	Ernie Banks, Jim Gentile, 5
Most Walks, Season:	Babe Ruth, 170
Most Stolen Bases, Career:	Rickey Henderson, 973 (at press time)
Most Stolen Bases, Season:	Rickey Henderson, 130
Most Strikeouts, at Bat:	Reggie Jackson, 2459
Most Walks, at Bat:	Babe Ruth, 2056

Pitching

Most Games, Career:	Hoyt Wilhelm, 1070
Most Complete Games, Career:	Cy Young, 751
Most Games Won, Career:	Cy Young, 511
Most Games Won, Season (since 1900):	Jack Chesbro, 41
Most Consecutive Games Won:	Carl Hubbell, 24
Most No-Hitters, Career:	Nolan Ryan, 7
Most Strikeouts, Season:	Nolan Ryan, 383
Most Strikeouts, Career:	Nolan Ryan, 5076
Most Strikeouts, Game:	Roger Clemens, 20

Basketball Records

Most Games, Career:	Kareem Abdul-Jabbar, 1560
Most Complete Games, Season:	Wilt Chamberlain, 79
Most Points, Career:	Kareem Abdul-Jabbar, 38,387
Most Points, Season:	Wilt Chamberlain, 4029
Most Points, Game:	Wilt Chamberlain, 100
Most Personal Fouls, Career:	Kareem Abdul-Jabbar, 4657
Most Assists, Career:	Oscar Robertson, 9887
Most Field Goals, Career:	Kareem Abdul-Jabbar, 15,837

Hockey Records

Most Games, Career:	Gordie Howe, 1767
Most Points, Career:	Wayne Gretzky, 1979 (through 1990 season)
Most Goals, Career:	Gordie Howe, 801

Football Records

Most Seasons, Active Player:	George Blanda, 26
Most Seasons, Head Coach:	George Halas, 30
Most Points, Career:	George Blanda, 2002
Most Points, Season:	Paul Hornung, 176
Most Touchdowns, Career:	Jim Brown, 126
Most Touchdowns, Season:	John Riggins, 24
Most Touchdowns, Game:	Gale Sayers, William Jones, Eric Nevers, 6
Most Field Goals, Career:	Jan Stenerud, 373
Most Yards Gained, Career:	Walter Payton, 16,726
Most Yards Gained, Season:	Eric Dickerson, 2105
Most Yards Gained, Game:	Walter Payton, 275
Most Passes Attempted, Season:	Dan Marino, 623
Most Passes Attempted, Game:	George Blanda, 68
Most Passes Completed, Career:	Fran Tarkenton, 3686
Most Passes Completed, Season:	Dan Marino, 378
Most Passes Completed, Game:	Richard Todd, 42
Most Passes Received, Career:	Steve Largent, 819
Most Passes Received, Season:	Art Monk, 106
Most Passes Received, Game:	Tom Fears, 18

Sports Trophies

America's Cup:	yachting championship
Calder Trophy:	professional hockey's outstanding rookie
Davis Cup:	world tennis championship (awarded to a nation's team)
Grey Cup:	Canadian Football League Championship
Hart Trophy:	professional hockey's Most Valuable Player
Heisman Memorial Trophy:	outstanding college football player
Lady Byng Trophy:	professional hockey, for best sportsmanship
Vince Lombardi Trophy:	winner of football's Superbowl
James Norris Trophy:	professional hockey's leading defenseman
Art Ross Trophy:	professional hockey's leading scorer
Ryder Cup:	winner, U.S. vs. British professional golf team match
Stanley Cup:	professional hockey championship
Vezina Trophy:	professional hockey's leading goalkeeper
World Cup:	world soccer championship (held every four years)
Cy Young Award:	professional baseball's outstanding pitchers (one from each league)

The Olympics

Years in Which Both Olympics Were Held in the Same Country

1924: France
1932: United States
1936: Germany

OLYMPIC SITES (WINNERS)

	Winter	Summer
1896	—	Athens (US)
1900	—	Paris (US)
1904	—	St. Louis (US)
1908	—	London (US)
1912	—	Stockholm (US)
1920	—	Antwerp (US)
1924	Chamonix, France (Norway)	Paris (US)
1928	St. Moritz, Switz. (Norway)	Amsterdam (US)
1932	Lake Placid, N.Y. (US)	Los Angeles (US)
1936	Garmisch-Partenkirchen, Germany (Norway)	Berlin (Germany)
1948	St. Moritz, Switz. (Sweden)	London (US)
1952	Oslo (Norway)	Helsinki (US)
1956	Contina d'Ampezzo, Italy (USSR)	Melbourne (USSR)
1960	Squaw Valley, California (USSR)	Rome (USSR)
1964	Innsbruck, Austria (USSR)	Tokyo (US)
1968	Grenoble, France (Norway)	Mexico City (US)
1972	Sapporo, Japan (USSR)	Munich (USSR)
1976	Innsbruck (USSR)	Montreal (USSR)
1980	Lake Placid (E. Germany)	Moscow (USSR)
1984	Sarajevo, Yugoslavia (USSR)	Los Angeles (US)
1988	Calgary, Alberta (USSR)	Seoul, South Korea (USSR)
1992	Albertville, France	Barcelona, Spain
1994	Lillehammer, Norway	—
1996	—	Atlanta

Note: 1992 is the last year that the Winter and Summer Olympics will be held in the same year. The following Winter Olympics will be in 1994, and the Summer Olympics in 1996, and thereafter they will always be two years apart.

Cities That Have Hosted More Than One Olympics

Innsbruck, Austria: 1964, 1976
Lake Placid: 1932, 1980
London: 1908, 1948
Los Angeles: 1932, 1984
Paris: 1904, 1924
St. Moritz, Switzerland: 1928, 1948

Founder of the Modern Olympics:

Baron Pierre Coubertin

Track

First 4-Minute Mile:

Roger Bannister (1954)

Horse Racing

Triple Crown

The Triple Crown consists of:

Kentucky Derby ("The Run for the Roses"), Churchill Downs, Kentucky
Preakness ("The Run for the Black-Eyed Susans"), Pimlico Racetrack, Maryland
Belmont Stakes ("The Run for the Carnations"), Belmont Racetrack, New York

Triple Crown Winners

1919: Sir Barton
1930: Gallant Fox
1935: Omaha
1937: War Admiral
1941: Whirlaway
1943: Count Fleet
1946: Assault
1948: Citation
1973: Secretariat
1977: Seattle Slew
1978: Affirmed

- One of the most famous horses ever, Man o' War, did not win the Triple Crown. He won the Preakness and Belmont but was not entered in the Kentucky Derby.

Boxing

Only boxer to win heavyweight title three times

Muhammad Ali

Only heavyweight champ to retire undefeated

Rocky Marciano

Longest reign as heavyweight champ

Joe Louis (June 1937–March 1949)

Soccer

Soccer ("Football" to everyone but the United States and Canada) holds its championship, the World Cup, every four years. It was first held in 1930. The most recent World Cup was held in Italy in 1990, with West Germany winning. The 1994 World Cup will be held in the United States.

Players' Nicknames

Many sports figures have colorful nicknames. Here is a potpourri, arranged by sport.

Basketball

Bill Bradley:	Dollar Bill
Wilt Chamberlain:	Wilt the Stilt, The Big Dipper
Julius Erving:	Dr. J
Earvin Johnson:	Magic
Pete Maravich:	Pistol Pete
Earl Monroe:	Earl the Pearl
Oscar Robertson:	The Big O

Baseball

Hank Aaron:	Hammerin' Hank
Dennis Boyd:	Oil Can
Ty Cobb:	The Georgia Peach
Joe DiMaggio:	Joltin' Joe, The Yankee Clipper
Leo Durocher:	Leo the Lip
Lou Gehrig:	The Iron Horse
Dwight Gooden:	Doc, Dr. K ("K" is how a strikeout is scored)
Jim Hunter:	Catfish
Walter Johnson:	The Big Train
Reggie Jackson:	Mr. October
Willie Mays:	The Say Hey Kid
Pete Rose:	Charlie Hustle
Babe Ruth:	The Sultan of Swat, The Bambino
Tom Seaver:	Tom Terrific
Casey Stengel:	The Perfesser
Ted Williams:	The Splendid Splinter
Carl Yastrzemski:	Yaz
"Murderers Row":	the heart of the 1927 Yankees, batting order, which included Ruth, Gehrig, Tony Lazzeri, Bob Meusel and Mark Koenig

Boxing

Muhammad Ali:	The Louisville Lip, The Greatest
James J. Corbett:	Gentleman Jim
Jack Dempsey:	The Manassa Mauler
Joe Louis:	The Brown Bomber
John L. Sullivan:	The Great John L.

Football

Alan Ameche:	The Horse
Sam Baugh:	Slingin' Sammy
Paul Bryant:	Bear
Red Grange:	The Galloping Ghost
Joe Greene:	Mean Joe Greene

Lou Groza:	The Toe
George Halas:	Papa Bear
Elroy Hirsch:	Crazy Legs
Paul Hornung:	The Golden Boy
Joe Namath:	Broadway Joe
William Perry:	Refrigerator
O. J. Simpson:	Juice
"The Four Horsemen":	name given by sportswriter Grantland Rice to 1922–24 Notre Dame backfield (Harry Stuhlduher, Don Miller, Jim Crowley, Elmer Layden).

Golf

Jack Nicklaus:	The Golden Bear
Greg Norman:	Great White Shark
Sam Snead:	Slammin' Sammy

Hockey

Wayne Gretzky:	The Great One
Bobby Hull:	The Golden Jet

Tennis

Rod Laver:	Rocket
Ilie Nastase:	Nasty

Quiz 13: SPORTS

Clues:

1. This team has bounced from Boston to Milwaukee to Atlanta.
2. The Green Wave can be found at this Southern school.
3. They're on the field when the Bucs meet the Bums.
4. The Ryder Cup is given in this sport.
5. The only sport whose divisions are named for people, not locations.
6. A successful season for the Hamilton Tiger Cats would yield this trophy.
7. Site of the only Winter Olympics ever held in Asia.
8. The Rose Bowl brings together the champs of these two conferences.
9. As a boy, he played hoops as Lew Alcindor.
10. It's the "House that Ruth built."

Answers:

1. Who are the Braves?
2. What is Tulane?
3. Who are the Pittsburgh Pirates and L.A. Dodgers?
4. What is golf?
5. What is hockey?
6. What is the Grey Cup (Canadian Football Championship)?
7. What is Sapporo, Japan?
8. What are the Pac 10 and the Big 10?
9. Who is Kareem Abdul-Jabbar?
10. What is Yankee Stadium?

CHAPTER 14

Royalty

Basically, **Jeopardy!** concentrates on British Royalty, which apparently fascinates most Americans and still has some political and emotional ties for the Canadian viewers. So, we've spent more time on British Royalty than on other houses, but we've thrown those in as well.

British Royalty

Royal Lines

House of Normandy

William I (the Conqueror)
William II
Henry I

House of Blois

Stephen

House of Plantagenet

Henry II
Richard I, Lion Heart
John (Lackland)
Henry III
Edward I
Edward II

House of Plantagenet

Edward III
Edward IV
Richard II

House of Lancaster

Henry IV
Henry V
Henry VI

House of York

Edward IV
Edward V
Richard III

House of Tudor

Henry VII
Henry VIII
Edward VI
(Lady Jane Grey: uncrowned Queen for nine days)
Mary I (Bloody Mary)
Elizabeth I

House of Stuart

James I

House of Stuart

Charles I (beheaded)
Charles II
James II

House of Orange

William III and Mary II

House of Stuart

Anne

House of Hanover

George I
George II
George III
George IV
William IV

House of Saxe-Coburg-Gotha

Victoria
Edward VII

House of Windsor*

George V
Edward VIII (abdicated)
George VI
Elizabeth II

*Note: The House of Saxe-Coburg-Gotha changed its name to Windsor during World War I to get away from the German associations of the original name.

The Reigning Royal Family

Queen Elizabeth II (succeeded 1952)
  Prince Philip (Mountbatten), her husband
Prince Charles (Prince of Wales; heir to the throne)
  Diana, Princess of Wales (née Spencer), his wife

Prince William and Prince Henry (their sons, second and third in line to the throne)
Prince Andrew (Duke of York; fourth in line)
Sarah, Duchess of York (née Ferguson), his wife
Prince Edward
Princess Anne
Mark Phillips (her husband, separated)
Princess Margaret (the Queen's sister; divorced from Anthony Armstrong-Jones, Viscount Linley)
Mary, the Queen Mother (or "Queen Mum" as most of Britain affectionately calls her)

Facts about Other British Royals

Longest Reign: Queen Victoria, 1837–1901
Longest Male Reign: George III, 1760–1820
Uncrowned Monarchs:
Edward V (killed in the Tower of London as a child)
Lady Jane Grey (put on the throne, for nine days, after the death of Edward VI)
Edward VIII (abdicated before coronation)
Wives of Henry VIII:
Catherine of Aragon (divorced; mother of Mary I)
Anne Boleyn (beheaded; mother of Elizabeth I)
Jane Seymour (died; mother of Edward VI)
Anne of Cleves (divorced)
Catherine Howard (beheaded)
Catherine Parr (outlived Henry)

(There's a ditty to help you remember the fate of Henry's wives: "Divorced, beheaded, died; divorced, beheaded, survived.")

Other Monarchies (Current)

Besides Britain, several other countries still have crowned heads of state. These are listed by house, followed by the monarch's title and name.

Belgium

Saxe-Coburg: King Baudouin

Denmark

Amalienborg: Queen Margrethe II

Japan

(no name): Emperor Akihito (longest continuous dynasty in the world)

Jordan

Hashemites: King Hussein

Kuwait

Al Sabah: Sheikh Jabr al-Ahmad Al Sabah

Luxembourg

Orange Nassau: Grand Duke Jean

Monaco

Grimaldi: Prince Rainier

Morocco

Cherifi Alaoui: King Hassan II

Nepal

Shah: Birendera Bir Bikram Shah

Netherlands

Orange: Queen Beatrix

Norway

(no name): King Harald V

Saudi Arabia

Al Saud: King Fahd

Spain

Bourbon: King Juan Carlos

Sweden

Bernadotte: King Carl XVI Gustaf (descended from one of Napoleon's marshals)

Thailand

Chakkri: Bhumibol

Other countries with hereditary rulers: Liechtenstein, Lesotho, Swaziland, Bahrain, Qatar, Oman, Tonga, Brunei, Malaysia, Bhutan

Famous Past Dynasties

For these royal houses, we've given the last monarch to sit on the throne, along with the year the reign ended.

Austria

Hapsburgs: Emperor Karl (Charles) (1918)

Egypt

King Farouk (1952)

Ethiopia

Emperor Haile Selassie (1974)

France

Capets: King Philip VI (1350)
Valois: King Louis XII (1515)
Bourbon: King Charles X (1830)
Orleans: King Louis-Philippe (1848)
Bonaparte: Emperor Napoleon III (1870)

Greece

Danish line: King Constantine (1967)

Iran (Persia)

Qajars: Ahmad (1925)
Pahlavis: Mohammad Reza Shah Pahlavi (1979)

Italy

Savoy: King Humbert II (Umberto) (1946)

Portugal

Braganzas: King Manoel II (1910)

Prussia, Germany

Hohenzollerns: Kaiser Wilhelm II (1918)

Romania

Hohenzollern-Sigmaringen: King Michael (1947)

Russia

Romanovs: Tsar Nicholas II (1917)

Spain

Hapsburgs: King Charles II (1700)

Quiz 14: ROYALTY

Clues:

1. More British kings have had these names than any other.
2. This should be William and Mary's school color.
3. When Prince Charles becomes king, this will be his number.
4. This Iranian dynasty produced only two Shahs.
5. The House of Orleans' first and last king.
6. Britain's first four Georges all belonged to this royal house.
7. Before they ruled all of Germany, the Hohenzollerns ruled here.
8. Charles II's wife, Catherine of Braganza, came from this kingdom.
9. The longest continuous ruling house is here.
10. He was the British "King who lost America."

Answers:

1. What are Henry and Edward?
2. What is orange (the House of Orange)?
3. What is Charles III?
4. What is Pahlavi?
5. Who is Louis-Philippe?
6. What is Hanover?
7. What is Prussia?
8. What is Portugal?
9. What is Japan?
10. Who is George III?

CHAPTER 15

U.S. and Foreign Currency

Here's an everyday sort of thing that provides a wealth of information that **Jeopardy!** loves to mine.

U.S. Currency Facts

COINS

Coins	**Front** (obverse)	**Back** (reverse)	**Year Introduced**
1 ct	Lincoln	Lincoln Memorial	1909 (reverse changed, 1959)
5 ct	Jefferson	Monticello	1938
10 ct	F. D. Roosevelt	Torch	1946
25 ct	Washington	Eagle	1932

Coins	Front (obverse)	Back (reverse)	Year Introduced
50 ct	Kennedy	Presidential seal	1964
$1	Eisenhower	Moon landing (Eagle on Moon)	1971–78
$1	Susan B. Anthony	Moon landing	1979–81

Mottoes on Coins

Front: In God We Trust, Liberty
Back: E Pluribus Unum ("Out of Many, One")

Retired Coins

1 ct: Indian head
5 ct: Indian head; buffalo reverse
10 ct: Mercury head
25 ct: Standing Liberty
50 ct: Benjamin Franklin; Liberty Bell reverse

BILLS

Bills:	Front	Back
$1	Washington	Great Seal of the United States
$2	Jefferson	Signing of the Declaration of Independence
$5	Lincoln	Lincoln Memorial
$10	Hamilton	U.S. Treasury
$20	Jackson	White House
$50	Grant	U.S. Capitol
$100	B. Franklin	Independence Hall
(no longer in circulation)		
$500	McKinley	($500)
$1000	G. Cleveland	($1000)

Bills:	Front	Back
$10,000	Salmon P. Chase	($10,000)
$100,000	Woodrow Wilson	($100,000)

Mottoes on Great Seal, Dollar Bill

Novus Ordo Seclorum: "A new order for the ages."
Annuit Coeptis: "He looks favorably on our undertaking."

Foreign Exchange

It may be just pocket change, but do you know where you'd be if you were spending shekels? Drachmas? Rands? How many countries other than the U.S. use the term "dollars"?

Argentina:	austral
Australia:	dollar
Austria:	schilling (made up of 100 groschen)
Belgium:	franc
Brazil:	cruzeiro
Britain:	pound (made up of 100 pence; Britain no longer has shillings, farthings, ha'pennies or guineas)
Canada:	dollar
Chile:	peso
China:	yuan
Colombia:	peso
Czechoslovakia:	koruna
Denmark:	krone
Ecuador:	sucre
Egypt:	pound, guinea
Finland:	mark
France:	franc (made up of 100 centimes)

Germany:	mark (made up of 100 pfennigs)
Greece:	drachma
Hong Kong:	dollar
Hungary:	forint
India:	rupee
Indonesia:	rupiah
Iran:	rial
Iraq:	dinar
Ireland:	punt
Israel:	shekel
Italy:	lira
Japan:	yen
Jordan:	dinar
Kenya:	shilling
Lebanon:	pound
Malaysia:	ringgit
Mexico:	peso (made up of 100 centavos)
Morocco:	dirham
Netherlands:	guilder
New Zealand:	dollar
Nigeria:	naira
Norway:	krone
Pakistan:	rupee
Paraguay:	guarani
Peru:	new sol
Philippines:	peso
Poland:	zloty
Portugal:	escudo
Romania:	leu
Saudi Arabia:	riyal
Singapore:	dollar
South Africa:	rand
South Korea:	won
Spain:	peseta
Sweden:	krona
Switzerland:	franc
Syria:	lira, pound
Thailand:	baht
Turkey:	lira
USSR:	ruble

United Arab Emirates:	dirham
Uruguay:	peso
Venezuela:	bolivar
Vietnam:	dong
Yugoslavia:	dinar
Zaire:	zaire

Quiz 15:
U.S. CURRENCY AND OTHERS

Clues:

1. The largest U.S. bill now in circulation.
2. Total value of money featuring George Washington.
3. The English translation of the currency most common to Scandinavia.
4. The only building to appear on a U.S. coin *and* bill.
5. These make up French francs.
6. These two European countries both use lira.
7. One "Grant" equals this many "Hamiltons."
8. This African country's currency is the same as its name.
9. Poland's currency is the last, alphabetically.
10. This preceded the Lincoln penny.

Answers:

1. What is $100?
2. What is $1.25?
3. What is "crown"?
4. What is the Lincoln Memorial?
5. What are centimes?
6. What are Italy and Turkey?
7. What is 5 ($50 = five $10 bills)?
8. What is Zaire?
9. What is the zloty?
10. What is the Indian head penny?

CHAPTER 16

Classical Music and Opera

Like rock and roll, some of you already know this and some don't. Bascially, it's a question of knowing who composed what. Who wrote 104 symphonies? Whose "Unfinished" symphony is famous? Which Italian composer used Shakespeare as a source for many of his operas? These are not all the works by all the composers, but a good list of the most famous by the most famous.

Classical Music

Bach (German)

Brandenburg Concertos

Samuel Barber (British)

Overture, *School for Scandal*

Bela Bartok (Hungarian)

Miraculous Mandarin

Ludwig von Beethoven (German)

Emperor Concerto
Missa Solemnis
Overtures
Egmont
Fidelio
Leonore
Symphonies (nine total)

No. 3: "Eroica"
No. 6: "Pastoral"
No. 9: "Choral"

Hector Berlioz (French)

Damnation of Faust
Harold in Italy
Romeo and Juliet
Overtures
Beatrice and Benedict
Benvenuto Cellini
King Lear
The Roman Carnival

Aaron Copland (U.S.)

Appalachian Spring

Claude Debussy (French)

Images
La Mer
Nocturne
Prelude, *Afternoon of a Faun*

Antonin Dvorak (Czech)

Symphony No. 9: "New World"

Franz Joseph ("Papa") Haydn (Austrian)

Symphonies (104 total)
No. 22:"The Philosopher"
No. 26: "Lamentation"
No. 31: "Horn Signal (Lookout)"
No. 45: "Farewell"
No. 48: "Maria Theresa"
No. 60: "Il Distratto"
No. 82: "L'Ours"
No. 83: "La Poule"
No. 85: "La Reine" ("The Queen")
No. 92: "Oxford"
No. 94: "Surprise"
No. 96: "Miracle"
No. 100: "Military"
No. 101: "The Clock"
No. 103: "Drumroll"

Charles Ives (U.S.)

Central Park in the Dark
The Unanswered Question

Franz Liszt (Hungarian)

A Faust Symphony
Mazeppa

Gustav Mahler (German)

Song of the Earth
Symphonies
No. 2: "Resurrection"
No. 8: "Symphony of a Thousand"

Felix Mendelssohn (German)

Overtures
The Hebrides (Fingal's Cave)
Ruy Blas
A Midsummer Night's Dream
Symphonies
No. 3: "Scottish"
No. 4: "Italian"
No. 5: "Reformation"

Wolfgang Amadeus Mozart (Austrian)

Symphonies (Köchel numbers)
No. 25: "Little G Minor"

Mozart (cont.)

No. 31: "Paris"
No. 35: "Haffner"
No. 36: "Linz"
No. 38: "Prague"
No. 41: "Jupiter"

Sergei Prokofiev (Russian)

Peter and the Wolf
Romeo and Juliet
Scythian Suite

Maurice Ravel (French)

Bolero
Daphnis and Chloe
Mother Goose
Spanish Rhapsody
La Valse

Ottorino Respighi (Italian)

The Pines of Rome
The Fountains of Rome

Nikolay Rimsky-Korsakov (Russian)

Scheherazade
Overture: *The Great Russian Easter*

Camille Saint-Saëns (French)

Danse Macabre

Franz Schubert (German)

Symphony No. 4: "Tragic"
No. 8: "Unfinished"

Robert Schumann (German)

Symphonies
No. 1: "Spring"
No. 3: "Rhenish"

Richard Strauss (German)

Don Juan
Don Quixote
Metamorphosis
Salome
Till Eulenspiegel
Thus Spake Zarathustra
Death and Transfiguration

Igor Stravinsky (Russian)

Card Game
Firebird
Petrushka
Rite of Spring
Song of the Nightingale

Peter Tchaikovsky (Russian)

Capriccio Italien
Symphonies
No. 2: "Little Russian"
No. 6: "Pathetique"
1812 Overture

Opera

Now this gets a little more complex, because there are not only composers and their works, but also characters, plots and famous arias.

Opera lovers will tell you that the plots are not the main point. Probably so; in fact, some of the plots largely defy synopsis. But **Jeopardy!** still draws a lot of its opera questions from specific information beyond who wrote what.

Bela Bartok

Bluebeard's Castle

Ludwig von Beethoven

Fidelio

Alban Berg

Lulu
Wozzeck

Hector Berlioz

Benvenuto Cellini
Damnation of Faust
Les Troyens ("The Trojans")
Beatrice and Benedict

Georges Bizet

Carmen

Aleksandr Borodin

Prince Igor

Benjamin Britten

Peter Grimes
The Rape of Lucretia
Billy Budd
Gloriana

Gaetano Donizetti

Lucia di Lammermoor
L'Elisir d'Amore
Lucrezia Borgia
Daughter of the Regiment
Don Pasquale

Christoph Glück

Orpheus and Eurydice
Alcestis
Iphigenia in Aulis
Iphigenia in Taurus

Ruggero Leoncavallo

I Pagliacci ("The Strolling Players")

Pietro Mascagni

Cavalleria Rusticana ("Rustic Chivalry")

Jules Massenet

Manon
Don Quixote

Modest Moussorgsky

Boris Godunov

Wolfgang Mozart

Idomeneo
Abduction from the Seraglio
Marriage of Figaro
Don Giovanni
Cosi fan tutte
The Magic Flute

Jacques Offenbach

Orpheus in the Underworld
The Tales of Hoffman

Amilcare Ponchielli

La Gioconda

Giacomo Puccini

Manon Lescaut
La Boheme
Tosca
Madame Butterfly
La Fanciulla del West ("Girl of the Golden West")
Turandot

Gioacchino Rossini

La Cenerentola ("Cinderella")
Semiramide
William Tell

Johann Strauss

Die Fledermaus ("The Bat")

Richard Strauss

Salome
Elektra
Der Rosenkavalier
Ariadne auf Naxos
The Woman Without a Shadow
Intermezzo

Igor Stravinsky

La Rossignol ("The Nightingale")
The Rake's Progress

Peter Tchaikovsky

Eugene Onegin
The Queen of Spades

Giuseppe Verdi

Nabucco
Macbeth
Rigoletto
Il Trovatore ("The Troubadour")
La Traviata ("The Lost One")
The Sicilian Vespers
The Masked Ball
The Force of Destiny
Don Carlos
Aïda
Otello
Falstaff

Richard Wagner

Rienzi
The Flying Dutchman
Tannhäuser
Tristan and Isolde
Die Meistersinger von Nurnberg
The Ring of the Nibelungen
  Das Rheingold
  Die Walküre
  Siegfried
  Götterdämmerung
Parsifal

Operas Based on Shakespeare

Berlioz: *Beatrice and Benedict* (*Much Ado About Nothing*)
Verdi: *Falstaff* (*Henry IV*, Parts I and II; *Merry Wives of Windsor*), *Macbeth*, *Otello*

"Don" Operas

Massenet: *Don Quixote*
Mozart: *Don Giovanni*
Verdi: *Don Carlos*

Operas Set in Seville

Beethoven: *Fidelio*
Bizet: *Carmen*
Mozart: *Don Giovanni, The Marriage of Figaro*
Rossini: *The Barber of Seville*

Opera Synopses

Beethoven: Fidelio

(Setting: Seville)

Main characters:

Florestan, *a freedom fighter;* Leonore, *his wife;* Pizarro, *his political enemy.*

Plot:

Florestan is arrested by Pizarro. Leonore disguises herself as a young man, calling herself Fidelio, to see Florestan in prison. In the end, justice triumphs; Florestan is freed and Pizarro is arrested.

Bizet: Carmen

(Setting: Seville)

Main characters:

Don Jose, *a guardsman;* Carmen; *a gypsy;* Escamillo, *a toreador (bull fighter).*

Plot:

Don Jose is led astray by his love for the fickle Carmen; Escamillo is his rival for her affection. In the end, Jose kills Carmen. Two famous arias: Carmen's "Habanera"; Escamillo's "Toreador Song."

Donizetti: The Daughter of the Regiment

(Setting: The Tyrol, 1815)

Main characters:

Marie, *a canteen manager in a French regiment;* Tonio, *her lover;* Countess of Berkenfeld.

Plot:

Marie has been raised in the regiment; she loves Tonio, whose life she saves. Marie is revealed to be, first, the niece and then the daughter of the Countess, who tries to marry off Marie to a nobleman. The regiment's soldiers intervene, allowing Marie to wed Tonio.

Donizetti: Lucia di Lammermoor

(Setting: 17th-century Scotland)

Main characters:

Lucia; Lord Enrico Ashton of Lammermoor, *her brother;* Edgardo of Ravenswood, *her lover.*

Plot:

Lord Ashton treacherously disrupts Lucia's romance with Edgardo in order to force her marriage to rich Lord Bucklaw. Lucia goes mad and kills Bucklaw (the famous "Mad Scene") and later dies; Edgardo kills himself. Based on Sir Walter Scott's novel, *The Bride of Lammermoor*.

Leoncavallo: I Pagliacci

(Setting: village of Montalto)

Main characters:

Canio, *head of a theatrical company;* Nedda, *his wife;* Tonio, *a clown;* Silvio, *a villager.*

Plot:

Nedda is unfaithful to Canio, who sings the famous aria *Vesti la giubba,* despairing deeply while playing a comedy role. During the performance of a comedy, Canio, playing the role of Pagliaccio, kills Nedda and Silvio on stage.

Massenet: Manon

Puccini: Manon Lescaut

(Setting: 18th century France—Amiens, Paris, Le Havre)

Main characters:	**Plot:**
Count de Grieux; Manon, *an adventuress.*	Two operas about the tempestuous affair between the Count and the sometimes fickle Manon. Eventually, Manon is forced into exile (for prostitution, by Massenet; for thievery, by Puccini); she falls ill and dies in the Count's arms.

Mozart: Abduction from the Seraglio (Die Entfuhrung aus dem Serail)

(Setting: 16th-century Turkey)

Main characters:	**Plot:**
Constanze; Blonde, *her maid;* Belmonte; Pasha.	Belmonte helps Constanze and Blonde escape from the Pasha's seraglio (harem), where they were sold by pirates. Mozart's first stage work after settling in Vienna.

Mozart: Don Giovanni (Don Juan)

(Setting: Seville)

Main characters:	**Plot:**
Don Giovanni; Dona Anna; the Commandant; Don Pedro.	Don Giovanni is a scandalous rake, whose libertine ways lead to his consignment to hell by the statue of the Commandant. Don Giovanni had killed him in a duel and later invited the statue to dinner. This is often called Mozart's finest opera.

Mozart: The Marriage of Figaro (Le Nozze di Figaro)

(Setting: 17th-century Seville)

Main characters:

Figaro, *a valet;* Count Almaviva, *his master;* Susanna, *Figaro's betrothed.*

Plot:

A typical "opera bouffe," with lovers and would-be lovers, and mistaken identities. Like *The Barber of Seville,* based on plays by Beaumarchais.

Offenbach: Tales of Hoffmann

(Setting: 19th-century Nuremberg, Venice and Munich)

Main characters:

Hoffmann, *a poet; his three loves,* Olympia, Giulietta, Antonia; Coppelius, *a magician in different guises.*

Plot:

Hoffmann, in a tavern, narrates three unfortunate affairs and his recurrent rivalry with Coppelius. After telling his story, Hoffmann loses his latest love, Stella, to his rival, Linsdorf. Offenbach died before this opera was ever performed.

Puccini: La Boheme

(Setting: 19th-century Paris)

Main characters:

Rodolfo, *a poet,* and Mimi, *a seamstress;* Marcello and Musetta.

Plot:

The turmoils of love among Parisian artists and their friends, ending with Mimi's death in their attic. Leoncavallo wrote a similar opera with the same name.

Puccini: Girl of the Golden West

(Setting: Gold Rush California)

Main characters:	Plot:
Minnie, *owner of the Polka Saloon;* Sheriff Jack Rance; Dick Johnson, *an outlaw.*	Minnie strives to protect Johnson (a.k.a. the outlaw Ramerrez) from the law: once, she cheats at poker with Rance to save Johnson's life; in the end, she talks lynchers out of hanging him.

Puccini: Madame Butterfly

(Setting: Nagasaki in the early 1900s)

Main characters:	Plot:
Cio-Cio-San (Madame Butterfly), *a geisha;* Lt. Pinkerton, *a U.S. naval officer.*	Pinkerton has a cavalier affair with Butterfly, who loves him deeply. After his ship sails, she waits faithfully for him. He returns with his American wife, who asks Butterfly to relinquish the son she had with Pinkerton. She agrees and commits suicide. Famous aria: "Un Bel Di." Ironically, this classic opera had a disastrous premier and had to be revised by Puccini.

Puccini: Tosca

(Setting: Rome, 1800)

Main characters:	Plot:
Floria Tosca, *an opera singer;* Mario, *her lover;* Scarpia, *chief of police.*	Tosca and Mario's love, against the background of Napoleon's invasion of Italy. Scarpia arrests Mario and tries to woo Tosca, who gives herself to him

to save Mario's life. Tosca kills Scarpia, but Mario's supposedly phony execution turns out to be real. Tosca throws herself from a prison parapet.

Puccini: Turandot

(Setting: Ancient Peking)

Main characters:

Princess Turandot; *the servants* Ping, Pang, Pong; Prince Calaf, the Unknown Prince; Liu, *a slave girl.*

Plot:

Turandot poses three riddles to her would-be suitors and executes each who fails to answer. Calaf succeeds and Turandot tries to renege on her pledge to marry; he agrees to release her if she can discover his identity. Liu, who loves Calaf, commits suicide rather than reveal that he is a prince of the Tartar enemy. Turandot realizes she loves Calaf. Puccini's last opera; he died before finishing it. Although another composer completed *Turandot,* the conductor Toscanini, per Puccini's wish, stopped the premiere performance at the point at which Puccini had left off.

Rossini: The Barber of Seville

(Setting: Seville)

Main characters:

Figaro, *a barber;* et al.

Plot:

One of the great Italian comic operas ("opera bouffe"), with conspiring lovers and mistaken identities. Like Mozart's *Marriage of Figaro,* based on plays by Beaumarchais. *Barber*'s premiere in Rome was a disaster.

Smetana: The Bartered Bride

(Setting: 19th-century Bohemia)

Main characters:

Marie; Hans; Wenzel; Kezal, *a marriage broker.*

Plot:

Marie is betrothed to Wenzel but loves Hans, who apparently is bribed to give her up (hence the "bartered bride"), but only as a trick to actually gain her. First important Bohemian folk opera.

Richard Strauss: Der Rosenkavalier (The Cavalier of the Rose)

(Setting: 18th-century Vienna)

Main characters:

The Feldmarshallin (Princess von Werdenberg); Baron Ochs; Octavian, *the Princess' lover;* Sophie, *loved by the Baron.*

Plot:

The Baron falls for Octavian, disguised as a maid. The Princess uses Octavian to convey a silver rose, the Baron's love token, to Sophie. Octavian and Sophie fall in love. After various intrigues and mistaken identities, the Princess blesses the marriage of Octavian and Sophie.

Verdi: Aïda

(Setting: Ancient Egypt)

Main characters:

Aïda, *an Ethiopian slave;* Radames, *captain of the guard;* Amneris, *daughter of Pharaoh;* King of Ethiopia, *Aida's father.*

Plot:

Amneris wants to marry Radames, who loves Aïda. Radames betrays Egypt's strategy against Ethiopia to Aïda and is condemned to be buried alive; Aïda joins him for his entombment. Opera was written to celebrate opening of the Suez Canal in 1869, but performance was postponed until after Franco-Prussian war.

Verdi: A Masked Ball (Un ballo in maschera)

(Setting: 18th-century Sweden)

Main characters:

King Riccardo; Renato, *his secretary;* Amelia, *Renato's wife;* Ulrica, *a fortune-teller.*

Plot:

Riccardo and Amelia are in love; jealous Renato kills the King at a masked ball. Based on the assassination of King Gustavus III in 1792; because its regicide theme was politically dangerous in the 19th century, the opera was initially presented as being set in colonial Massachusetts.

Verdi: Nabucco

(Setting: Ancient Babylonia)

Plot:

Story of the Israelites in exile in Babylon, and their yearning for their homeland. Famous chorus: *Va pensiero.* One of Verdi's earliest operas, and seen as a political metaphor for the growing Italian desire for unification.

Verdi: Rigoletto

(Setting: 16th-century Mantua)

Main characters:

Rigoletto, *a hunchback court jester;* Gilda, *his daughter;* Duke of Mantua.

Plot:

Rigoletto helps the Duke with his various love affairs, until Gilda becomes the Duke's next desire. Rigoletto's plot to kill the Duke results in Gilda's death instead. Famous arias: *"La donna è mobile"; "Caro nome."*

Verdi: La Traviata (The Lost One)

(Setting: Paris, 1840)

Main characters:

Violetta Valery, *a courtesan;* Alfredo Germont, *her lover.*

Plot:

Based on Dumas' *La Dame aux Camelias* (*Camille*). Alfredo loves Violetta despite his father's protest about her status. At last, she breaks off the affair for Alfredo's sake, without telling him why. They are reconciled just as she dies of tuberculosis. This opera was considered a failure when first produced.

Verdi: Il Trovatore (The Troubador)

(Setting: 15th-century Biscay and Aragon)

Main characters:

Manrico; Count di Luna, *his rival;* Leonara; Azucena, *a gypsy.*

Plot:

The rivalry of Manrico and the Count for Leonora, complicated by the machinations of the gypsy Azucena, who knows the two men are actually brothers. Famous chorus: "The Anvil Chorus."

Wagner: The Flying Dutchman

(Setting: 18th-century Norwegian village)

Main characters:

Vanderdecken, *a sailor;* Daland, *a sea captain;* Senta, *his daughter*; Eric, *her lover.*

Plot:

For challenging heaven and hell, Vanderdecken must sail the seas forever on his ship, "The Flying Dutchman," until he is redeemed by the love of a faithful woman. Senta gives up Eric for Vanderdecken, who now fears that she will betray him as well. Vanderdecken sails away; Senta, still faithful, throws herself into the sea.

Wagner: Löhengrin

(Setting: 10th-century Antwerp)

Main characters:

Löhengrin, *a Knight of the Holy Grail;* Elsa of Brabant.

Plot:

Löhengrin is the son of Parsifal (*see below,* Wagner's *Parsifal*). He arrives in a swan-drawn boat, saves Elsa's life and marries her. She promises never to attempt to discover his true identity, but betrays this promise, which forces them to part.

Wagner: The Mastersingers of Nuremberg (Die Meistersinger von Nürnberg)

(Setting: 16th-century Nuremberg)

Main characters:

Pogner, *a goldsmith;* Eva, *his daughter;* Walther von Stolzing, *a knight;* Hans Sachs, *a cobbler.*

Plot

Pogner offers Eva in marriage to the winner of a song contest. Walther hopes to win, but doesn't know the contest rules. Hans recognizes Walther's talent and helps Walther win. Wagner's only comedy; similar in plot to his Tannhauser (*see below*).

Wagner: Parsifal

(Setting: The Castle of Montsalvat)

Main characters:

Parsifal; various Knights of the Holy Grail; Klingsor, *a magician*.

Plot:

Wagner's last drama, concerning the Knights of the Holy Grail, the Grail itself and the Spear that pierced Jesus at the crucifixion. (*See* Wagner's *Löhengrin, above*, about Parsifal's son.)

Wagner: The Ring of the Nibelungen

Wagner's four-part "Ring Cycle." Wagner actually wrote them in reverse order, over a period of 25 years. (Setting: Ancient times)

1. The Rhinegold (Das Rheingold)

Main characters:

Wotan, *ruler of the gods;*
Fasolt and Fafner, *giants;*
Rhine Maidens; Alberich, *King of the Nibelungs;*
Mime, *his brother*.

Plot:

The Rhine Maidens guard magic gold; whoever makes it into a ring could rule the world if he renounces love. Alberich does so. Wotan reneges on giving Fafner and Fasolt his sister in marriage as the price for their building his palace; he offers them Alberich's ring instead. Mime creates the helmet *Tarnhelm,* which allows the wearer to change form. Fafner kills Fasolt to get the ring.

2. The Valkyrie (Die Walküre)

Main characters:	**Plot:**
Brunhilde, *Wotan's daughter;* Siegmund *and his twin sister* Sieglinde, *Wotan's children by a mortal.*	Siegmund and Sieglinde, unaware of their relationship, become lovers. Siegmund steals the sword *Nothung;* together they flee her husband, Hunding. Brunhilde helps them despite Wotan's orders. Siegmund is killed, his sword broken. Brunhilde is deprived of her divinity and put to sleep in a ring of fire; the man who penetrates this ring will be her husband.

3. Siegfried

Main characters:	**Plot:**
Siegfried, *son of Siegmund and Sieglinde.*	Mime tells Siegfried of his parentage and tries to repair the sword *Nothung* for Siegfried to use against Fafner, who is now a dragon and has the Ring. Siegfried slays Fafner; Alberich and Mime argue over the treasure. Siegfried enters the circle of flame and takes Brunhilde. Siegfried slays Fafner.

4. The Twilight of the Gods (Die Götterdämmerung)

Main characters:	**Plot:**
Gunther, *chief of the Gibichungs;* Hagen, *his brother;* Gutrune, *their sister.*	Siegfried gives Brunhilde the Ring. Hagen wants Gunther to marry Brunhilde and Gutrune to marry Siegfried. Siegfried is given a potion that erases his memory; he forgets Brunhilde and agrees to marry Gutrune. When his memory is restored, Hagen kills him.

Hagen kills Gunther over the Ring. Brunhilde dies on Siegfried's funeral pyre. The Rhine floods and the Rhine Maidens retrieve the Ring; Valhalla, the home of the gods, crumbles in flames, destroying the gods.

Wagner: Tannhäuser

(Setting: 13th-century Thuringia)

Main characters:	**Plot:**
Tannhäuser, *a minstrel knight;* Elizabeth, *niece of the landgrave.*	Tannhäuser enters a song contest, the subject of which is love, to win Elizabeth's hand. Offending everyone by singing a sensual song about Venus, he is banished and joins a pilgrimage to Rome. He returns having failed to receive absolution (it will come when the Pope's staff sprouts), and dies as Elizabeth's funeral bier passes by. Later pilgrims bring news that the Pope's staff has sprouted, i.e., Tannhäuser is absolved at last.

Wagner: Tristan and Isolde

(Setting: Cornwall and Brittany)

Main characters:	**Plot:**
Tristan; King Mark of Cornwall, *his uncle;* Isolde, *Princess of Ireland.*	Via a love potion, Tristan and Isolde fall in love as he conveys her to marry Mark. After the wedding, Mark traps the lovers; Tristan is wounded and flees to Brittany. Isolde joins him before he dies, then falls dead over his body.

Ballet

Some classical music is intended to set your toes a-tapping, or at least is composed specifically for ballet. Here are some of the more famous.

Adolph-Charles Adam

Giselle

Georges Bizet

Assembly Ball
Carmen

Claude Debussy

Afternoon of a Faun
Ballade

Serge Prokofiev

Cinderella
Prodigal Son
Romeo and Juliet

Nikolay Rimsky-Korsakov

Capriccio Espanol
Scheherazade

Richard Rodgers

Slaughter on 10th Avenue

Gioacchino Rossini

The Fantastic Toyshop

Charles Camille Saint-Saëns

Dying Swan

Robert Schumann

Carnaval

Igor Stravinsky

Agon
Apollo
The Fairy's Kiss
Firebird
Orpheus
Petrouchka
Rite of Spring

Peter Tchaikovsky

Sleeping Beauty
Swan Lake

Quiz 16:
CLASSICAL MUSIC

Clues:

1. You don't need a detective to know he was Madame Butterfly's lover.
2. Alexander Dumas' *Camille* was the inspiration for this Verdi opera.
3. Ping, Pang and Pong are featured in Puccini's "unfinished" opera.
4. He was Parsifal's son.
5. This composer can be said to "pine for Rome."
6. He provided the plot of Donizetti's *Lucia di Lammermoor.*
7. The tenor best known for the role of the crying clown of *I Pagliacci.*
8. This Verdi opera was based on an actual royal assassination in Sweden.
9. He led a "Danse Macabre."
10. This Stravinsky ballet caused a scandal at its premiere.

Answers:

1. Who is Lt. Pinkerton?
2. What is *La Traviata*?
3. What is *Turandot*?
4. Who is Löhengrin?
5. Who is Respighi?
6. Who is Sir Walter Scott?
7. Who is Enrico Caruso?
8. What is *The Masked Ball*?
9. Who is Saint-Saëns?
10. What is *The Rite of Spring*?

CHAPTER 17

Canada

There are lots of reasons to know some facts about Canada. After all, it is our neighbor to the north; millions of Canadians watch **Jeopardy!**, and—oh, yes—Alex Trebek was born there.

Geography

PROVINCES AND CITIES

Province	Capital	Largest City
Alberta	Edmonton	Calgary
British Columbia	Victoria	Vancouver
Manitoba	Winnipeg	Winnipeg
New Brunswick	Fredericton	St. John
Newfoundland	St. John's	St. John's
Nova Scotia	Halifax	Halifax
Prince Edward Island	Charlottetown	Charlottetown

Province	**Capital**	**Largest City**
Quebec	Quebec	Montreal
Ontario	Toronto	Toronto
Saskatchewan	Regina	Regina
Territory		
Northwest Territories	Yellowknife	Yellowknife
Yukon	Whitehorse	Whitehorse

Most Populous Province

Ontario (9,000,000)

Least Populous Province

Prince Edward Island (125,000)

Largest Province

Quebec

Smallest Province

Prince Edward Island

"Birthplace of Canada"

Charlottetown, Prince Edward Island

Provinces Named for People

Alberta: Princess Louise Caroline Alberta, fourth daughter of Queen Victoria
British Columbia: Columbus
Prince Edward Island: Edward, Duke of Kent

Politics

First Members of Confederation (1867)

Upper Canada (Ontario), Lower Canada (Quebec), Nova Scotia, New Brunswick

Last Province to Join Canada

Newfoundland (1949)

Parliament

House of Commons and Senate

Political Parties

Liberal
Progressive Conservative
New Democrats

First Prime Minister

Sir John A. MacDonald

First French-Canadian Prime Minister

Sir Wilfrid Laurier

Quiz 17: CANADA

Clues:

1. The last province to join Canada.
2. Canada's southernmost province, dipping below the surrounding U.S. border.
3. This is Canada's largest city.
4. This provincial capital is North America's only walled city.
5. Its capital means "Queen" in Latin.
6. These two generals both died in the battle that gave Canada to Britain.
7. The 1990 pact that failed to cement a unified Canada.
8. Canada's poet of the Yukon, his verse serves well.
9. Symbol in the Canadian flag.
10. It's at 24 Sussex Drive, Ottawa.

Answers:

1. What is Newfoundland?
2. What is Ontario?
3. What is Toronto?
4. What is Quebec?
5. What is Saskatchewan (Regina)?
6. Who are Wolfe and Montcalm (at the Plains of Abraham)?
7. What is the Meech Lake Accord?
8. Who is Robert Service?
9. What is the maple leaf?
10. What is the Prime Minister's official residence?

CHAPTER 18

Explorers and Discoverers

This subject is a combination of geography and history. We've included in this the exploration of space, which is another **Jeopardy!** favorite.

Global Exploration

Vikings: Labrador, Nova Scotia, Newfoundland and New England ca. A.D. 1000. They named their settlements Helluland, Markland and Vineland.

Prince Henry the Navigator: Great Portuguese patron of exploration; expeditions financed by Henry explored the Madeiras, the Azores, the Canaries and the West African coast.

Bartolomeu Dias: First to pass the Cape of Good Hope, 1488, for Portugal.

Christopher Columbus: Italian; discovered America for Spain, 1492. He made four voyages and discovered many of the major Caribbean islands (Cuba, Puerto Rico, Jamaica, Hispaniola). Born Christopher Colombo; known in Spanish as Cristoforo Colon.

John Cabot: Newfoundland or Nova Scotia, northeast coast of North America, for England, 1497–98. Cabot was born Giovanni Caboto.

Vasco da Gama: First to reach India, 1498, for Portugal.

Pedro Cabral: Brazil, for Portugal, 1513.

Vasco Nunez de Balboa: Pacific Ocean, for Spain, 1513.

Juan Ponce de Leon: Florida, for Spain, 1513; also searched for the fabled Fountain of Youth.

Hernando Cortez: Conquered Aztec Empire of Mexico, for Spain, 1519.

Ferdinand Magellan: First circumnavigation of the globe, for Spain, 1519–20. Expedition discovered Straits of Magellan and the Philippines, where Magellan was killed. His crew finished the voyage afterward.

Giovanni Verrazano: New York harbor, for France, 1524. The Verrazano-Narrows Bridge connecting Brooklyn and Staten Island across the mouth of New York harbor is named for him.

Francisco Pizarro: Conquered Inca Empire of Peru, for Spain, 1524.

Jacques Cartier: Gulf of St. Lawrence, etc., for France, 1532.

Hernando de Soto: Mississippi River, for Spain, 1539–41.

Francisco de Coronado: Expedition across much of what is now the southwest United States, for Spain, in search of Cibola, the Seven Cities of Gold, 1540.

Samuel de Champlain: Canada, and Lake Champlain, for France, 1603–09.

Henry Hudson: Hudson River, for Holland; Hudson Bay, for England, 1609–10.

Jacques Marquette, Louis Joliet: Explored Mississippi River, for France, 1673.

Sieur de La Salle: Length of the Mississippi River, for France, 1682; laid claim to all lands touching the river, which he called Louisiana for King Louis XIV.

Vitus Bering: Dane; discovered Bering Strait, Alaska, for Russia, 1728, 1741.

James Cook: Three voyages of exploration across the Pacific for Britain, 1768–79. He discovered the east coast of Australia, was the first to sail across the Antarctic Circle, and also discovered Christmas Island and the Hawaiian (Sandwich) Islands, where he was killed.

Alexander Mackenzie: Canadian northwest, for Britain, 1789.

Mungo Park: Explored the Gambia and Niger Rivers, 1795–98, 1805, for Britain.

David Livingstone: Crossed Africa, discovered Victoria Falls, for Britain, 1853–1856.

Richard Burton, John Speke: Exploration of Nile, including source of the White Nile, for Britain, 1858–59.

Henry Stanley: Anglo-American, led expedition to find David Livingstone, 1871.

Robert Peary: First to reach North Pole, for the United States, 1909; there is now some question as to whether he actually reached the Pole. Accompanied by black American explorer, Matthew Henson.

Roald Amundsen: First to reach South Pole, for Norway, 1912, beating the British expedition led by Robert Falcon Scott, all of whose members perished.

Richard Byrd, Floyd Bennett: First flight over the North Pole, for the United States, 1926.

Richard Byrd: First flight over South Pole, for the United States, 1929.

Space Exploration

Firsts and Other Records

First Man in Space: Yuri Gagarin, USSR, 1961

First American in Space (suborbital): Alan Shepard, 1961

First American in Space (orbital): John Glenn, 1962

First Woman in Space: Valentina Tereshkova, USSR, 1963

First American Woman in Space: Sally Ride, 1983

First Space Walk: Aleksei Leonov, USSR, 1965

First U.S. Space Walk: Edward White, 1965

First Flight to the Moon (no landing): Apollo 8 (Frank Borman, Jim Lovell, William Anders), 1968

First Moon Landing: Apollo 11 (Neil Armstrong, first man on the moon, and Edwin Aldrin; Michael Collins orbited in the command module), 1969

Soviet Space Program

Vostok (1 cosmonaut, 6 missions)
Voshkod (2–3 cosmonauts, 2 missions)
Soyuz (1–3 cosmonauts, 8 missions)
Salyut (3 cosmonauts, 1 mission)
Mir (permanent manned space station)

U.S. Space Program

Mercury (1 astronaut, 6 missions) (Mercury capsule with Atlas booster)
Gemini (2 astronauts, 9 missions) (Gemini capsule with Titan booster)
Apollo (3 astronauts, 12 missions) (Apollo capsule with Saturn booster)
Skylab (3 astronauts, 3 missions)
Space Shuttle: First shuttle, Columbia, April 21, 1981
Other shuttles: Challenger (exploded, January 28, 1986); Atlantis, Discovery, Enterprise (prototype, never flown), Endeavor (never flown).

Joint U.S.–Soviet Missions

Apollo 18–Soyuz 19 (3 astronauts, 3 cosmonauts), 1975

Moon Exploration

Number of Moon Landings: 6 (Apollo 11, 12, 14–17) 1969, 1971, 1972
Number of Men to Walk on Moon: 12

Quiz 18:
EXPLORERS AND DISCOVERERS

Clues:

1. Canada's longest river, named for the man who first crossed Canada to the Pacific.
2. We presume you know these two explorers met dramatically in Ujiji, Tanganyika, in 1871.
3. Born Giovanni Caboto in Italy, he did his exploring for England.
4. This pioneering spacecraft crashed to Earth in Australia in 1979.
5. In Russian, it means "star," the first Soviet spacecraft.
6. Robert Peary's black co-explorer of the Arctic.
7. Titan boosters lifted this two-man U.S. space capsule.
8. Meaning of "Mir," the Soviet permanent space station.
9. Discoverer of New York Harbor.
10. He destroyed Atahualpa's empire (the Incas).

Answers:

1. What is the Mackenzie?
2. Who are Stanley and Livingstone?
3. Who is John Cabot?
4. What is Skylab?
5. What is Vostok?
6. Who is Matthew Henson?
7. What is the Gemini?
8. What is "peace"?
9. Who is Giovanni Verrazano?
10. Who is Francisco Pizarro?

CHAPTER 19

Holidays and Observances; the Calendar

Everyone looks forward to holidays, except **Jeopardy!** players. This category trips up lots of players as they try to remember which holidays fall when and which months "hath 30 days."

U.S. Public Holidays

These are the public holidays celebrated in the United States, the days set aside for them, and the only dates on the calendar on which they can occur—all facts that **Jeopardy!** loves to use.

New Year's Day: January 1

Martin Luther King's Birthday: 3rd Monday in January (January 15–21 are the only possible dates)

Presidents Day: 3rd Monday in February (February 15–21 are only possible dates; this is a combination of the holidays celebrating Lincoln's Birthday, Feb. 12, and Washington's Birthday, Feb. 22). Note: Washington was born Feb. 11, 1731, on the old-style

Julian—as in Julius Caesar—calendar. In 1752, when calendars were switched to the more accurate Gregorian, 11 days were added, changing Washington's birthday to February 22. Also, the first day of the year was changed from March 1 to January 1, moving Washington's birthday from 1731 to 1732.

Memorial Day: last Monday in May (May 25–31 are only possible dates; also called Decoration Day)

Independence Day: July 4

Labor Day: 1st Monday in September (September 1–7 are only possible dates)

Columbus Day: 2nd Monday in October (October 8–14 are only possible dates; Columbus actually landed on October 12, 1492; in some locations this is also called Discoverers' Day or Pioneers' Day)

Election Day: the 1st Tuesday after the 1st Monday (November 2–8 are only possible dates; whether this is an actual holiday depends on the individual state)

Veterans' Day: November 11 (originally called Armistice Day, it commemorated the end of World War I on November 11, 1918 at 11:00 A.M., the "11th hour of the 11th day of the 11th month")

Thanksgiving: 4th Thursday in November (November 22–28 are only possible dates; the first Thanksgiving was proclaimed by President Lincoln)

Christmas Day: December 25

Other Holidays

Groundhog Day: February 2 (Punxsutawney, Pa. is home of the most celebrated ground hog)
Valentine's Day: February 14
St. Patrick's Day: March 17
Easter: sometime in March or April

Months with No Holidays

4 (March, April, June, August)

Months with More Than One Holiday

January (2); November (2–3, depending on Election Day)

Some State Holidays

Seward's Day:	Alaska
Patriots' Day:	Massachusetts
San Jacinto Day:	Texas
King Kamehameha I Day:	Hawaii

Calendar and Seasons

Equinox: the two days when day and night are of equal length (12 hrs.) and the beginnings of spring and autumn

Solstice: the two days when the Sun is at its extreme northern position (at the Tropic of Cancer, first day of summer) or southern position (at the Tropic of Capricorn, first day of winter)

Vernal (Spring) Equinox (about March 21)
Summer Solstice (about June 21)
Autumnal Equinox (about September 23)
Winter Solstice (about December 21)

The only months entirely in Spring:	April, May
The only months entirely in Summer:	July, August
The only months entirely in Autumn:	October, November
The only months entirely in Winter:	January, February

Names of the Months

The months' names are Roman in origin. Note that September, October, November and December are numerical names, but that they now fall two months later than their names would suggest, due to the insertion of July and August.

January: Janus, a Roman god
February: Februalia, a Roman period of sacrifices to atone for sins
March: Mars, Roman god of war
April: from the Latin, "to open," as in new growth (*aperire*)
May: Maia, Roman goddess of growing plants
June: from Latin for "youth" (*juvenis*)
July: Julius Caesar
August: Emperor Augustus
September: seventh month
October: eighth month
November: ninth month
December: tenth month

Names of the Days of the Week

The names of the days in English are derived from the Saxon names, which used the names of Norse gods.

Sunday: Sun's Day
Monday: Moon's Day
Tuesday: Tiw's Day (also call Tyr, god of war)
Wednesday: Woden's Day (Woden is the same as Odin, the chief Norse god)
Thursday: Thor's Day (Odin's son, god of thunder)
Friday: Frigg's Day (wife of Odin, queen of the gods)
Saturday: Seterne's Day (apparently derived from the Latin god Saturn)

Quiz 19: HOLIDAYS AND OBSERVANCES; THE CALENDAR

Clues:

1. These four federal holidays always occur on the same date.
2. The longest stretch between federal holidays separates these two dates.
3. The two months named for historical figures.
4. The newest federal holiday.
5. The month with the longest name.
6. Wednesday is named for him.
7. It used to be Armistice Day.
8. The days of the Sun's extreme northern and southern positions.
9. The February hero of Punxsutawney, Pennsylvania.
10. Seward's Day is celebrated here.

Answers:

1. What are New Year's, July 4, Veterans Day and Christmas?
2. What are Presidents' Day and Memorial Day?
3. What are July (Julius Caesar) and August (Emperor Augustus)?
4. What is Martin Luther King's Birthday?
5. What is September?
6. Who is Woden?
7. What is Veterans' Day?
8. What are the solstices?
9. What is the groundhog (Punxsutawney Phil)?
10. What is Alaska?

CHAPTER 20

Weights and Measures

Do you measure up? Sure, most of the world is metric, but not the U.S. **Jeopardy!** players have to know both systems, as well as how to convert some of them.

U.S. Weights and Measures

Linear Measurement

12 inches = 1 foot
3 feet (or 36 inches) = 1 yard
5½ yards (or 16½ feet) = 1 rod
40 rods (or 660 feet or 220 yards) = 1 furlong
8 furlongs (or 5,280 feet or 1,760 yards) = 1 mile
3 miles = 1 league (the definition of a league has varied over time)

Note: The statute mile (5,280 feet, etc.) is *shorter than* the international nautical mile (over 6,076 feet).

Area Measurement

144 square inches = 1 square foot
9 square feet = 1 square yard
4840 square yards = 1 acre
640 acres = 1 square mile

Surveyors' Measurement

7.92 inches = 1 link
100 links = 1 chain
80 chains = 1 statute mile

Liquid Measurement

4 gills = 1 pint
2 pints = 1 quart
4 quarts = 1 gallon

Liquid Volume

8 ounces = 1 cup
2 cups (16 ounces) = 1 pint
2 pints (32 ounces) = 1 quart
4 quarts (128 ounces) = 1 gallon

Note: The U.S. gallon (4 quarts, or 128 ounces) is *smaller than* the Imperial gallon.

Dry Measurement

2 pints = 1 quart
8 quarts = 1 peck
4 pecks = 1 bushel

Weight Measurement

437.5 grains = 1 ounce
16 ounces = 1 pound
2,000 pounds = 1 ton

Note: The ton (or net or short ton, 2,000 lbs.) is *lighter than* the metric ton (over 2,204 lbs.).

The Metric System

The metric system of weights and measures was created in France during the French Revolution, as part of an overall break with the past. It is a simple system, based on units of increasing or decreasing factors of 10.

Metric Prefixes

Fractions

one tenth	deci
one hundredth	centi
one thousandth	milli
one millionth	micro
one billionth	nano
one trillionth	pico
one quadrillionth	femto
one quintillionth	atto

Multiples

ten times	deka
one hundred times	hecto
one thousand times	kilo
one million times	mega
one billion times	giga
one trillion times	tera
one quadrillion times	peta
one quintillion times	exa

Note: In many countries, the word "milliard" is used for one thousand million (i.e., one billion in the United States) and "billion" is used for what we call "trillion."

Linear Measurement

10 millimeters (mm) = 1 centimeter (cm)
10 centimeters = 1 decimeter (dm)
100 centimeters (or 10 decimeters) = 1 meter
1,000 meters = 1 kilometer

Area Measurement

100 square millimeters = 1 square centimeter
10,000 square centimeters = 1 square meter
100 square meters = 1 are
100 ares (or 10,000 square meters) = 1 hectare
100 hectares (or 1,000,000 square meters) = 1 square kilometer

Weight Measurement

10 milligrams (mg) = 1 centigram (cg)
10 centigrams = 1 decigram
100 centigrams = 1 gram (g)
1,000 grams = 1 kilogram (kg)
1,000 kilograms = 1 metric ton (t)

Liquid Measurement

10 milliliters = 1 centiliter
100 centiliters = 1 liter
1,000 liters = 1 kiloliter

Conversions

And then there's the nasty business of converting between the U.S. system and the metric system.

1 inch = 2.54 centimeters
1 yard = 0.9 meters
1 meter = 39.37 inches
1 kilometer = 0.6 miles or 3,281 feet
1 mile = 1.6 kilometers
1 acre = 0.4 hectare
1 hectare = 2.4 acres
1 quart = .946 liters
1 liter = 1.05 quarts
1 gallon = 3.785 liters
1 pound = .45 kilograms
1 kilogram = 2.2 pounds

Or, to put it another way:

An *inch* is longer than a *centimeter*.
A *meter* is longer than a *yard*.
A *mile* is longer than a *kilometer*.
A *hectare* is larger than an *acre*.
A *liter* is larger than a *quart*.
A *kilogram* is larger than a *pound*.

Other Measurement Facts

Barrel: not a fixed measure; different substances have different standard sizes of barrels. For example, a barrel of oil = 42 U.S. gallons.

Kilogram: not a measure of weight, but of mass. (Thus, your weight on Earth is less on the moon, but your mass, i.e., bulk, in kilograms is the same.)

Knot: not a distance, but a rate of speed, equal to 1 nautical mile per hour

Light Year: not a measure of time, but distance—the distance light travels in 1 year (5.8 trillion miles)

Temperature

Finally, there is the measurement of temperature. Again, there are two different scales, Fahrenheit and Celsius or centigrade.

	Fahrenheit	**Celsius/ Centigrade**
Freezing Water	32°	0°
Boiling Water	212°	100°
Average Human Temperature	98.6°	37°

To convert Fahrenheit into Celsius:

Subtract 32, multiply by 5, divide by 9 (or subtract 32 and multiply by 5/9)

To convert Celsius into Fahrenheit:

Multiply by nine, divide by 5, add 32 (or multiply by 9/5 and add 32)

The Fahrenheit and Celsius scales intersect at −40°

Quiz 20: WEIGHTS AND MEASURES

Clues:

1. The prefix "micro" means this.
2. Horse players know a mile has this many furlongs.
3. Your normal body temperature, in centigrade.
4. Of yards and meters, the longer.
5. "Links" and "chains" are used in this profession.
6. Jules Verne's "20,000 leagues" would be this many miles.
7. Where the metric system was invented.
8. In the love song "a bushel and a peck," the number of pecks.
9. This prefix means "one billion times."
10. Britain's Imperial one is bigger than the U.S. measure.

Answers:

1. What is "one millionth"?
2. What is eight?
3. What is 37°?
4. What is a meter?
5. What is surveying?
6. What is 60,000 miles?
7. What is France?
8. What is five pecks?
9. What is "giga"?
10. What is the gallon?

CHAPTER 21

Potent Potables

This classic **Jeopardy!** category shows up fairly frequently, testing your knowledge of spirituous drinks. We've listed them by major types of liquor and some of the more famous cocktails derived from them. Bottoms up!

Absinthe: a licorice-flavored aperitif (*see below*) that was banned because of the presumed harmful effects of one of its ingredients, oil of wormwood

Ale: made from brewed and fermented malt (*see below*) or malt and cereal

Amaretto: almond-flavored Italian liqueur

Aperitif: classification of drinks; literally, an "appetizer." Popular aperitifs include Dubonnet, ouzo, absinthe, vermouth.

Beer: brewed and fermented grain, often malted barley and hops

Brandy: a liqueur distilled from wine, or from other fermented fruit juices

BRANDY ALEXANDER: brandy, creme de cacao, heavy cream

SIDECAR: brandy, liqueur, lemon juice

STINGER: brandy, white creme de menthe

Champagne: a sparkling wine; the priest Dom Perignon is credited with "inventing" champagne, i.e., discovering how to keep it effervescent

Claret: red Bordeaux wine

Drambuie: a liqueur of scotch, honey and spices; associated with Scotland's Bonnie Prince Charlie

Gin: distilled grain (i.e., alcohol), with other "botanicals" added, often juniper berries

DRY MARTINI: gin and vermouth; the less vermouth, the "drier" the martini

GIMLET: gin (or vodka) and lime juice

TOM COLLINS: gin, lemon juice, sugar, club soda. There are many varieties of a Collins, with other liquors.

Kahlua: a Mexican coffee-flavored liqueur

Kvass: Russian beer

Lager: means "to store"; a beer, usually dry and light in color

Liqueur: classification of after-dinner drinks, including brandy and a variety of cordials (Drambuie, Kahlua, Amaretto, Sabra, Armagnac, etc.)

Malt: barley or grain steeped in water

Mead: fermented honey and herbs

Ouzo: licorice-flavored Greek aperitif; called Araq ("sweat") in Arab countries, Raki in Turkey

Port: a wine named for Oporto, Portugal

Porter: rich sweet ale

Rum: distilled, fermented juice of sugarcane; comes either light or dark (i.e., with caramel added for color)

DAIQUIRI: rum, lime juice, sugar, liqueur; named for a town in Cuba

PINA COLADA: rum, pineapple juice, coconut creme, sugar

PLANTER'S PUNCH: rum, lime juice, sugar; associated with Jamaica

Sabra: an Israeli chocolate- and orange-flavored liqueur. "Sabra" is the Israeli term for one who is Israeli-born; the name comes from a local prickly-pear cactus.

Sake: Japanese rice wine (pronounced "sah-key")

Shandy: a mixture of beer and ginger ale

Sherry: fortified wine; name derived from Jerez in Spain.

Stout: very dark, sweet ale

Tequila: fermented juice of maguey plant; also called mezcal.

MARGARITA: tequila, lime juice, salt

Vermouth: white wine, flavored with herbs, roots, etc.

Whisky/Whiskey: a number of liquors distilled from grain, including bourbon, rye, scotch

HOT TODDY: whiskey, sugar, clove, lemon, boiling water; often a favored cold remedy

MANHATTAN: a cocktail of whiskey, vermouth and bitters

MINT JULEP: a cocktail of bourbon, sugar, mint, lemon and water; often associated with the Kentucky Derby

OLD FASHIONED: a cocktail of whiskey, sugar, bitters, lemon peel, water

SAZERAC: a cocktail of bourbon, sugar, bitters, absinthe; often associated with New Orleans

WHISKEY SOUR: whiskey, lemon juice, sugar

Vodka: Russian liquor, originally distilled from wheat; can also be made from other cereals or from potatoes

BLACK RUSSIAN: vodka and Kahlua

BLOODY MARY: vodka, tomato juice, spices

BULLSHOT: vodka, beef bouillon

SCREWDRIVER: vodka, orange juice

VIRGIN MARY: Bloody Mary without the vodka, i.e., spiced tomato juice

Quiz 21:
POTENT POTABLES

Clues:

1. The drink to have at "the Run for the Roses."
2. This scotch-based liqueur is the drink to toast Bonnie Prince Charlie.
3. The less of this, the "drier" the martini.
4. The maguey plant is the source of this Mexican liquor.
5. This drink is named for a Cuban town.
6. Juniper berries are an additive for this drink.
7. Distill wine, and you get this.
8. A Viking favorite, made with fermented honey.
9. He is credited with "inventing" champagne.
10. Its taste is licorice; its name means "sweat" in Arabic.

Answers:

1. What is a mint julep (at the Kentucky Derby)?
2. What is Drambuie?
3. What is vermouth?
4. What is tequila?
5. What is the daiquiri?
6. What is gin?
7. What is brandy?
8. What is mead?
9. Who is Dom Perignon?
10. What is Araq?

CHAPTER 22

Astronomy and Astrology

It's a big universe out there, but you only have to remember a very small slice of it for **Jeopardy!** There are the various planets and their moons, the constellations, and then the influence that they may all have on our daily lives: astrology, a topic that comes up with some regularity.

The Solar System

The Planets and Their Moons (in Order from the Sun)

Mercury (0 moons)
Venus (0 moons)
Earth (1 moon)
Mars (2 moons)
Jupiter (16 moons)
Saturn (21+ moons)
Uranus (15 moons)
Neptune* (8 moons)
Pluto* (1 moon)

*Note: Pluto's orbit is irregular, sometimes bringing it inside Neptune's orbit, as is now the case. Thus, for the remainder of this century, Pluto will actually be closer to the Sun than Neptune.

The Planets in Size Order (Largest to Smallest)

Jupiter
Saturn
Uranus
Neptune
Earth
Venus
Mars
Mercury
Pluto

Planets with Rings

Jupiter (extremely faint)
Saturn
Uranus
Neptune

Stars

These are the 20 brightest stars in the sky (in descending order), and the constellations in which they appear.

Sirius: Canis Major
Canopus: Carina
Alpha Centauri: Centaurus
Vega: Lyra
Capella: Auriga
Arcturus: Bootes
Rigel: Orion
Procyon: Canis Minor
Archernar: Eridanus
Beta Centauri: Centaurus
Altair: Aquila
Betelgeuse: Orion
Aldebaran: Taurus
Spica: Virgo
Pollux: Gemini
Antares: Scorpius

Fomalhaut: Piscis Austrinus
Deneb: Cygnus
Regulus: Leo
Beta Crucis: Crux

THE CONSTELLATIONS

There are 88 recognized constellations (* indicates those in the Southern Hemisphere).

Name	Meaning
Andromeda	Chained Maiden
Antila*	Air Pump
Apus*	Bird of Paradise
Aquarius	Water Bearer
Aquila	Eagle
Ara	Altar
Aries	Ram
Auriga	Charioteer
Bootes	Herdsman
Caelum*	Chisel
Camelopardalis*	Giraffe
Cancer	Crab
Canes Venatici*	Hunting Dogs
Canis Major	Great Dog
Canis Minor	Little Dog
Capricornus	Sea-goat
Carina*	Keel
Cassiopeia	Queen
Centaurus	Centaur
Lacerta*	Lizard
Leo	Lion
Leo Minor*	Little Lion
Lepus	Hare
Libra	Balance, Scales
Lupus	Wolf
Lynx*	Lynx
Lyra	Lyre
Mensa*	Table
Microscopium*	Microscope
Monoceros*	Unicorn
Musca	Fly
Norma*	Square (rule)
Octans*	Octant
Ophiuchus	Serpent Bearer
Orion	Hunter
Pavo*	Peacock
Pegasus	Flying Horse
Perseus	Hero

Name	Meaning	Name	Meaning
Cepheus	King	Phoenix	Phoenix (bird)
Cetus	Whale	Pictor*	Painter
Chamaeleon*	Chameleon	Pisces	Fishes
Circinus*	Compasses (art)	Piscis Austrinus	Southern Fish
Columba*	Dove	Puppis*	Stem (deck)
Comas Berenices*	Berenice's Hair	Pyxix*	Compass (sea)
Corona Australis	Southern Crown	Reticulum*	Reticle
Corona Borealis	Northern Crown	Sagitta	Arrow
Corvus	Crow	Sagittarius	Archer
Crater	Cup	Scorpius	Scorpion
Crux*	Cross (Southern)	Sculptor*	Sculptor
Cygnus	Swan	Scutum*	Shield
Delphinus	Dolphin	Serpens	Serpent
Dorado*	Goldfish	Sextans*	Sextant
Draco	Dragon	Taurus	Bull
Equuleus	Little Horse	Telescopium*	Telescope
Eridanus	River	Triangulum	Triangle
Fornax*	Furnace	Triangulum Australe*	Southern Triangle
Gemini	Twins	Tucana*	Toucan
Grus*	Crane (bird)	Ursa Major	Great Bear
Hercules	Hercules	Ursa Minor	Little Bear
Horologium*	Clock	Vela*	Sail
Hydra	Water Snake (female)	Virgo	Maiden
Hydrus*	Water Snake (male)	Volans*	Flying Fish
Indus*	Indian	Vulpecula*	Fox

The Zodiac

Twelve of the constellations comprise the Zodiac (from the Greek, meaning "circle of the signs"), the astrological signs that some believe determine character and influence fate. Unfortunately, the signs do not correspond exactly to the months of the calendar.

Mar. 21–Apr. 19: **Aries,** the Ram
Apr. 20–May 20: **Taurus,** the Bull
May 21–June 20: **Gemini,** the Twins
June 21–July 22: **Cancer,** the Crab
July 23–Aug. 22: **Leo,** the Lion
Aug. 23–Sept. 22: **Virgo,** the Maiden
Sept. 23–Oct. 22: **Libra,** the Balance or Scales
Oct. 23–Nov. 22: **Scorpio,** the Scorpion
Nov. 23–Dec. 21: **Sagittarius,** the Archer
Dec. 22–Jan. 19: **Capricorn,** the Sea-goat
Jan. 20–Feb. 18: **Aquarius,** the Water Bearer
Feb. 19–Mar. 20: **Pisces,** the Fishes

Quiz 22:
ASTRONOMY AND ASTROLOGY

Clues:

1. These two planets have no moons.
2. The "birthday sign" of the USA.
3. The only planet not named for a god.
4. These three animal constellations come "Great" and "Little."
5. The brightest star in Aquila (Eagle), its name means "the bird" in Arabic.
6. She's the Chained Maiden.
7. The smallest planet.
8. By Jove, it's the planet with the red spot.
9. The asteroid belt lies between these two planets.
10. He's the Archer.

Answers:

1. What are Mercury and Venus?
2. What is Cancer (the Crab)?
3. What is Earth?
4. What are the Dog, Lion and Bear?
5. What is Altair?
6. Who is Andromeda?
7. What is Pluto?
8. What is Jupiter?
9. What are Mars and Jupiter?
10. Who is Sagittarius?

CHAPTER 23

The Bible

As with other major literary sources, the Bible offers many categories from which questions can be formed, such as people, quotes and stories. You don't have to be devout to learn the basic information.

Old Testament

GENESIS: Creation; Adam and Eve, et al.; Noah and the Flood; Tower of Babel; Sodom and Gomorrah; Abraham, Isaac and Jacob; Joseph

EXODUS: Moses; Departure from Egypt; Ten Commandments

LEVITICUS

NUMBERS: Balaam and the ass

DEUTERONOMY

The books above constitute the Torah (also called the Pentateuch or the Five Books of Moses)

JOSHUA: Battle of Jericho

JUDGES: Gideon defeats the Midianites; Samson and Delilah

SAMUEL: Part I: David and Goliath; Part II: David and Bathsheba

KINGS: Part I: Solomon; Part II: Elijah, Elisha

DANIEL: Handwriting on the wall; Daniel in the lions' den

Days of Creation

FIRST DAY: heavens and earth; separation of light from darkness

SECOND DAY: separation of waters, sky

THIRD DAY: land, sea, plants

FOURTH DAY: celestial bodies

FIFTH DAY: birds and sea creatures

SIXTH DAY: land animals, man

SEVENTH DAY: rest

Ten Commandments

1. Thou shall have no other God before me.
2. Thou shall not make no graven images, bow down to them, nor serve them.
3. Thou shall not take the name of the Lord in vain.
4. Remember the Sabbath day, keep it holy.
5. Honor thy father and mother.
6. Thou shall not kill.
7. Thou shall not commit adultery.
8. Thou shall not steal.
9. Thou shall not bear false witness.
10. Thou shall not covet thy neighbor's house, wife, slave, ox, donkey, etc.

People in the Old Testament

Major Prophets: Isaiah, Jeremiah, Ezekiel, Daniel

Minor Prophets:

Hosea	Obadiah	Nahum
Haggai	Joel	Jonah
Habakkuk	Zechariah	Amos
Micah	Zephaniah	Malachi

The Twelve Tribes:

Asher	Issachar	Naphtali
Benjamin	Joseph	Reuben
Dan	Judah	Simeon
Gad	Levi	Zebulun

The Patriarchs and Matriarchs

Abraham and Sarah
Isaac and Rebecca
Jacob and Rachel, Leah

Main Figures:

AARON: brother of Moses; first High Priest

ABEL: son of Adam and Eve; killed by brother Cain, first homicide

ABRAHAM: first Jew, first Patriarch; husband of Sarah, father of Isaac (by Sarah) and Ishmael (by Hagar)

ABSALOM: son of David, killed leading a revolt against his father

AHAB: king of Israel, husband of Jezebel

BALAAM: prophet rebuked by donkey for cursing God

BATHSHEBA: wife of Uriah, then wife of David and mother of Solomon

BOAZ: husband of Ruth

CAIN: son of Adam and Eve; killed his brother Abel

CALEB: spy sent by Moses into Canaan

DANIEL: prophet; saved from the lions' den

DAVID: son of Jesse; slayer of Goliath; king of Israel after Saul; father of Solomon by Bathsheba

DEBORAH: prophetess who helped Israelites conquer Canaan

DELILAH: Philistine mistress of Samson, who betrayed him

ELIJAH: prophet, opposed to the idolatrous Ahab; went to heaven in a chariot of fire

ELISHA: prophet, successor to Elijah

ENOCH: son of Cain, father of Methuselah

ESAU: son of Isaac; sold his birthright to younger brother Jacob for a "pottage (soup) of lentils" (usually referred to as a "mess of pottage")

ESTHER: Jewish wife of Persian King Ahasuerus; saved Jews from evil Vizier Haman, which is celebrated in the holiday Purim

GIDEON: judge; defeated Midianites

GOLIATH: Philistine soldier, a giant, slain by David

HAGAR: servant of Sarah, concubine of Abraham; mother of Ishmael by Abraham

HAM: son of Noah; legendary father of the Africans

HAMAN: chief minister of Persian king Ahasuerus; his plot to destroy the Jews foiled by Esther

HIRAM: king of Tyre, friend of King Solomon

ISAAC: son of Abraham and Sarah, second Patriarch; almost sacrificed to God by Abraham; half-brother to Ishmael and father of Jacob and Esau by Rebeccah

ISHMAEL: son of Abraham and Hagar; half-brother of Isaac

JACOB: third Patriarch, son of Isaac and Rebeccah; wrestled with an angel; later called Israel, the twelve tribes were descended from his sons by Leah and Rachel.

JAPHETH: son of Noah

JESSE: father of David

JETHRO: priest of the Midianites; father of Zipporah, father-in-law of Moses

JEZEBEL: Phoenician princess, wife of King Ahab; worshipper of Baal

JOB: patient sufferer of afflictions; his friends were Bildad, Elihu, Eliphaz and Zophar

JONAH: prophet who doubted his mission; fled from Nineveh to Tarshish; cast into sea and swallowed by a great fish

JONATHAN: son of Saul, close friend of David; slain in battle along with his father

JOSEPH: Jacob's youngest son, and only son by Rachel; sold into slavery in Egypt by his jealous brothers, he rose to become second in power to Pharaoh

JOSHUA: son of Nun, successor to Moses, who led Israelites into Canaan after Moses' death

JUDITH: slayer of Babylonian general Holofernes

LABAN: father of the matriarchs Rachel and Leah, wives of Jacob

LEAH: Matriarch, wife of Jacob, sister of Rachel, his other wife; mother of all of Jacob's sons except Joseph

LOT: Abraham's nephew; survived destruction of Sodom; his wife was turned to a pillar of salt when she looked around to view the destruction

METHUSELAH: oldest man in the Bible, 969 years, son of Enoch

MIRIAM: sister of Moses and Aaron

MORDECAI: uncle of Esther, joined with her to save the Jews from Haman's plot

MOSES: prophet and lawgiver; led Jews out of Egypt, received the Ten Commandments; only person in Old Testament to speak to God "face to face"; husband of Zipporah

NAOMI: mother of Boaz, mother-in-law of Ruth

NATHAN: prophet, rebuked David for causing Uriah's death to free his wife Bathsheba for marriage

NEBUCHADNEZZAR: King of Babylon, destroyer of Jerusalem

NIMROD: famed hunter

NOAH: Patriarch who escaped the flood in an ark; father of Shem, Ham, Japheth

POTIPHAR: Egyptian official who bought Joseph to serve in his house

RACHEL: Matriarch, wife of Jacob, sister of Leah, his other wife; mother of Joseph

REBECCAH: second Matriarch; wife of Isaac, mother of Jacob

REHOBOAM: son of Solomon; during his reign the united kingdom of Israel split into rival kingdoms of Israel (north) and Judah (south)

RUTH: non-Jew, who married Boaz and converted; great-grandmother of David

SAMSON: judge of Israel; fabled strongman, betrayed to Philistines by Delilah

SAMUEL: last judge; anointed Saul as first king of Israel

SARAH: wife of Abraham, mother of Isaac; first Matriarch

SAUL: first king of Israel; slain in battle with Philistines and succeeded by his friend and later enemy, David

SETH: Adam and Eve's third son

SHEM: son of Noah; legendary father of the Semites

SOLOMON: son of David and Bathsheba; king of Israel; builder of the first Temple

URIAH: warrior, husband of Bathsheba; sent to his death in battle by David to free her for marriage

ZIPPORAH: daughter of Jethro, wife of Moses

Quotes from the Old Testament

Genesis

"In the beginning God created the heaven and the earth.
And the earth was without form, and void; and darkness was upon the face of the deep.
And the Spirit of God moved upon the face of the waters.
And God said, Let there be light: and there was light."

"And the evening and the morning were the first day."

"And God said, Let us make man in our image, after our likeness."

"And the Lord God formed man of the dust of the ground, . . ."

"The tree of life is also in the midst of the garden."

"But of the tree of the knowledge of good and evil, thou shalt not eat of it: . . ."

"Now the serpent was more subtle than any beast of the field."

"In sorrow thou shalt bring forth children."

"And Adam called his wife's name Eve; because she was the mother of all living."

"Am I my brother's keeper?" (said by Cain)

"And Cain went out . . . and dwelt in the land of Nod."

"There were giants in the earth in those days."

Exodus

"I have been a stranger in a strange land."

"Behold, the bush burned with fire, and the bush was not consumed."

"A land flowing with milk and honey."

"Let my people go."

"And the Lord went before them by day in a pillar of a cloud to lead them the way; and by night in a pillar of fire, . . ."

Leviticus

"Thou shalt love thy neighbor as thyself."

"Proclaim liberty throughout all the land unto all the inhabitants thereof." (inscribed on the Liberty Bell)

Numbers

"What hath God wrought!" (also the first message sent by Morse via telegraph)

Deuteronomy

"Man doth not live by bread only, . . ."

Book of Ruth

"Whither thou goest, I will go; and where thou lodgest, I will lodge; thy people shall by my people, and thy God my God."

Book of Samuel

"Saul has slain his thousands, and David his ten thousands."

Book of Job

"Naked came I out of my mother's womb, and naked shall I return thither: the Lord gave, and the Lord hath taken away; . . ."

"I am escaped with the skin of my teeth."

"The price of wisdom is above rubies."

Psalms

"The Lord is my shepherd; I shall not want." (23rd Psalm)

"The meek shall inherit the earth." (37th Psalm)

"The days of our years are threescore years and ten;" (90th Psalm)

"By the rivers of Babylon, there we sat down, yea we wept, when we remembered Zion." (137th Psalm)

"If I forget thee, O Jerusalem, let my right hand forget my cunning." (137th Psalm)

"Put not your trust in princes." (146th Psalm)

Proverbs

"A soft answer turneth away wrath."

"Pride goeth before destruction, and an haughty spirit before a fall."

"Open rebuke is better than secret love."

"Who can find a virtuous woman? for her price is far above rubies."

Ecclesiastes (The Preacher)

"Vanity of vanity, saith the Preacher, vanity of vanities; all is vanity."

"The sun also riseth."

"To everything there is a season, and a time to every purpose under heaven. A time to be born, and a time to die; . . ."

"A man hath no better thing under the sun, than to eat, and to drink, and to be merry."

"Cast thy bread upon the waters."

Isaiah

"Come now, and let us reason together . . ." (often quoted by President Lyndon Johnson)

"They shall beat their swords into plowshares, and their spears into pruninghooks: nation shall not lift up sword against nation, . . ."

"I am holier than thou."

Daniel

"And this is the writing that was written, MENE, MENE, TEKEL UPHARSIN." [Translation: "God hath numbered thy kingdom, and finished it. Thou art weighed in the balances, and art found wanting. Thy kingdom is divided, and given to the Medes and Persians." This is the "handwriting on the wall."]

New Testament

The Gospels: Matthew, Mark, Luke John

People in the New Testament

The Apostles:

Andrew	James the Greater	Jude (or Thaddeus)
Barnabas	James the Lesser	Matthew
Bartholomew	Judas Iscariot	Matthias*

Paul*	Philip	Thomas (Didymus)
Peter	Simon	

*Note: There were originally 12 Apostles. Matthias replaced the disgraced Judas Iscariot. Paul, a later convert, was added later.

Main Figures:

ANANIAS: (1) false Christian in Jerusalem, name became synonymous with lying; (2) baptizer of Saul (Paul) in Damascus; (3) high priest and chief judge at trial of Paul

ANDREW: fisherman Apostle; patron saint of Scotland

BALTHAZAR: one of the Three Magi (traditional name, not used in the Bible)

BARABBAS: criminal released at demand of the crowd in preference to Jesus

CAIAPHAS: Jewish high priest, presided at trial of Jesus

CASPAR: one of the Three Magi (traditional name, not used in the Bible)

ELIZABETH: cousin of Mary and mother of John the Baptist; wife of Zechariah

GABRIEL: one of seven archangels; appeared to Mary

HEROD: name of several Jewish kings. *Herod the Great* was king at the time of Jesus' birth, met with the three Wise Men and ordered massacre of children. *Herod Antipas* was Herod the Great's successor, ordered the execution of John the Baptist, and interrogated Jesus after his arrest.

JAMES: brother or half-brother of Jesus

JOHN THE BAPTIST: son of Zechariah and Elizabeth; baptized Jesus; killed by Herod at request of Salome

JOHN THE DIVINE: author of the Book of Revelation, written in Patmos, Greece

JOHN THE EVANGELIST: author of the fourth Gospel, possibly one of the Apostles

JOSEPH: father of Jesus

JOSEPH OF ARIMATHEA: member of Sanhedrin sympathetic to Jesus; provided tomb for Jesus

JUDAS ISCARIOT: disciple of Jesus, who betrayed him for 30 pieces of silver

LAZARUS: brother of Martha and Mary, raised from the dead by Jesus

LUKE: author of third Gospel and Book of Acts; said to be a physician

MAGI: Caspar, Balthazar, Melchior (traditional names, not named in the Bible)

MARK: author of second Gospel

MARY: mother of Jesus, daughter of Joachim and Anne

MARY MAGDALENE: possibly sister of Lazarus; first witness of Jesus' resurrection

MATTHEW: author of first Gospel; a tax collector who became one of the Apostles

MELCHIOR: one of the Three Magi (traditional name, not named in the Bible)

NICODEMUS: Pharisee, defended Jesus in the council

PAUL: originally Saul, converted to Christianity on the road to Damascus; wrote many books of the New Testament

PETER: "Simon called Peter"; Apostle who denied Jesus three times on the night he was arrested. The first pope; he asked to be crucified upside-down out of deference to Jesus.

PONTIUS PILATE: Roman procurator of Judea, tried and condemned Jesus

SALOME: daughter of Herodias; did the "Dance of the Seven Veils" for Herod Antipas and received execution of John the Baptist as a reward

STEPHEN: disciple of Jesus, stoned to death

THOMAS: Apostle who doubted resurrection until Jesus appeared to him (hence the phrase "Doubting Thomas")

TIMOTHY: companion and messenger of Paul

ZECHARIAH: husband of Elizabeth, father of John the Baptist

Quotes from the New Testament

Matthew's Gospel

"The voice of one crying in the wilderness."

"Follow me, and I will make you fishers of men."

"Blessed are the poor in spirit: for theirs is the kingdom of heaven. . . .
Blessed are the meek: for they shall inherit the earth. . . .
Blessed are the peacemakers: for they shall be called the children of God."

"Ye are the salt of the earth."

"Ye are the light of the world. A city that is set on a hill cannot be hid."

"The light of the body is the eye."

"No man can serve two masters."

"Ye cannot serve God and mammon."

"Judge not, that ye be not judged."

"Neither cast your pearls before swine."

"Ask, and it shall be given you; seek, and ye shall find; knock, and it shall be opened unto you."

"By their fruits ye shall know them."

"He that is not with me is against me."

"A prophet is not without honor, save in his own country."

"Thou art Peter, and upon this rock I shall build my church; and the gate of hell shall not prevail against it.
And I will give unto thee the keys of the kingdom of heaven."

"Get thee behind me, Satan."

"It is easier for a camel to go through the eye of a needle, than for a rich man to enter into the kingdom of God."

"Many that are first shall be last; and the last shall be first."

"Many are called, but few are chosen."

"Render unto Caesar the things which are Caesar's; and unto God the things that are God's."

"Thou shalt love thy neighbor as thyself."

"Verily I say unto you, that one of you shall betray me."

"It had been good for that man [Judas] if he had not been born."

"O Father, if it be possible, let this cup pass from me."

"And Peter remembered the word of Jesus . . . Before the cock crow, thou shalt deny me thrice."

"My God, my God, why hast thou forsaken me?"

Mark's Gospel

"If a house be divided against itself, that house cannot stand."

"My name is Legion: for we are many."

"I bring you tidings of great joy, . . ."

"Physician, heal thyself."

"The laborer is worthy of his hire."

"Father, forgive them; for they know not what they do."

"Father, into they hands I commend my spirit."

John's Gospel

"In the beginning was the Word, and the Word was with God, and the Word was God."

"The Word was made flesh, and dwelt among us . . . full of grace and truth."

"Behold the Lamb of God, which taketh away the sin of the world." (spoken by John the Baptist)

"God so loved the world, that he gave his only begotten Son, that whoever believeth in him should not perish, but have everlasting life."

"He that is without sin among you, let him first cast a stone at her."

"I am the light of the world: he that followeth me shall not walk in darkness, but shall have the light of life."

"The truth shall make you free."

"Greater love hath no man than this, that a man lay down his life for his friends."

"Whither goest thou?" (Latin: *Quo vadis?*)

"Behold the man!" (Latin: *Ecce homo*; spoken by Pontius Pilate.)

Acts

"Saul, Saul, why persecutest thou me?"

"Immediately there fell from his eyes as it had been scales."

"God is no respecter of persons."

"It is more blessed to give than to receive."

"The wages of sin is death; but the gift of God is eternal life."

First Corinthians

"It is better to marry than to burn."

First Timothy

"The love of money is the root of all evil."

Revelation

"The first beast was like a lion, and the second beast like a calf, and the third beast had a face as a man, and the fourth beast was like a flying eagle."

"A book . . . sealed with seven seals."

"Behold a pale horse: and his name that sat on him was Death, and Hell followed with him."

"I am Alpha and Omega, the beginning and the end, the first and the last."

Quiz 23:
THE BIBLE

Clues:

1. This patriarch married two matriarchs, sisters.
2. He was killed in battle to free Bathsheba for marriage to King David.
3. He provided a tomb for Jesus.
4. Alphabetically, the first of Israel's Twelve Tribes.
5. Author Robert Heinlein took the title *Stranger in a Strange Land* from this book of the Bible.
6. His foray into Canaan was the first recorded spy caper.
7. Matthias replaced this Apostle.
8. His parents were Zechariah and Elizabeth.
9. He said "Ecce homo."
10. Of Elisha and Elijah, the elder.

Answers:

1. Who is Jacob?
2. Who is Uriah?
3. Who is Joseph of Arimathea?
4. What is Asher?
5. What is *Exodus*?
6. Who is Caleb?
7. Who is Judas Iscariot?
8. Who is John the Baptist?
9. Who is Pontius Pilate?
10. Who is Elijah?

CHAPTER 24

Mythology

A good game of **Jeopardy!** depends on luck or, as the ancients would say, "It is in the lap of the gods." So you might as well learn who the gods are, or were, just in case they come up—or in case you feel the need to invoke them. We've divided this up into biographical entries, some important family trees, and a chart comparing the Greek and Roman gods.

Graeco-Roman Mythology

Main Mythological Figures

Achilles: By dipping him in the River Styx, this Greek warrior was made invulnerable, save for his heel ("Achilles' heel"), by which his mother held him. Chose a short, glorious life over a long, dull one. Homer's *Iliad* tells of his quarrel with Agamemnon during the Trojan War. In that war Achilles killed Hector and was slain in turn by Paris, via an arrow to his heel.

Adonis: youth famed for his beauty, loved by Aphrodite and Persephone. Killed by a boar, after which Zeus decreed he spend half of the year with each goddess.

Aeneas: Trojan prince, son of Aphrodite and a mortal. He and his followers escaped Troy as it fell, fleeing west where he became the ancestor of the Romans. Hero of Virgil's *Aeneid.*

Agamemnon: King of Mycenae, leader of the Greeks against Troy. Slain after the war by his wife, Clytemnestra, and her lover. Avenged by his son, Orestes.

Ajax: petulant Greek warrior against Troy, who killed himself when armor of dead Achilles was awarded to Odysseus.

Amazons: female warriors, allied to Troy. Their name is said to mean "without breasts," referring to the belief that they cut off their breasts to allow them to use bows and arrows. Their queen, Hippolyta, was captured by and married to Athens' King Theseus (*see* Shakespeare's *A Midsummer Night's Dream*).

Andromeda: Ethiopian princess, chained to a cliff to be devoured by a monster; rescued by Perseus. A constellation is named for her, containing a galaxy among the closest to our own Milky Way.

Antigone: daughter of Oedipus by Jocasta, his mother. Hanged herself. Subject of a play by Sophocles.

Aphrodite: Greek goddess of love and beauty (Roman: Venus). Born from the severed member of Cronus. Unfaithful wife of Hephaestus, mother of Eros (Roman: Cupid). Started the Trojan War by allowing Paris to take Helen from her husband.

Apollo: son of Zeus. God of poetry, games, healing, prophecy. Later associated with Helios (the Sun). The only major god to have the same name in Greece and Rome. (Third series of U.S. manned spacecraft named for him.)

Arachne: she bested Athena in a weaving contest and was turned into a spider for her pride ("hubris"). Her name, which means spider, was given to the class of animals, arachnids, that includes spiders.

Ares: son of Zeus, Greek god of war (Roman: Mars, from which comes the term "martial"). Father of Eros.

Argo: ship used by Jason in his search for the Golden Fleece.

Argus: 100-eyed monster slain by Hermes.

Ariadne: daughter of Crete's King Minos, she helped Theseus through the labyrinth to slay the Minotaur. Theseus abandoned her on island of Naxos, where she became a devotee of Dionysus. Subject of opera by Richard Strauss. Also name given to European space program (French "Ariane").

Artemis: (Roman: Diana) goddess of hunting, fertility, chastity; a virgin; later associated with the moon; twin sister of Apollo.

Asclepius: mortal son of Apollo, slain by Zeus for raising the dead. Later deified as god of medicine. One of Socrates' last remarks was to remind his followers that he "owed a cock to Asclepius."

Astraea: goddess of justice.

Atalanta: princess who outran each of her would-be suitors in a race. She was defeated when Hippomenes (or Melanion) dropped golden apples given him by Aphrodite, which Atalanta stopped to retrieve.

Athena: (Roman: Minerva) goddess of wisdom. Zeus' daughter, she sprang full-grown from his brow. Her symbol was an owl.

Atlas: a Titan, son of Iapetus, condemned to support the earth (or the sky) on his shoulders for warring against Zeus.

Atreus: king of Mycenae, father of Agamemnon and Menelaus. (*See* family chart *below*.)

Aurora: (Greek: Eos) Roman goddess of the dawn.

Bellerophon: hero who killed the Chimera with the help of the winged horse Pegasus.

Calliope: muse of epic poetry.

Calypso: sea nymph who kept Odysseus captive on her island for seven years. (Jacques Cousteau named his oceanographic research vessel *Calypso*.)

Cassandra: daughter of King Priam of Troy; given the gift of prophecy by Apollo, but condemned not to be believed after she spurned him.

Centaurs: half-human/half-horse creatures. The most famous was Chiron, who tutored Achilles.

Ceres: (Greek: Demeter) Roman goddess of harvest, agriculture. (Source of the word "cereal." Also, the largest asteroid is named Ceres.)

Charon: boatman who ferries dead souls across the River Styx to Hades. Greeks were buried with coins on their eyes to pay Charon's fare. (The planet Pluto's moon is named Charon.)

Charybdis: undersea monster opposite Scylla, she created whirlpool which threatened passing ships, in the *Odyssey*.

Chimera: female monster with the head of a lion, body of a goat and tail of a serpent; slain by Bellerophon.

Chronos: personification of time (as in "chronology"). Not to be confused with Cronus—*see below*.

Circe: enchantress who kept Odysseus and his men captive on her island for many years, turning many of the Greeks into swine.

Clio: muse of history.

Clytemnestra: Agamemnon's wife; with her lover Aegisthus she killed Agamemnon in his bath after his return from Troy, to avenge his sacrifice of their daughter Iphigenia. The killers were slain by her son, Orestes.

Cronus: (Roman: Saturn) leader of the Titans, god of the harvest. Son of Uranus and Gaea, father of Zeus and his brothers, who dethroned Cronus in a great war (the Titanomachia).

Cupid: (Greek: Eros) god of love, son of Aphrodite and Ares.

Cyclops: one-eyed giants in the *Odyssey*. Odysseus outsmarted the cyclops Polyphemus, blinding him.

Daedalus: master inventor and craftsman. Built the labyrinth on Crete for Minos. Father of Icarus. Daedalus fashioned waxen wings for them to escape from Crete.

Danae: mother of hero Perseus by Zeus, who came to her as shower of gold.

Demeter: (Roman: Ceres) goddess of agriculture and harvest, mother of Persephone.

Dido: legendary queen of Carthage, who committed suicide when Aeneas left her (*see* Virgil's *Aeneid*), thus accounting for the future rivalry of Carthage and Rome.

Dionysus: (Greek: Bacchus) Roman god of wine and ecstasy.

Dioscouri: the twins Castor and Pollux, sons of Leda and Zeus, who came to her as a swan. Brothers to Helen of Troy. The Romans called them the Gemini.

Echo: nymph who loved Narcissus; she pined away when he ignored her, leaving only her voice.

Electra: daughter of Agamemnon and Clytemnestra, sister of Orestes. She urged him to kill their mother after the murder of Agamemnon. Subject of a play by Sophocles, and a version by Eugene O'Neill (*Mourning Becomes Electra*).

Erato: muse of love poetry.

Eros: god of love, son of Aphrodite and Ares. Also known as Cupid or Amor.

Eris: goddess of strife; she helped instigate the Trojan War by throwing a golden apple inscribed "To the Fairest" amid three goddesses. Paris awarded it to Aphrodite, who gave him Helen.

Euterpe: muse of music.

Fates: the Moirae, goddesses who determine mortals' lives. Clotho spins the thread of life; Lachesis determines the length; Atropos cuts the thread.

Fauns: Roman deities of woods and groves (Greek: satyrs).

Flora: Roman goddess of flowers.

Furies: the Eumenides, avenging spirits.

Gaea: goddess of the Earth; daughter of Chaos, wife of Uranus, mother of the Titans.

Galataea: statue of a maiden carved by Pygmalion; Aphrodite brought her to life. (The musical *My Fair Lady* is based on Shaw's *Pygmalion*.)

Ganymede: beautiful youth who succeeded Hebe as the gods' cupbearer. (Name of the largest moon of Jupiter.)

Gemini: Roman name for the Dioscouri, Castor and Pollux. (Name of the United States' two-man space capsules.)

Gorgons: three female monsters with snakes for hair, whose gaze turned mortals to stone. The gorgon Medusa was slain by Perseus, who used a mirror to avoid her eyes.

Graces: the Charities, beautiful goddesses of joy; daughters of Zeus.

Hades: god of the underworld, brother of Zeus. Abducted Persephone to be his queen.

Harpies: monsters with women's heads and birds' bodies.

Hebe: goddess of youth; daughter of Zeus and Hera; original cupbearer of the gods; later married to Hercules when he was made immortal.

Hecate: goddess of witchraft, magic, crossroads.

Hector: son of King Priam of Troy, Troy's leading warrior, slain by Achilles.

Hecuba: queen of Troy, wife of Priam. A main character in Euripides' *The Trojan Women*.

Helen: daughter of Zeus and Leda; the most beautiful woman in the world. She was seduced by Paris, a Trojan prince, who took her from her husband, King Menelaus of Sparta. Helen's was "the face that launched a thousand ships."

Helios: personification of the Sun, often associated with Apollo (Roman: Sol).

Hephaestus: (Roman: Vulcan) lame son of Zeus and Hera. God of fire, smith to the gods. Husband of Aphrodite.

Hera: (Roman: Juno) wife (and sister) of Zeus; queen of heaven, goddess of marriage and childbirth. Every year she bathed in a spring on Argos to renew her virginity. Her symbol was a peacock.

Hercules: mortal son of Zeus, performed the twelve labors. Later made one of the gods. (Gibraltar and an opposite mountain in Morocco are called "The Pillars of Hercules.")

Hermes: (Roman: Mercury) son of Zeus, messenger of the gods, god of commerce, travel, thieves. Patron of physicians, whose symbol, the staff entwined with snakes ("caduceus"), was Hermes' staff. (Word "hermetic," meaning completely sealed, is derived from a seal said to be invented by Hermes.)

Hero: a priestess of Aphrodite. Her lover Leander swam the Hellespont to meet her; when he drowned in a crossing, she killed herself.

Hesperus: personification of the evening star.

Hubris: Greek concept of overly large pride or conceit, which leads to nemesis (retribution).

Hydra: nine-headed monster slain by Hercules.

Icarus: son of Daedalus, he flew too close to the Sun on the waxen wings his father made, falling to his death in the sea. (Name given to a large asteroid that approaches the Sun.)

Ichor: fluid that flowed in the gods' veins.

Io: a mortal loved by Zeus, who turned her into a heifer to hide her from jealous Hera. Hera had Io tormented by a gadfly. (A moon of Jupiter is called Io; it is the most volcanically active body in the solar system.)

Iphigenia: daughter of Agamemnon, who offered her as a sacrifice at Aulis to Artemis. Subject of two plays by Euripides.

Janus: two-faced Roman god of gates and doors. The month January is named for him.

Jocasta: mother of Oedipus, who unwittingly became his wife, and committed suicide when this was revealed.

Jupiter: Roman version of Zeus.

Laocoon: Trojan priest who warned against bringing the Trojan horse into the city. Athene sent a serpent to destroy him and his sons. Subject of a famous sculpture now in the Vatican.

Lares: Roman household gods, usually linked with the Penates, a similar group of deities.

Leander: lover of Hero, he drowned in the Hellespont swimming to meet her.

Mars: (Greek: Ares) Roman god of war (as in "martial"). Fourth planet from the Sun; Mars' minions Phobos (Fear) and Deimos (Terror) are Martian moons.

Medea: sorceress who helped Jason obtain the Golden Fleece. Jason abandoned her for Creusa; Medea killed the children she had borne Jason, and also her rival, via a poisoned robe. Subject of a play by Euripides.

Menelaus: King of Sparta, brother of Agamemnon, husband of Helen.

Mercury: (Roman: Hermes) First U.S. manned spacecraft were named Mercury.

Midas: King of Phrygia, given gift of golden touch. Also given ass's ears by Apollo, when Midas voted against the god in a musical contest.

Minos: King of Crete; son of Europa and Zeus, who came to her as a bull.

Minotaur: ("Minos-bull") half-man/half-bull, kept by Minos in the labyrinth. Slain by Theseus.

Morpheus: god of sleep, dreams. (Source of the word "morphine.")

Mt. Olympus: home of Zeus and the other gods.

Muses: nine daughters of Zeus and Mnemosyne (Memory); goddesses of the arts. (Source of "museum," home of the Muses.)

Narcissus: youth loved by Echo. As punishment for spurning her, he was made to fall in love with his own reflection (as in "narcissism"). (Also the name of a flower.)

Nemesis: goddess of retribution. A punishment for hubris (pride).

Neptune: Roman name for Poseidon, god of the sea. Eighth planet from the Sun.

Nestor: king of Pylos; wisest Greek leader in the Trojan War.

Nike: goddess of victory. (Name given to a U.S. defensive missile system.)

Odysseus: also known as Ulysses. King of Ithaca, husband of Penelope, father of Telemachus. One of the Greek leaders against Troy, he thought up the Trojan horse. Forced to wander ten years en route home to Ithaca after the war, as told in Homer's *Odyssey*.

Oedipus: unwittingly killed his father, Laius, and married his mother, Jocasta, becoming King of Thebes. Also solved the riddle of the Sphinx. When Oedipus discovered the truth of his parentage, he blinded himself. Father of Antigone. Subject of two plays by Sophocles.

Orestes: son of Agamemnon and Clytemnestra, brother of Electra. He slew his mother and her lover after they killed Agamemnon, and was then pursued by the Furies. Subject of the "Oresteia" trilogy by Aeschylus, and a play by Euripides.

Orion: hunter slain by Artemis, placed in the sky as a constellation.

Orpheus: famed musician, son of Apollo. Tried to bring his wife back from the Underworld, but lost her when he turned to see if she was following, which he had been warned not to do.

Pan: son of Hermes; a wood nymph, with goat's legs and horns. God of forests, fields, flocks and shepherds. ("Panic" derives from Pan, for the fear he can instill.)

Pandora: the first woman. Out of curiosity she opened a box, releasing all the ills on the world; only Hope was left in the box.

Paris: son of King Priam of Troy; he awarded Eris' golden apple of discord to Aphrodite, who gave him Helen, starting the Trojan War. He killed Achilles with an arrow to his vulnerable heel. Also called Alexander.

Pegasus: winged horse ridden by Bellerophon when he slew the Chimera. (Corporate symbol of Mobil Oil and Tri-star Pictures.)

Penelope: wife of Odysseus, who stayed faithful to him although besieged by suitors during his long absence.

Persephone: daughter of Zeus and Demeter. Goddess of growing grain. Abducted to the underworld by Hades, she was allowed to return above ground annually, thus bringing spring. Romans called her Proserpina.

Perseus: son of Zeus and Danae; he slew the Gorgon Medusa, and rescued Andromeda.

Pleiades: daughters of Atlas, transformed into a group of stars. (In Japanese, Pleiades is equivalent to "Subaru," a company whose symbol is seven stars.)

Pluto: Roman name for Hades (also called Dis). Ninth planet from the Sun.

Pomona: Roman goddess of fruit.

Poseidon: (Roman: Neptune) Greek god of the sea; brother of Zeus. Bringer of earthquakes. His symbol was a horse.

Priam: King of Troy. Husband of Hecuba. Father of Hector, Paris.

Procrustes: he placed people on a bed, and either stretched them or cut their legs to make them fit. Slain by Theseus. (Source of the term "Procrustean bed," meaning an overly restrictive form or process.)

Prometheus: titan who stole fire from heaven for man. Zeus punished him by having him chained to a rock, where his liver was devoured by a bird each day, growing back again each night. Subject of a play, *Prometheus Bound*, by Aeschylus and a poem, "Prometheus Unbound," by Shelley.

Proteus: sea god who could change his form at will. (Source of the word "protean," meaning multi-faceted.)

Pygmalion: king of Cyprus who carved a beautiful statue of a maiden,

Galatea, brought to life by Aphrodite. (Title of play by Shaw, later made into *My Fair Lady*.)

Pyramus: Babylonian youth who loved Thisbe through a hole in a wall. He killed himself when he erroneously thought she had been killed by a lion. Their story is the play within Shakespeare's *A Midsummer Night's Dream*.

Python: giant serpent slain by Apollo.

Remus: brother of Romulus: Romulus killed Remus when he mocked Romulus' initial wall that would become Rome.

Romulus: founder of Rome; he and his brother Remus were abandoned and suckled by a wolf.

Satyrs: (Roman: fauns) half-goat demigods, woodland spirits, noted for their lust.

Scylla: monster who occupied a rock opposite the whirlpool of Charybdis; found in the *Odyssey*.

Selene: (Roman: Luna) personification of the moon. (Element 34, Selenium, is named for her.)

Sirens: singing goddesses who lured sailors to their doom. Odysseus listened to their song lashed to his mast; his sailors' ears were plugged with wax, making them impervious to the songs.

Sisyphus: king of Corinth, condemned to push a stone endlessly to the top of a hill for trying to outwit Death. Subject of an essay by Camus, *The Myth of Sisyphus*.

Sphinx: monster with the head of a woman and body of a lion. She devoured those could not answer her riddle: "What walks in the morning on four legs, in the afternoon on two, in the evening on three?" When Oedipus answered, "Man," the Sphinx killed herself.

Tantalus: for trying to serve his son to the gods as a meal, he was punished by being kept in a neck-deep lake with fruit overhead.

When he reached for the fruit, it blew upward; when he stooped to drink, the lake ebbed. (Source of the word "tantalize"; Element 73, Tantalum, is named for him.)

Telemachus: Odysseus' son.

Terpsichore: muse of song and dance.

Thanatos: god of death.

Theseus: King of Athens; he killed the Minotaur; captured and married the amazon Queen Hippolyta.

Thisbe: lover of Pyramus, she killed herself when she learned of his death.

Titans: elder gods, the children of Uranus and Gaea; overthrown by Zeus and his siblings. (The largest moon of Saturn, the only moon with a substantial atmosphere, is called Titan.)

Triton: son of Poseidon, a sea demigod. (Name of Neptune's largest moon.)

Ulysses: Roman name for Odysseus.

Uranus: personification of the heavens. Husband of Gaea, father of the Titans, who was dethroned by his son Cronus. (Name of the seventh planet from the Sun.)

Venus: Roman name for Aphrodite. (Source of the word "venereal"; name of the second planet from the Sun.)

Vulcan: Roman name for Hephaestus. (Home planet of "Star Trek" 's Mr. Spock.)

Zeus: son of Cronus and Rhea; chief of the gods (Roman: Jupiter). God of thunder and lightning; husband of Hera, but father of many via numerous love affairs.

GREEK AND ROMAN GODS COMPARED

Greek Name	Roman Name	Attributes
Zeus	Jupiter (Jove)	Chief god; sky god; symbol is an eagle
Hera	Juno	Queen of the gods; symbol is a peacock
Apollo	Apollo	Sun
Artemis	Diana	Moon
Ares	Mars	War
Athena	Minerva	Wisdom; symbol is an owl
Poseidon	Neptune	Oceans; symbol is a horse
Hades	Pluto	Underworld, Death
Aphrodite	Venus	Love
Hephaestus	Vulcan	Craftsman, smith of the gods
Hermes	Mercury	Messenger of the gods
Demeter	Ceres	Agriculture
Persephone	Proserpina	Fertility
Dionysus	Bacchus	Wine
Eros	Cupid, Amor	Love

GRAECO-ROMAN FAMILY TREES

The Gods

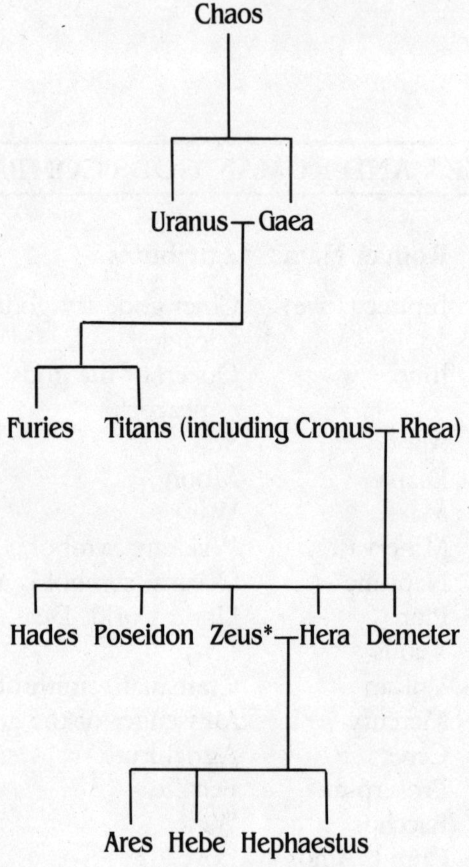

*Zeus fathered Apollo, Hermes, et al. by other mothers; Athena sprang full-grown from his brow.

The House of Atreus (the Atreides)

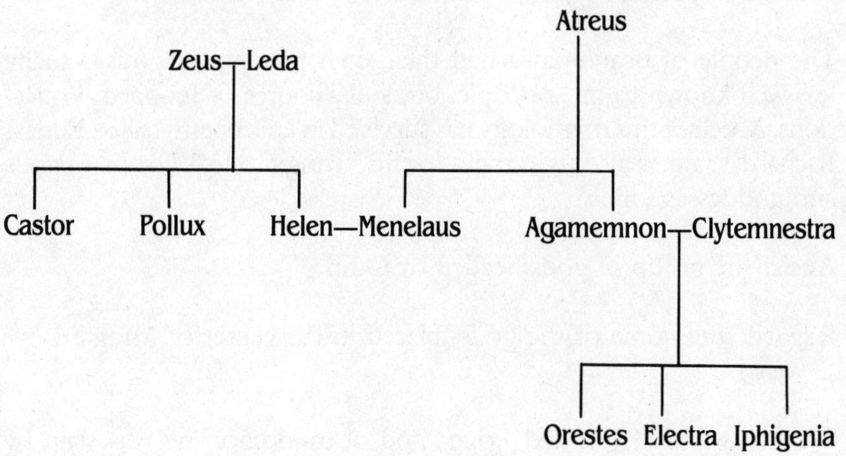

Royal House of Thebes

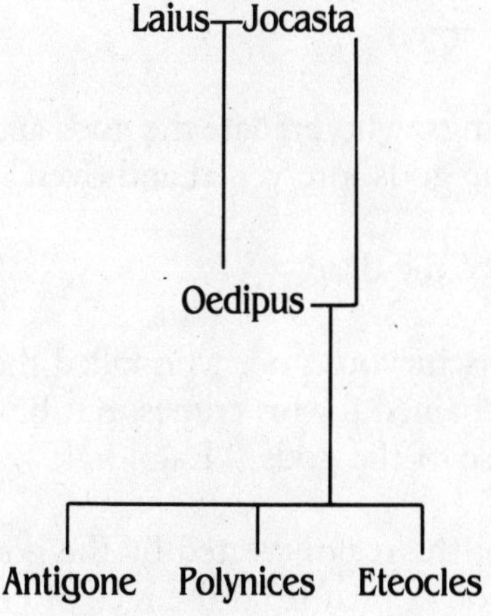

Norse Mythology

The people of Scandinavia had their own panoply of gods, usually less well known to most people, but still a source of **Jeopardy!** questions. Much of this mythology has survived in epic poems called Eddas; Richard Wagner also used them for his "Ring Cycle." The main gods and goddesses follow.

Aesir: the group of gods headed by Odin.

Asgard: the home of the gods, placed in the center of Midgard (*see below*).

Balder: son of Odin and Frigg; god of innocence; he was slain by the evil god Loki, using an arrow of mistletoe, the one substance that Frigg had forgotten to ask for a promise not to harm her son. Balder would return from the dead after the final destruction of all things in Ragnorak (*see below*), to help Odin create a new, happy race of men.

Fenrir: the monster wolf, a child of Loki. He will devour Odin in the final battle of the gods and giants ("Ragnorak").

Freya: goddess of love and beauty; daughter of Tyr. She is often confused with Frigg, Odin's wife.

Frigg: Odin's wife, queen of the gods. Mother of Balder. (Friday derives from her name.)

Giants: primeval beings, who predate the gods and came into conflict with mankind. The gods intervened and overcame the Giants.

Hel: female keeper of the dead.

Loki: an evil and mischievous god, who killed the good god Balder. Eventually, he is chained for his crimes, but he escapes, instigating the final apocalypse of the gods ("Ragnorak").

Midgard: the Earth; the realm created by the gods in the middle of the universe to protect men from the race of Giants.

Midgard Serpent: a giant serpent, a child of Loki, that coiled around Midgard.

Nifelheim: the realm of the deepest cavern of darkness.

Odin: father of the gods and man, ruler of the world. He sacrificed one of his eyes to gain knowledge. He was married to Frigg. Odin is also known as Wotan or Wodin. (Wednesday derives from his name.)

Ragnorak: "doom of the gods," the final apocalyptic battle between the gods and the Giants, in which all would be destroyed. Richard Wagner, in his Ring Cycle, altered this into "Götterdämmerung," or "twilight of the gods."

Thor: son of Odin; god of thunder; protector of man against the Giants. Thor's weapon was his hammer.

Tyr: one-handed god of war. Tuesday is named for him.

Valhalla: "hall of the slain," where the Valkyries bring the dead heroes who will serve Odin in his final battle.

Valkyries: "choosers of the dead," female spirits sent by Odin to bring him heroes slain in battle. The heroes are taken to Valhalla.

Yggdrasill: a giant ash tree that spread over all the realms of the world; it was the greatest shrine of the gods. The seasonal changes of the tree represented the changing fate of the universe.

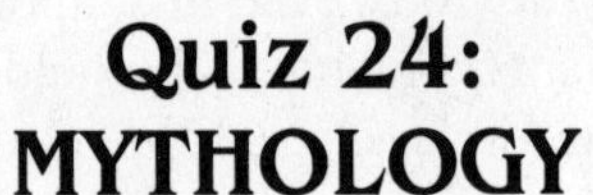

Quiz 24: MYTHOLOGY

Clues:

1. Hippolyta was their queen.
2. She helped Theseus kill the Minotaur.
3. They brought slain heroes to Valhalla.
4. The only major god with the same name in Greece and Rome.
5. Odysseus' home island.
6. Her regal symbol was the peacock.
7. The "evil doer" of Norse myth.
8. Carthage's legendary queen, deserted by Aeneas.
9. The total number of Muses.
10. They are the Gemini.

Answers:

1. Who are the Amazons?
2. Who is Ariadne?
3. Who are the Valkyries?
4. Who is Apollo?
5. What is Ithaca?
6. Who is Hera (Juno)?
7. Who is Loki?
8. Who is Dido?
9. What is nine?
10. Who are Castor and Pollux?

A FINAL WORD

There you have it. This is not the sum total of human knowledge and we may have omitted one of the less frequent categories that is a favorite of yours. But you do have most of what you need to be a more informed **Jeopardy!** player, either in the studio or at home. And remember, the number of those who prefer to play at home far outnumbers those who really want to try out their skills on the air.

We have found that most of the people who enjoy the show—in either location—also enjoy just reading odd bits of information. After all, as:

> This author wrote in *Tristam Shandy:* "The desire of knowledge, like the thirst of riches, increases ever with the acquisition of it."
>
> (Who is Laurence Sterne?)